TRAVELS WITH TINKERBELLE

6,000 Miles Around France

SUSIE KELLY

blackbird
blackbird-books.com

Blackbird Digital Books publication, 2018 © Susie Kelly 2018
ISBN 9781916426801
This work is a revision of "*A Perfect Circle*" previously published by Transworld
Publishers in 2006
First published in 2006 by Transworld Publishers Ltd.
The moral right of the author has been asserted
Cover art: Auguste Renoir (Limoges 1841–1919 Cagnes-sur-Mer)
Robert Lehman Collection, 1975, Creative Commons New York Met Museum

PROLOGUE

There's a reason the inhabitants of the Poitou-Charentes are affectionately known as *cagouilles* – snails. It's rare to see anybody moving faster than a cautious walking pace. Only mad foreigners jog. A common denominator in the obituaries is the great age of the departed – mid to late 90s is pretty much the norm. Some of our French neighbours have never been more than 30 miles from the village where they were born. Their needs and wants can generally be found in small local towns; why should they go further afield?

The same indolence affects us. With quaint villages, traffic-free lanes, limitless acres of fields, forests and rivers, long hot summers, sufficient hostelries to cater for our tastes, and the pure pleasure of sitting in the garden surrounded by our animals, listening to the birds, we live in our own little heaven.

But in this paradise there is a sly serpent, and its name is Wanderlust. When it whispers I feel a craving to be on the move.

"Shall we take Tally," (our dog) "and a tent, and drive all round France? Just drive around and see what we can discover?" I suggested one autumn day while we were collecting chestnuts.

"When?" Terry asked.

"Late spring, early summer?"

"How long for?"

"About six weeks?"

"All right. Find somebody to come and look after the animals, and we'll go."

What could be simpler? All we needed was a house-pet-sitter and a tent.

I contacted our lovely American friend, Jennifer Shields who had taken care of our animals and house some years previously when I had walked across France. She'd be delighted to come back, so that was one thing ticked off our list.

"Do you think," I asked, "that Tally will get bored being in the car for so long? Should we get a small companion for him?" Yes, we agreed, that would be a good idea. And so we collected a small black puppy of unknown origin who looked like the kind of small black puppy who would grow to be a small black dog. His huge ears, instant devotion and tireless efforts to please reminded me of Dobby the house-elf in Harry Potter, and so that's what we called him.

Two months before our departure date, things began to go awry.

Firstly Jennifer badly injured her leg and had to cancel her visit.

Secondly, Dobby grew, and grew, and grew. In no time at all he was the size of a new-born calf. He wasn't going to fit in our car with Tally, all our camping gear, and us. We were going to have to buy a far larger vehicle. One that we couldn't afford.

In a serendipitous stroke of fate, my old schoolfriend from Kenya, Vivien Prince, won a raffle prize – an open-ended return flight from Kenya to Paris. She enthusiastically volunteered to step into Jennifer's shoes.

Buying a vehicle large enough to accommodate our equipment and canine entourage, and that was within our means, was more difficult. With Vivien already here, and only six days before our departure date, we still hadn't found anything we could afford. At the eleventh hour, somebody introduced us to an ageing Talbot van converted to a campervan. She was beautifully fitted with hand-made oak cabinets and seemed mechanically sound. She cost more than twice what we had budgeted for, but she was our only option. We were ready to roll.

FRANCE

Note to reader: There were too many places of interest to include on a page this size. At the end of the book you'll find a list of links to places of specific interest we encountered on our travels. These are underlined in the text.

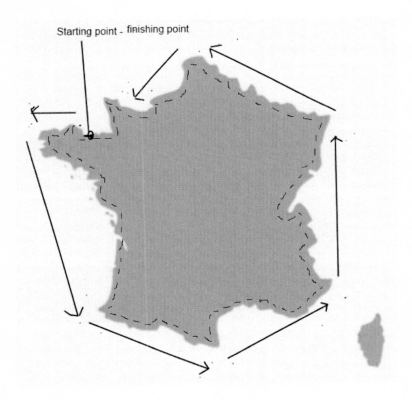

Starting point - finishing point

1

Northern Brittany

Ille et Vilaine

We are starting our trip from Cancale on the Brittany coast, and will travel 6,000 miles anti-clockwise around the perimeter of France until we arrive back where we began.

On a chilly day in May we wave farewell to Vivien and head north from our home in south-west France. It is 250 miles to Cancale, and we reach a campsite near there late at night after a pleasant and uneventful journey, apart from Terry finding that the clutch is rather stiff. We quietly park Tinkerbelle, drink cups of instant soup, wrap the dogs and ourselves in duvets, and fall asleep.

The first morning of our trip is off to a sublime start. At 8.00am the sun is already hot. From a gentle incline on the Pointe du Grouin north of Cancale, we overlook the sapphire waters of the bay of Mont-Saint-Michel to the east and the gulf of St Malo to the west. Just offshore a babbling mass of gulls and cormorants flap and hop about on the Île des Landes.

I join a queue of cheerful French folk in dressing gowns and slippers as we wait to wash our dishes in the communal facilities. There is a single topic of conversation – the glorious weather. A small, nut-brown man wearing a striped blue-and-white jumper and tiny white shorts pronounces with an air of authority that we are witnessing the beginning of a long hot summer. We all gaze at him with the reverence that the faithful in St Peter's Square might regard the Pope.

Although the inside of Tinkerbelle, as we have named the campervan, is a muddled mess, we will sort it out later. First things first: this is a holiday. We take the dogs to walk along the cliff top. They are astonished by their first sight of the sea, undecided whether to rush back and forth on the path or scale the cliffs down to the water that lies below, as flat

1

and still as a blue sheet of glass. This is the Brittany coastline at its most docile and beguiling, bearing no resemblance to the familiar postcard scenes of titanic waves engulfing lighthouses and ships.

With the dogs sprawling comfortably on our bed in the back of the van, we point Tinkerbelle towards St Malo. On the way we stop at a perfect sandy beach where the only other occupants are a couple with a small child and a golden retriever. Tally rushes over to play, but Dobby is entranced by his first introduction to the sea. He lies down in it and gulps mouthfuls of salt water for several minutes before joining the two dogs racing around the rocks and kicking up the sand. Half an hour later the quantity of sea-water he's drunk has a predictably unsettling effect upon his digestion.

After he's recovered we continue on our way, until we notice a sign to 'Les Rochers Sculptés' at Rothéneuf. We pick our way down a twisty, stony path to a colony of monsters, smugglers and corsairs sprawling in the sun on a windy hillside overlooking the ragged Emerald Coast. These strange creatures are the work of a 19th century local priest. For 25 years this lonely man passed his spare time here sculpting from the granite several hundred intricate figures, based upon the legend of a powerful 16th century Rothéneuf family of pirates and smugglers. There are sea-calves, serpents, stern watchmen, and figures eroded past recognition. My favourite is a rectangular tableau showing what looks like a couple of dwarves against a background of palm trees. The male dwarf appears to be simultaneously pulling off the lady's headdress and kicking her up the backside.

Old photographic postcards show the Abbé's handiwork in its heyday, before time and tide and the tramp of feet had taken their toll. I wonder what he'd been thinking as he chipped away for all those years, and how long his lonely labour of love will last before the elements obliterate it.

The cobbled streets and battlements of St Malo are crammed with vehicles and holidaymakers. Flags swoon limply in the still heat. We will not stay here overnight; it's too busy. We are looking for somewhere remote and quiet, where the dogs can run free. Tinkerbelle's gears are making a horrible grinding noise, and there is a loud rattling coming from somewhere beneath the bodywork.

Côtes d'Armor

Until 1959 the *département* in which we are now was called the Côtes-du-Nord – the northern coast. Bretons felt it was misleading and damaging to tourism, which after agriculture is their main source of revenue. 'Nord' suggested cold, but the Bretons regard their climate as mild; and whilst it is indisputable that Brittany is in the northern region of France, it does lie to the west. And so the Côtes-du-Nord became the more seductive Côtes-d'Armor. Pale blue sky, pink stones, bleached white sands. Yachts clinking and jingling on their moorings. Collections of quaint stone cottages nestling in clumps of rhododendrons and semi-tropical vegetation. The tide is far out, and gulls poke about for morsels in an inlet of glossy mud.

Every turn in the road reveals another glorious beach of pristine sand tickled by a silky turquoise sea. Beside the lighthouse at Cap Fréhel we are nearly blown off our feet and the edge of the cliff by the ferocity of a wind that arrives from nowhere, and which is not only ferocious but also freezing, but Tally and Dobby are oblivious as they gallop around through the beautiful moorland heather and wild flowers.

We pass the small town of Minihy-Tréguier where St Yves, patron saint of lawyers, was born into a noble family. After training as a priest he studied law and devoted himself to helping the underprivileged. Defending a poor man sued for having the impudence to stand outside a kitchen enjoying the cooking smells, for which the smells' owner felt he was entitled to payment, Yves rattled a coin. The noise, he said, paid for the smell. I like that! It is almost 7.00pm when we reach Ploumanac'h, where there are, according to an apparently reliable directory, three open campsites. The first two are closed. Terry is tired and irritable after wrestling all day with Tinkerbelle's gearbox which is becoming exceedingly temperamental and will no longer engage reverse, and we are both hungry. We've driven several times up and down and round and round in Ploumanac'h and are barely speaking by the time we eventually stumble upon the third campsite. Terry finds the traffic too slow, the signs useless and the other drivers idiots, and apparently it's entirely my fault. While we set up the awning, feed and walk the dogs I maintain a righteous frosty silence until Terry invites me to a meal at Trégastel-Plage.

Terry enjoys oysters followed by *moules* and *frites*, while my prawns, salmon and chilled rosé perfectly match the pink blush of the boulders squatting on the beach in the final rays of the sun. The Pink Granite Coast is at its very pinkest, and its rosy beauty melts away our irritability. It's a perfect evening.

The following morning we discover that during the night Dobby has eaten Tally's collar. A cold wind (it is definitely cold despite the mild Breton climate) lashes an improbably green sea into curly white-tipped waves, on which a lone yacht rocks and bobs. We cross the *départementale* boundary into Finistère, literally 'the end of the earth'.

Finistère

According to an article in the Brittany Tourist Board's magazine, the town of Morlaix prides itself on being the home of possibly the oldest chili palm in Europe, even the world, standing 65ft. tall and bearing 12ft. long leaves. We imagine the palm rearing up over the town like a vast parasol, but there is no sign of it. We go to ask about it at the Tourist Office, which closes for lunch as we arrive at its door.

There's a small créperie in a sheltered sunny square facing a row of tall houses, where gulls dance among the self-sown plants on saggy slate roofs. After lunching on Breton *galettes* and golden Breton cider, we wander down a quaint cobbled alley and into l'Echoppe Artisanale, a hat shop of extraordinary beauty. Confections of straw and ribbons, chiffon and silk, flowers, artificial fruits and jewels, so light, so colourful, so luscious that they'd be at home in a Parisian *patisserie*. If you want a beautiful hat, try this shop first.

At 2.00pm we head back to the Tourist Office.

"We'd like to see your famous chili palm," I explain to the girl at the counter. "Could you tell us where to find it, please?"

"Ah yes, there are many chili palms. You can see them in Roscoff."

"We'd like to see the one in Morlaix – the one mentioned in your brochure." I show her the magazine article from the *Comité Départemental du Tourisme du Finistère* mentioning the great palm. She reads it, looking nonplussed.

"Well, I don't know where that palm is," she says, "so it's probably privately owned and not open to the public."

"Are you sure? Could you possibly find out whether we can go and see it?"

"No, I'm afraid not." She turns her attention to a pile of booklets on a shelf behind her.

"We've come quite a long way especially to see the tree. Perhaps you could suggest how we can find out how to view it?"

"Yes," she replies. "Go to Roscoff."

Back in Tinkerbelle, the traffic lights turn red as we approach. Terry brakes, and Tinkerbelle gives a despairing shudder and makes a very bad clunking sound.

"Oh, hell," I say. "Has somebody hit us, or have we burst a tyre?" Terry climbs out and walks round to the back, where he stands looking perplexed. In the rear-view mirror I see the driver of the car behind us waving to him, and pointing. Terry lies down in the road and vanishes under Tinkerbelle, shortly reappearing with a length of exhaust pipe. The lights change to green and cars behind hoot, their drivers smiling and waving as they pass.

My heart sinks. On the second day of our trip, there is already a gearbox problem, a clutch problem and now a broken exhaust. We have bought a mechanical wreck! Is the entire vehicle going to fall to bits? The unexpected need to buy a camping car because of the small black puppy has already eaten up nearly all the funds we had put aside for our journey. There is no margin for major emergencies.

"Don't worry, it's no problem," Terry reassures me in his characteristically positive way. "We'll just keep going for now, and as soon as we find a breaker's yard we'll pick up a used part." Off we drive, noisily. The lush vegetation, narrow winding lanes, pretty stone cottages and Celtic road signs are reminiscent of Cornwall. To our right the inshore waters of the beautiful bay of Morlaix are palest turquoise, darkening by shades into the distance to a deep aquamarine.

Local place names beginning with Plou-, Tré-, and Lan- reflect the fact that the Breton language is a sister to Welsh and Cornish. Between the 5th and 7th centuries Christians fleeing Anglo-Saxon persecution in England came to Armorique, the land of the sea. They called their new home Brittany, or Little Britain. That's why England, Scotland and Wales became known, in the 17th century, as Great Britain.

Terry mentions that Tinkerbelle's gearbox seems to have eased up. However, he adds casually, the brakes aren't quite as effective as they should be. He says I shouldn't worry, so I try not to. We drive past fields of artichokes and potatoes stretching right to the horizon, and to the horizon beyond that.

Roscoff is quaint and picturesque, touristy but charming, the harbour front lined with slate-roofed stone cottages. People drift around in the sunshine through narrow streets, and a bridge disappears into the sea. We drive around looking in vain for giant chili palms, before giving up and driving to Sainte-Marguerite on the Coast of Legends, where we find a stunningly beautiful location in the dunes of the Abers. Gulls float overhead, and a single red-sailed fishing boat skirts the rocks. We drop anchor for the night and take the dogs down to the beach, where patches of seaweed as red as the sail form a playground for legions of sand hoppers. A black Labrador on a lead watches wistfully as Tally and Dobby race across the sand and rocks, while we collect smooth, tactile pebbles in subtle colours. But we don't take them away, because I always feel that stones removed from their natural environment lose their soul, and never look as perfect anywhere else.

As dusk falls and the dogs have run until they can't run any more we make our way back from the beach. A well-camouflaged green and buff-coloured toad tuts indignantly as it scrambles clumsily out of our way on the sandy path.

Our morning and evening ritual is labour-intensive. During the day,

5

while we are travelling the dogs stay in the back of the van, sitting on what at night will become our bed. It's two benches facing each other, with a table between. The table collapses on request, and with some rearranging the cushions form a mattress that we cover with a thick blanket for the dogs. At night, they sleep in the cab. Once they are removed from the back, we can cook a meal, eat at the table, and then drag out from various drawers our bed linen and such other things as are necessary for our comfort. From whichever part of the van they are occupying we have to remove everything chewable: camera, maps, guide books, pens, mobile phones, ropes are all grist to Dobby's insatiable mill. It is an immutable fact that if it's within his reach he will eat it, despite the fact that we have brought with us sufficient dog toys to stock a small shop. In the three days since we left home he has devoured amongst other things a washing up bowl and sponge, a pair of socks and a plastic container screwed to the wall, as well as chewing Tally's collar into four sections. Each morning we stow away everything in the back, make up the bed with the dogs' blanket and their toys and put their water bowl down. They are happy to wrestle and snooze until the next opportunity for a run.

The night is still and silent, the darkness pierced by the white light of Europe's tallest lighthouse, the Phare de l'Île de la Vierge.

2

West & Southern Brittany

Finistère

Next morning is heralded not by the song of the larks, but by the persistent rapping of a woodpecker. The dogs leap from the cab, full of *joie de vivre* and hurtle straight into a neighbouring campervan that arrived during the night. A small angry poodle shocks them and sends them racing down to the beach. They spend the next hour chasing each other over the sands and through the dunes while we breakfast. They are like children in their delight at this new experience, running back to us every few minutes to make sure we are still here, and to tell us how much fun they are having. We rub off as much wet sand as we can before they jump back onto the bed and we set off for another day.

We've no plan other than to wander along the coast and see what we find. The villages have comic-book names – Ar Stonk, Kroaz Konk. Around every curve is a new paradise, the beaches of dreams, the beaches of childhood memories. No busy promenades, ice-cream vendors or deckchairs. Just pepper-fine silver sands patterned with birds' footprints and sprinkled with small, delicate shells, lapped by clearest waters beneath cloudless skies.

Bedding flutters from windows, taking advantage of the sunshine and nippy breeze. There's a hairdressing salon named Marine Hair, where the mermaids go when they need a new style. Platoons of cyclists in bright-coloured tight clothing whirr past as we chug for several miles down narrow lanes behind a tractor loaded with new potatoes and fragrant cattle-shed cleanout, a rural scent that I love, while appreciating that it's not for everyone.

We stop for coffee at a smart beach-side restaurant. The ladies' room is down some steep stairs in a narrow basement. A large lady on crutches is struggling to negotiate the steps, so another lady and I take her by the elbows and manoeuvre her to the bottom. While waiting for her to emerge, the other lady and I discuss the superb weather, wondering if it is too good to be true (it is), and whether it will last through the summer (it won't). All the time we are standing there the chef in his whites is hopping up and down the stairs collecting boxes of oysters from an open storage area next to the loo. Sometimes it's better not to see behind the scenes in restaurants.

Across the sea to our right lies the Île d'Ouessant, a haven for lighthouses and home to one with an interesting history, La Jument. In March of 1904 M. Charles Eugene Potron, who had survived a shipwreck, bequeathed a large sum of money for the erection of a lighthouse. It was to be of the highest quality and fitted with the finest equipment, and built on a rock in some of the most dangerous waters of the Atlantic coastline, off the Île d'Ouessant. M. Potron's Will stipulated that if the lighthouse wasn't completed within seven years, the legacy would become void and would pass instead to the Central Society for the Shipwrecked.

The site chosen for the new lighthouse was an area of one hundred square yards of rock, only accessible during calm weather and at low tide. Construction began in May 1904 in diabolical conditions, and during the first year only 51 hours of work were accomplished. The La Jument lighthouse was finally completed just before the seven year deadline. Twenty years later somebody noticed that it wasn't anchored to the rock, but simply perched on top and maintained in place by its own weight. Since then it has been secured by four high-tension cables.

It's market day in picturesque le Conquet, or if you prefer its funny Breton name, Konk Leon. The town is throbbing with holidaymakers and strutting dogs. Tinkerbelle splutters and farts through the crowded streets, startling shoppers at stalls selling strawberries, pillows, fish, cheeses and vegetables, fabrics and jewellery, and bread in every possible shape. Once she is tucked into a car park we take the dogs to explore the port where the morning's catch had been unloaded and despatched in the early morning. A few fishermen are picking out tiny crabs and small useless fish who have died needlessly in the awful nylon nets that have replaced traditional linen and cotton.

From Denis Lunven's *boulangerie* in Rue Clemenceau we buy two glossy slabs of *kuign aman* – literally 'butter cake', a Breton speciality made with lashings of butter, heaps of sugar and a teeny sprinkling of flour just sufficient to bind it together. We also buy a cake with a layer of seaweed in it. We like new tastes. Close by is a café/bar where we sit in the sun at a table on the pavement. Terry is drinking his coffee and I am sipping cider as we munch our way through the cakes. Seeing a small, self-important dog swaggering about bringing the traffic to frequent abrupt halts, heedless of its own safety and the irritation of drivers, Dobby makes a sudden lunge in a frenzied attempt to join in the fun, almost dragging us and our table into the middle of the road.

Saturated with buttery cakes we drive to St Mathieu's Point, where there's a ruined abbey, a lighthouse and a monument to sailors who have given their lives for France. Built by Benedictine monks, and facing Jerusalem in accordance with tradition, the abbey is dedicated to St Matthew, patron saint of tax collectors and accountants. Breton sailors brought a piece of his skull here from Ethiopia, where he either died naturally or was martyred in the course of squeezing taxes out of people. Nobody knows how he met his end. If you examine a set of apostle spoons you'll see that each of the apostles holds something in his hand. St Matthew holds an axe. Don't you think that's a strange tool for a tax collector? Elegant arches stand in the broken walls of the abbey, and granite pillars reach up searching for a roof that is no longer there. Even in its skeletal state the abbey retains a suggestion of its lost grandeur. Now pigeons nest in the dark and dank mossy walls of the dormitory. There's nobody here on this wild headland except us, and the air carries the haunting sadness of a once mighty place reduced to lonely emptiness. In a walled field where once the monks grew vegetables and fruit, medicinal plants and fodder for their animals, a blackbird feeds her fluttering baby amongst the buttercups.

50,000 ships pass here each year, through one of the world's busiest maritime crossroads. From the extreme edge of the cliffs and tucked up tight against the abbey, Saint Mathieu's lighthouse peers down, incongruously, through the open roof space. Nearby is the stone chapel of Notre Dame du Bout du Monde – Our Lady of the End of the World – a simple building with a high vaulted ceiling, plain stone walls, and pots of agapanthus and arum lilies on the altar before a statue of the Madonna. As we meander along we see a sign to a strawberry museum at Plougastel-Daoulas. I am intrigued to learn how a whole museum can be centred on a strawberry, but Terry drives past, apparently deaf to my suggestion. He's alternately pumping the clutch and brakes up and down. The spectacular bay of Douarnenez is the site of the legendary city of Ys, built by the king of Cornouailles for his evil daughter Dahut. Every night Dahut took a new lover whom she forced to wear a silken mask. At daybreak the mask turned into a horrible clawed creature that killed its wearer, whose body was thrown into the sea. Fittingly, Dahut died as a result of her treachery when she opened the gates of Ys and flooded the city. It's said that in March, when the tides reach their nadir, the ruins of palaces can be seen in the sands, and on a quiet night you may hear the city's bells tolling.

Heading towards Plogoff we find a simple campsite – just a small field behind the house – belonging to a dear old lady who keeps a public bar in her tiny front room. As well as alcohol she sells packets of

9

biscuits, jars of coffee, tins of vegetables, and very old postcards. We have a glass of cider with two locals who ask if we are going to visit the Pointe du Raz. We ask how far it is to walk, and the two customers and landlady all point in conflicting directions and give distances ranging from a quarter of a mile to six miles, and times ranging from ten minutes to four hours. We decide to postpone our visit until tomorrow, and to drive there, because we don't actually know exactly where we are, and if we leave on foot we might never find our way back. There is no road sign at either end of the hamlet, and when we ask its name they all talk at once and give different answers, and it sounds as if they are saying that the place doesn't actually have a name.

Apart from a young couple in a tent who look suspiciously like a pair of schoolchildren enjoying an illicit weekend together when their parents think they are studying at a friend's house, we have the campsite to ourselves. The only sounds are of a blackbird chattering in the hedge, and the methodical munching of cattle in a neighbouring field.

This morning our hostess asks us to walk down the lane to admire the quaint local chapel. It has just been rebuilt from a virtual ruin, she explains, paid for by fund-raising events organised by the local community who are immensely proud of it. It is a charming, simple little building with a smart new timber ceiling and decorated with naïve paintings. If only it had a name on it, we might be able to discover where we are. But it doesn't, so we are doomed never to know.

We drive about until we find a sign to the Pointe du Van, a site of unbelievable, unspoilt beauty carpeted in grasses and herbs, heathers and wild flowers. Granite boulders pierce clumps of pink scabious that perfectly complement the blues of the sea and sky. No words or photographs can capture the essence of its magical beauty. The sky and the sea are linked by a dozen shades of blue. Standing at the cliff's edge looking out at the Atlantic Ocean, on a perfect early summer day when the sea is calm and there's not another human being in sight, and the only sound is of lazy waves tickling the rocks, you'll believe you can fly.

Instead of their usual wild gallop the dogs move slowly, sniffing the air and staring around them in wonderment as we trace the path to the chapel of St They, which stands perilously close to the clifftops. This is mainland France's most westerly place of worship. Outside on a granite pillar two characters stand back to back, but the inscription has been worn away by time. Lizards scuttle round the stone window openings and over the lichen-covered slates of the roof. From its Gothic belfry the bell is said to toll by itself to warn boats in danger. According to legend, long ago the French fleet was being pursued and the bell of St They rang out to guide the ships to safety; but when the enemy fleet followed a strong current appeared, dashing many of their boats on to the rocks and

10

dispersing the rest out to sea.

St They's plain exterior gives no hint of its interior of ornate gilded columns and pillars and colourful plaster saints, one of them pointing to a nasty wound above his poor knee. This most maritime little church's turquoise arched wooden ceiling is reminiscent of an upturned boat; model boats stand in front of the two altars, and there's a lifebelt washed up from a shipwreck.

Cradled between the Pointe du Van and Pointe du Raz lies the Baie des Trépassés – the Bay of the Dead. Despite its forbidding name and macabre legends all to do with death, it's a glorious sandy beach where dead Druids were launched to the gateway to the other world on the Île de Sein. It's easy to see why they chose this as their final point of departure from the temporal world, because it would be difficult to find anywhere more naturally splendid. It's so beautiful that it hurts. In the 6th century Saint Guénolé built a bridge of ice to link the Île de Sein to the mainland. But the Devil walked over it and melted it with his hot little cloven feet. To this day there is no bridge, and the island can only be reached by sea.

Satiated with scenery, we go in search of lunch, following the coast until the village of Kérity. The 'le Doris' restaurant serves an excellent meal of succulent salmon with a generous selection of fresh vegetables, and not the customary uninspiring little castle of boiled rice that is so often plopped onto the plate. I'm addicted to watching people, and fascinated by an English couple at the next table. They nod to us when we arrive, and say "Hello." Then they eat their way through a five-course menu as if they are expecting to take an exam on it later. They savour each mouthful reverently, staring at it on their forks, inhaling its aroma, and smacking their lips; but during the entire meal they do not exchange a single word.

Afterwards we walk beside the bobbing flock of sailing boats in the small harbour, stopping to read a plaque on the wall: *'From this harbour, on 23 and 24 June 1940, in response to a call from General de Gaulle, our following compatriots sailed to England aboard Notre Dame de Bon Conseil to join French forces, and fought on all seas and all fronts for the honour of France and her liberty.'* There are eight names listed, and we wonder how many had returned safely to Kérity after the war.

We pass a lady cyclist with a small dog perched in a basket on her handlebars. She waves to stall-holders selling lacework and hot dogs, and seabirds poke around in puddles on the rocky beach.

Something rather awful happened in Saint Guénolé, where we arrive in mid-afternoon. In October 1870 the wife and daughter of Finistère's *préfet*, together with a friend, were swept off the rocks and drowned at the place known as the Hell Hole, or the Victims' Rock. Whatever was

11

the *préfet* doing allowing his wife and child to put themselves into such a perilous situation? It does make you wonder if he was fit for purpose. A superfluous notice warns that this is a dangerous place. Anybody can see that. Even on this calm day the waves are heaving and crashing violently on the rocks.

There's a sturdy iron rail designed to prevent people falling into the sea. Unbelievably, incredibly, ankle-deep in swirling foam on a small, wet, round rock stands a fisherman. He seems oblivious to the waters churning round him and sometimes over him as he calmly casts his line. When a couple of young men climb out of a car and into wetsuits and prepare to plunge into the sinister waters I drag Terry away before he has any crazy ideas.

After the last few days of doddling around deserted beaches and dozy villages, Concarneau comes as a shock. The streets are crowded, traffic almost stationary, and in oven-like heat the all-pervasive odour from France's third largest fishing port wafts into Tinkerbelle through every crevice and cranny. There's a funfair and shoals of squealing children swimming and splashing each other in the bay. Tally is astonished by the sudden change in our environment and climbs on top of the fridge for a better view. We continue to Pont-Aven where we drive round in circles looking for somewhere to park, past art galleries featuring seascapes and nudes, and more seascapes and nudes, until I suspect it is because of the multitudes of nude paintings that we are driving around, and not because we are lost.

Luckily we find a breakers' yard in Pont-Aven where we might be able to find a replacement exhaust system to stifle Tinkerbelle's roars. Unluckily it closes just as we arrive at the gates. Never mind, we'll be back tomorrow.

By sheer chance and great good fortune we arrive at a small, pretty car park in a grove of trees just a few metres from the beach at nearby Port-Manec'h. A friendly French couple come over to tell us that campervans are allowed to park here overnight. They have been here four days, but are now leaving. We must be very careful, they warn, because two nights ago a gang of drunken youths had attacked them. No damage was done, *mais quand même* .....

On the beach two dozen blue and white bathing huts stand like sentry boxes in a row. A few of them seem tired and are leaning on their neighbours. There are a couple of yachts anchored in the aquamarine water. It's easy to imagine Gauguin and his friends at their easels here, catching their pipe smoke with the brims of their straw hats, and dabbing idly at their canvasses.

When the dogs have had a run I put a couple of salmon steaks in the oven, and Terry and I stroll along a footpath through a copse leading to a cumbersome stone building standing on a small headland. A lean, lanky man appears wearing a checked shirt and faded blue jeans halfway down his snake-thin hips. Large spectacles magnify his bright-blue eyes, and an unlit aromatic pipe juts from beneath a walrusy moustache.

What are we doing, he asks. Without waiting for a reply he offers us a glass of wine and some oysters. We haven't any money with us, and I don't eat oysters if I can possibly avoid them, so we decline politely. He introduces himself - his name is Hervé – and vanishes inside the building. When he returns he's carrying two glasses of wine, a fistful of oysters and a sharp knife with which he points us to a table. A deafening noise is blasting from the building – I think it's the Ride of the Valkyries playing at thunderous volume on a radio that isn't precisely tuned to the station. Hervé won't have a drink himself, but expertly stabs open an oyster and holds it out to me. I hide my reluctance behind a gracious mask, and gulp down the vile thing. Terry finishes the rest. Hervé and his pipe sit between us. Quite what he is talking about we aren't sure, because all his tales taper off before reaching their finale. He is much given to elbow digging and long meaningful stares whose meaning we cannot grasp, and all the while the Valkyries are galloping more frenziedly through the radio's static crackling.

I begin to worry about the salmon in the oven and make getting-up-to-go moves; but Hervé signals me with his sharp knife to sit down while he regales us with a story featuring Admiral Donitz, some English submarines, and the barbarity of the Ukrainian soldiers who'd massacred the Port-Manec'h locals.

"When the Resistance – you know about the Resistance, don't you?" he jabs me with his elbow, and I nod – "When the Resistance caught the Ukrainians, you know what they did to them?"

"Killed them? Shot them?"

He puts his wide blue eyes close to my face, and says slowly and clearly:

"They cut out their tongues and dug out their eyes, and filled the holes with wire netting!"

"Why?"

"And you know why oysters are so expensive in England, don't you?"

No, I don't. I'm still waiting to learn about the wire netting. At the same time Terry is trying to keep up with the conversation in his minimal French, while I fill in the parts he can't get, without really understanding them myself.

"Well, I'll tell you." Hervé stares silently at me for several minutes, and I stare back like a rabbit hypnotised by a snake. I am seriously worried in case the salmon catches fire and burns the van down with the

13

dogs in it.

"You want some more oysters, don't you?" No, I say, thank you very much, we really don't want any more oysters. I don't add that if I never ate another oyster for the rest of my life I'd be perfectly happy. We do not know what our relationship with Hervé is, if we are his guests, or his customers and are going to be presented with a bill that we don't have the means to pay. Ignoring our refusal, he goes away and returns with another fistful of oysters and puts them in front of Terry, who raises his hands in a gesture that says "No thank you." Hervé pushes them at him forcefully. Terry opens and eats them.

Now Hervé wants to arm-wrestle with Terry.

"Well, what a pity we must leave," I say. "We have a long way to go." This is of course untrue. Hervé is a delightful man, but I am worried that if he knows we are staying in the nearby car park he might spend all night, to the accompaniment of the furious Valkyries, telling us stories that don't end and we can't understand, and forcing upon us oysters I don't want and we don't have the wherewithal to pay for. We all stand up, and Hervé kisses me six times; Terry receives one kiss and another arm-wrestle. Hervé writes his and my name on a piece of paper, and gives me six more kisses. Terry asks him how we can pay for the oysters. Hervé casually indicates a battered box on his table, and Terry empties into it all the loose change from his pocket, which didn't amount to very much at all.

We never learn why oysters are so cheap in France and so expensive in England, nor why the dead Ukrainians were filled with wire netting.

By the time we get back to Tinkerbelle the salmon steaks are almost but not quite beyond redemption. In the late evening we sit reading and watching a melange of blue tits, robins and chaffinches hoovering up the charred remains of our meal. A small green caterpillar humps itself ticklishly up my leg. The night passes peacefully; we are not attacked by intoxicated adolescents, but merely assailed by the pervading odour of burnt fish.

From now on, we agree, we will just have a cup of coffee in the morning rather than a proper breakfast, because by the time we've cooked, eaten, cleared up and organised the dogs in the back of the van half the morning has gone.

We set off early for the breaker's yard at Pont Aven to find an exhaust for Tinkerbelle. The industrial estate is strangely deserted. The factories are all closed and the only sign of life comes from two noisy German shepherds hurling themselves at the fence. After several moments of bewilderment and indignation, we realise that today is the third of four public holidays in France during May this year. We rattle away to our next destination.

The countryside becomes tamer, more sophisticated; grander houses in tropical gardens replace the chocolate-box cottages of northern Brittany.

Morbihan

In Guidel the church bells are ringing merrily, the market is lively, and there's a show-jumping competition on the beach. Licking ice-creams, we watch horses bouncing over obstacles, and occasionally knocking them down like spillikins. Then we take the dogs to the beach where riders are cooling their sweating mounts. Seeing a creature similar in size to himself, Dobby joyfully bounds towards a horse and rider already teetering on the edge of control. The horse almost turns a somersault at the sight of the slathering black creature with a foot-long floppy tongue galloping towards it through the waves.

Next stop Lorient, where Terry is looking forward to visiting the submarine base, but there are no guided tours today because of the public holiday. However, a friendly young man at the gate says we are free to wander around and explore.

I find it a profoundly horrible place, a conglomeration of submarine pens, sinister concrete buildings with walls several yards thick. Even the few weeds struggling for life out of cracks in the concrete have a hopeless air. From here German U-boats crept out to attack Allied shipping in the Atlantic during the WWII. I break out in a sweat when I think of men locked inescapably in the ghastly vessels.

A single submarine sits at the dockside, a shiny black capsule reeking of stealth, death and claustrophobia. I want to escape from this awful place, but Terry is in his element, fascinated, ready to clamber into a submarine, submerge and sail off in it if he gets the chance. Then something else attracts his attention: a man working on a trimaran up on a trestle. He commands me to ask the man to invite him aboard, which I obediently do mentioning that Terry is an experienced ocean racer who navigated a winning British Admiral's Cup team yacht.

Soon Terry is up on deck with a charming and handsome Portuguese gentleman called Miguel, who speaks fluent English. He tells Terry the trimaran once belonged to France's greatest yachtsman, Eric Tabarly, who sadly fell overboard and disappeared at sea in 1998. Tabarly's boats were usually named Pen Duick, but this trimaran is called Côte d'Or II because she was sponsored by the chocolate manufacturers. She has an unfortunate history, having been dismasted and overturned twice. Miguel has rescued her and been working to rebuild her for the last year, whilst living in a container at the submarine base.

Terry is completely enraptured, while I'm stranded on the cracked and

15

sweltering tarmac with the weeds and the horrible submarine, trying to keep the dogs cool. But soon I have a friend, a beautiful Spanish girl wearing a bikini and a huge smile, who rides up on a bicycle. Rosa speaks no English and little French, and I speak virtually no Spanish, but mostly due to her enthusiasm we find a common language. In between bouts of conversation she cycles round and round beside the boat, looking up at Miguel, and I think she's in love with him. She talks about him a great deal. He's her friend, and she comes from Spain to visit him several times a year. She stays at another friend's flat in Lorient. Miguel is in love with his boat, she says.

Rosa is outgoing: she tells me about her mother, who is from Asturia, and her father who is from Galicia. They're retired now and living in Asturia. She has a sister named Anjelica, who is a talented artist and is looking after Rosa's golden retriever while Rosa is visiting Miguel. Rosa comes from Corunna, a name that always takes me back to my schooldays when we giggled heartlessly as we recited 'The Burial of Sir John Moore after Corunna,' which at the time had seemed extraordinarily entertaining: *"We buried him darkly at dead of night, **The sods** with our bayonets turning, By the struggling moonbeam's misty light, And the lanthorn dimly burning."*

Since the Prestige oil tanker sank and flooded the Galician coast with twenty million gallons of oil, the local tourist industry is in decline, so Rosa is currently jobless. She doesn't mind, because she hates working in an office anyway.

Terry and Miguel are talking obsessively about sailing, and Rosa is cycling round in her bikini with her beautiful, tanned, slim body, gazing up at Miguel. She looks eighteen. She wants to take the dogs for a walk. She loves dogs, she says. We get them out of the van and they tow us around for fifteen minutes; then they're gasping so Rosa cycles off and brings back a bucket of water for them. I ask how old she is, and she astonishes me by replying that she's 33. I laugh and shake my head, and on a piece of paper write down 23? No, she laughs, writing down 33. Then she tells me about her boyfriend, who lives in Madrid and used to be an engineer, but now he has become an actor, which pleases her because it's a far more interesting career than engineering.

Is Miguel married, I ask tentatively, because he wears a wedding ring. Yes, she beams, his very beautiful wife is at home in Portugal, expecting their second baby in December. They're both very happy and she is happy for them.

She produces a digital camera and takes a photo of the two of us with our arms around each other. Finally I tear Terry away from Miguel and Côte d'Or II, and Rosa gives me a great hug, and I give her my bracelet. I'm totally charmed by this lovely girl who is content to spend weeks

16

cycling around this strange area while Miguel works on his boat, her boyfriend is acting in Madrid, and Miguel and his wonderful wife are joyfully expecting another baby in Portugal.

Terry is very excited; he hopes Miguel will launch the boat in July. He has invited Terry to sail with him, possibly across the Atlantic. Mentally Terry is already packing his ditty bag.

The Quiberon peninsula is one long stationary stream of traffic stretching into the distance, so we head for Carnac to visit the church of St Cornely, patron saint of Carnac and horned animals. Also we want to see the ranks of megaliths said to be legions of soldiers petrified by Cornely to stop them chasing him. But there is no parking space to be had. Everybody and his wife are here today taking advantage of the unseasonably hot weather. We decide to go to Vannes for the night, via the Gulf of Morbihan, where the inland sea, says legend, was created by the tears of the fairies driven from Merlin's enchanted forest, Brocéliande. They tossed into it garlands of flowers which became the islands of Houat, the duck, Hoédic, the duckling, and Belle-Île, the Isle of Beauty.

The largest island in the gulf is the Île aux Moines (Monks' Island), half a mile from the second largest, the Île d'Arz (Bear Island). According to local legend (Brittany is very strong on legends!) the two islets were once linked by a narrow causeway, but the two communities hated each other. One were sailors who considered themselves superior to the others who were mere fishermen. When a boy from the Île aux Moines fell in love with a girl from the Île d'Arz, his parents imprisoned him with the monks. Every day the lovesick Arz girl crossed the causeway to sing beneath the walls of the monastery. The girl was so beautiful that she literally took away the breath from the inhabitants of the Île aux Moines. Believing this the Devil's work, the Prior called upon God's help. His prayer was answered: the sea rose and submerged the causeway. The girl was drowned and the two isles were separated for ever. Most of the legends in Brittany seem to end tragically.

Vannes has some sensationally pretty timbered buildings and a quaint old-fashioned cinema with a fading fascia bedecked with plaster roses. While the municipal campsite has a spacious lawned area for tents and caravans, campervans are restricted to a bleak and crowded tarmac patch. Our neighbours are a friendly Dutch couple who kindly lend Terry a bike so he can pedal to the nearest shop to buy something for us to eat.

I greatly admire the Dutch lady. She is strong-willed, and knows exactly what she does and does not like. She most particularly doesn't like cooking, so she doesn't cook. Ever. No ifs. No buts. Fortunately her partner loves cooking, so while she sits and relaxes he happily takes care of the catering department. When I raise the subject with Terry he just

17

grunts.

Next morning we stop to let the dogs run at an unusually unpleasant beach of pebbles and coarse sand. Several giant beige-tinted jellyfish lie dead upon the beach, like transparent bowler hats. Dobby tries to eat one, but its size and resilient texture defeat him. After a while he gives up and joins Tally who is making inroads into a dead seagull.

For our breakfast we go to the historic Viking town of la Roche-Bernard in the Vilaine estuary. In the quiet square a life-sized silhouette of a kneeling man awaits the guillotine blade that will decapitate him. It's a reminder of the bloody Vendée rebellion when the revolting peasants and Chouans engaged in civil war against the Republicans. Nowadays la Roche-Bernard is a peaceful and lovely small town of cobbled streets, medieval buildings with brightly coloured shutters, and stone walls sprouting clumps of poppies and wild flowers. A most pleasant place to visit on a summery morning. Yachts relax in orderly ranks in the river, overlooked by two rusting cannons pointing at a row of beehives in a field of cornflowers. The guns are from the great 17th century warship La Couronne, a reminder that the town was once an important naval shipyard.

3

Pays de la Loire

Loire-Atlantique

Oh Brittany, what a wonderful experience you have given us, with your magnificent scenery, beautiful towns, glorious food, intriguing legends and tropical weather. Will any other part of France delight us as much, I wonder?

Now we are in the Loire-Atlantique, once part of Brittany and still regarded as such by many Bretons, but currently engulfed into the Pays-de-la-Loire region.

Wobbly foals filled with *joie de vivre* totter behind their mothers through marshy fields of buttercups in the Brière Regional Natural Park. We are on our way to le Croisic where a brochure says there is a splendid aquarium with a restaurant where the food is served by divers. The aquarium closes for lunch just as we arrive, so we go directly to the restaurant. The waiters and waitresses are ordinary terrestrial creatures, and not divers at all. We'd visualized them swimming to the tables somehow bearing trays of food and drink without it getting wet or floating away. Terry is irritated and insists I ask the manageress where the aquatic servers are. She looks at me blankly and plainly hasn't the least idea what I am talking about. Terry is hungry and not at his normally good-natured best. He wants me to cross-examine the lady, and force her to produce waterborne staff; but I am already sufficiently embarrassed by the strange looks she is giving me, so I say if he wants to get involved in that kind of contretemps he'll have to speak French, and the misunderstanding is probably due to translation error.

Despite being served by earthlings, our meal is excellent. We have *moules* with *frites*, followed by salted caramel *crépes*. The addition of a pinch of local salt does something very special to the caramel. We are washing it down with teacups of cider when suddenly the restaurant plunges into semi-darkness. There is much shouting and yelling, some laughter and a worried conversation. The power failure has knocked the credit-card payment machine out of action, and a person trying to pay for his meal claims to have no cash. The manageress has no intention of letting him escape without paying. After a few minutes he reluctantly admits that he has a chequebook, and settles up slightly sheepishly.

I am worried about the well-being of the fish if the electricity is going to be off for long, but our waiter says there is a generator for emergencies and the fish will be fine. The aquarium opens as we finish eating. It is a fabulous underwater world of infant oysters and baby lobsters – quarrelsome characters with their claws bound to prevent them mauling each other; infinitesimal plankton and cute young sturgeon with tip-tilted noses. Herbaceous borders of sea anemones waft their tentacles dreamily at spider crabs and the fearsome-looking but harmless wolf fish. A spiny lumpsucker with Brigitte Bardot lips and big eyes mouths silent messages to us through the glass. Sunflower stars almost three feet in diameter cheerily wave their numerous limbs.

Crossing a walkway to visit the Australian sharks and manta rays, we are shocked to see into a room where white-coated people are busily chopping up fish. However, this is not a massacre of the inhabitants, but lunch for the penguins who are swimming around excitedly in their pool.

Gurnards line up in an orderly row too with their sad faces and funny legs all round their heads. Ethereal jellyfish float around in a glass cylinder. We read that they are related to sea anemones, composed of 90 per cent water, extremely fragile, with a short lifespan. Not much going for them, really.

A large spider crab stands upright rubbing together what look like little hands, like Uriah Heep, while odd things in its mouth move up and down like piano keys. Next to the yellow feathery corals are incubating spotted dogfish eggs, huge things like stag beetles; they undergo an eight-month incubation period and we can clearly see the embryos moving inside the casings. Seahorses prance and hook themselves to coral branches with their curly little tails, and everywhere it seems as if the fish are watching us as much as we are watching them.

As well as the exotic residents are the more mundane, those normally destined to end up coated in batter and surrounded by fried potatoes. It is only small swivelling eyes on the floor of a tank that betray the presence of flatfish-like turbot and plaice camouflaged in the sand. The iridescent shoals of mackerel twisting in a perfectly choreographed aquatic ballet are such sensitive souls, explains a notice, that they cannot survive longer than ten seconds out of water, or being touched. And all cuckoo wrasse are born female, and pink, but as they mature some of them change into males, and turn blue! "Pink for a little girl, blue for a boy," in the words of the song. Amazing. Le Croisic aquarium is every bit as wonderful as it claims to be. It might be a while before we can eat fish without feeling uneasy.

We are going to Guérande next. Over the last twenty years a new generation of *paludiers* has been working to revitalise the industry for which the town was once renowned – salt. Alongside the road, workers use traditional wooden rakes to scrape the grey crust from the salt pans. The town is busy with holidaymakers flocking to the gift shops to buy bags of damp, coarse grey salt, or the finer and more expensive pure white "flowers of salt." We take the dogs for a walk through the walled medieval town. Tally spots a cat in an alley and catching Terry unawares almost jerks him off his feet as he tries to follow it. A cluster of camera-laden Japanese tourists scatter in panic.

After buying a small linen bag of salt to support the local industry, we splutter along in Tinkerbelle to the fine beach at Pornichet. Tally, whose manners are normally as impeccable as his breeding, runs down the sands to where a couple are peacefully relaxing. The man lies on his stomach, propped up on his elbows reading a newspaper. Beside him his wife is on her back soaking up the sun. Tally stops three feet from the newspaper-reading man's elbow, adopts an unmistakable posture, and proceeds to defecate copiously. There is only one thing I feel I can decently do, and that is to walk in the opposite direction acting as if Tally is nothing to do with me. From a safe distance I see Terry assess the situation. As he talks to the man I watch their body language to see how difficult the man is going to be. He hands Terry a sheet from his newspaper, and stands up. While Terry makes a neat parcel, the man makes a fuss of Tally. When Dobby joins the party the sunbathing lady plays with him and I feel it is safe to venture over and join them.

They breed German pointers, and declare they have fallen in love with both our dogs. Although Tally is the aristocrat and Dobby of unknown origins, it's usually Dobby who attracts the most attention. He is a very handsome animal, and people frequently ask what breed he is. I once heard Terry describing him as a *'braque noir,'* translating as a black pointer. Tally is what the French call a *'braque hongrois'* – a Hungarian Vizsla. I tell people that Dobby is a *'chien de carton'* – a cardboard box dog because he was found in one.

Our new friends keep stroking the two dogs and saying how beautiful they are, which is quite true. They are beautiful dogs. While we are talking and watching them play, Dobby runs back and urinates for what seems like eternity all over the lady's white fluffy beach towel. Mortification just doesn't describe how we feel, but they laugh and recall situations where their dogs had similarly embarrassed them. They send their daughter and her boyfriend back to their house – a few yards from the beach – to bring their own dogs out to play. While they chase each other into the sea, the man tells us he is a journalist on the local newspaper. They have spent the day on a replica sailing ship which is departing from Saint-Nazaire this evening. If we watch the headland we'll see it passing.

He urges us not to park in isolated places for the night; the days are gone when it was safe to do so. These are dangerous times: this morning the body of a young boy abducted some time previously was found in a lake in Guérande.

We drive on to the harbour at Saint-Nazaire, where a three-masted square-rigger named the Stadt Amsterdam is preparing to sail. People scramble about on her decks amid a jungle of ropes and blocks; they climb rope ladders and edge out on to the spars of her masts like circus performers, loosening the sails. The Dutch ensign flies from her stern, and a courtesy French tricolour from her standing rigging. Both flags are comprised of red, white and blue stripes; sailors say you can tell which is which because the Dutch do it lying down, and the French standing up. There is a small crowd watching, a dozen people at most, the men all enthralled and the women visibly bored and cold as the sun goes down and a nippy wind springs up.

"I hope they sail her out," says Terry, "and don't use her engine." We wait in the wind, and the ship waits for the wind. We wait, and she waits, until the tide had risen to the level of the water in the harbour and the lock gates open.

Terry is spellbound as the upper and lower topsails on her foremast and main mast unfurl and are sheeted in to trap the wind. Slowly gathering momentum, she glides out into the Atlantic Ocean towards the sunset, driven only by the wind. It's a scene from the romantic age of sail.

After the ship has disappeared into the distance we drive down to the docks to enjoy la Nuit des Docks. This is Saint-Nazaire's rather original idea of using clever lighting focused on various structures around the dockland to bring it to life at night. As dusk falls the lights came on; giant gantries and cranes twinkle, and the warehouse walls glow green and red, the lights reflecting in the black waters. The coloured spectrums change slowly, subtly, and more buildings emerge into the scene. By the time we leave the whole docklands have been transformed into a Technicolor post-apocalyptic scene.

It's late and we have no idea where to stay. Had we not met the journalist this afternoon we might have found a deserted place at the back of the docks for the night. We decide to heed his warning and drive until we find a car park opposite the Mairie at strangely-named Saint-Michel-Chef-Chef. The campervans have barely sufficient room between them to open the doors, but we squeeze in. It might not be very inviting, but it is at least safe.

Early next morning a wedding party arrives. The bride is magnificent, like a galleon in full sail, enormous but pretty, with pearls in her hair and a full-length billowing white satin dress trimmed with pink rosebuds. Her bridegroom is thin and looks bewildered. All their friends' cars are decorated with net posies and ribbons flying from their aerials, a tradition in France. Later they'll all drive in convoy hooting loudly in celebration. Terry asks me to go and talk to the owner of a nearby campervan similar to Tinkerbelle, to ask if he has problems with his gearbox. Tinkerbelle's gear lever has started flopping around limply. The man is talkative and friendly with a pencil-thin moustache and a worried-looking wife. I explain about Tinkerbelle's loose gear lever. He puts a hand on my arm, and in a sympathetic tone says that our gearbox is totally *foutou* – a French word that translates into English with varying degrees of vulgarity, but the bottom line means that it's had it. It's the worst possible thing to happen, he says, because it's impossible to repair and, worse still, impossible to find a replacement part. Very soon our gearbox will fail completely, just as his did in Angoulême last year. He asks his wife to corroborate the unfortunate episode. She nods briefly and looks away. Oh! What a horrible experience they'd had, he remembers: they had to abandon their vehicle and at hideous expense hire a car to get home to Saint-Nazaire. Then there was the exhausting hunt for a replacement; but nobody manufactures parts for these vehicles any more. He estimates we have perilously little time left before our gearbox gives up the ghost entirely. It is our *pignon baladeur* that has gone; he hopes we don't have far to go, because he very much doubts we'll get there. I listen in terrible dismay, translating to Terry and envisioning us stranded on the road hundreds of miles from home, with no *pignon baladeur*, two dogs and several thousand miles still to travel. Terry is frustrated because I don't know how to translate a *pignon baladeur* and anyway, he asks, how does the man know what the problem is if he hasn't even looked at Tinkerbelle's gearbox? I don't know, I say, all I'm doing is trying to translate.

The little man watches us with crafty eyes, and throws us a lifeline. It is our lucky day, because when he'd managed, at unspeakable cost and with unimaginable difficulty to locate the part for his own van, he'd bought not one, but two. The other, which was by far the better of the two and virtually new, is in his garage at this very moment, not twelve miles from where we stand. As you might guess, something of such rarity is worth a fortune, almost as much in fact as we paid for all of Tinkerbelle. His wife shuffles and looks anywhere but at us. We thank him and tell him it is too expensive and we will take our chances with our foutou gearbox. He shrugs, says *"Comme vous voulez,"* (It's up to you), climbs into his cab and drives away.

23

"Add a *pignon baladeur* to the list," says Terry, "and when we find a breaker's yard, we'll get one there." To add to the anxiety of Tinkerbelle's thundering exhaust, suspect brakes and temperamental clutch I add the fear that our adventure will be wrecked by whatever the *pignon baladeur* is.

The landscape on the Atlantic coast is flatter, and more open than Brittany. Bright white bungalows with blue shutters and pantiles take the place of stone cottages and slate roofs, and little coves become long straight beaches. Intermittent disused gun emplacements squat along the coast, an ugly reminder of the past. People dig in the seaweed-carpeted beach, poking things out of the sand. A chap wades into the sea in a wetsuit, while a couple paddle past in a canoe that looks about to sink. Two small boys pedal demonically through the traffic. It's the seaside in full swing.

Vendée

Skirting the Baie de Bourgneuf, where herds of fat ponies graze the salt marshes, we cross into the Vendée and the Marais Breton. The road leads through the muddy oyster- and mussel-producing port of le Collet, a flat area trembling in a violent easterly wind that whistles and wails through the masts of the boats in the harbour.

Tally has developed a proprietorial attitude regarding Tinkerbelle. He protests loudly, somewhat hysterically if cyclists, pedestrians or other dogs come anywhere near. Dobby tilts his head in puzzlement, unsure whether he should bark.

At Beauvoir-sur-Mer we follow a sign to *la Maison de l'Âne* (The House of the Donkey). Some fifty donkeys, mules and horses live here with a collection of assorted poultry. They're the children of a dark, handsome man called Paulo Dieumegard. When we arrive Paulo is perched on a three-legged stool in a cosy barn, milking a placid donkey mare into a plastic jug. Her foal is running up and down the next-door stall, yelling that his lunch is being stolen. Paulo assures us that the mares are only milked once a week, so their babies aren't deprived of their natural food. Donkey or asses' milk is pure white with a firm frothy head any beer could be proud of. It tastes, Paulo says, similar to coconut milk, and is rich in vitamins and minerals. Ideal for people with skin problems, but no good for making butter or cheese because it has a very low fat content. However, it makes an excellent soap and is a far more practical way of keeping the complexion up to scratch than trying to wallow about in a bathful like Cleopatra. And cheaper, too: asses' milk sells for something like £12 a pint. Paulo's passion is for saving rare breeds on the verge of extinction. We walk around meeting different

24

breeds of donkeys and petting their furry, fluffy foals with spindly legs and tiny jewel-like hooves, ears that are far too big and velvety muzzles that explore our fingers and clothing. The animals are clearly well-loved and cared for and in radiant good health. Paolo likes to feed his animals organically, and tells us they thrive on the coarse grass of the salty marshes. La Maison de l'Âne is not a commercial venture but a labour of true love. We buy a bar of lavender-scented asses' milk soap for Vivien who, every time I phone her is either cooking a meal for friends, bathing and grooming one of the animals, redesigning the garden or retiling a roof.

As it's low tide we are able to drive over the causeway and on to the Île de Noirmoutier. The roads are lined with stalls selling oysters, mussels and locally-produced sea salt, and almost every inch of the seven-mile causeway is filled with parked cars and dry seaweed. Gulls and egrets share the vast expanse of sand with scores of wellie-wearing people armed with buckets and plastic bags, all prodding around in the small pools of water to excavate the shellfish lurking there. Frequent signs warn of the danger of drowning when the tide comes in, but the sea is invisible, withdrawn to beyond the horizon. It's difficult to imagine how quickly it can cover the sands and the causeway. With no vehicles in sight, it's a seaside scene from an earlier century.

Our overnight stop is at Saint-Jean-de-Monts, a resort with a magnificent golden sandy beach, long seafront and wall-to-wall modern low-rise apartment blocks. A couple of hundred yards from the beach is the area allocated for campervans. It's cramped, with about 18" between each vehicle, and the campers already there are doing their utmost to discourage newcomers. One girl flails her arms around shouting *"C'est complet."* (It's full). Terry manages to squeeze past her and into a narrow slot, leaving just sufficient space for us to get in and out. It's not the most attractive place to spend an evening but it is free, and with Tinkerbelle critically in need of new parts we must make sacrifices where we can to establish the contingency fund we hadn't allowed for.

At sparrows' crack we're on the beach, which is raked by a bitter wind and empty apart from a scattering of vacant mussel and razor clam shells, and two more of the giant jellyfish. Dobby retrieves a dead seagull from the surf and runs around joyously with it. He stares reproachfully when Terry says he cannot bring it into the van and play with it on our bed.

Even this early in the morning there's heavy traffic on the Corniche. This is such a different world from the unspoilt wildness of Brittany. It is full of new houses and buildings, highly developed and geared for mass tourism, filled with camp sites, playgrounds, quad-biking parks, giant slides and pizza stands, and a mini-golf park dominated by a giant green plastic frog, several plastic penguins, and three life-sized skewbald plastic cows. Most appealing is the family of coypus playing among yellow irises on the river banks; least appealing is a sign advertising a three-star campsite named Pong.

Paulo at *la Maison de l'Âne* had recommended a visit to somewhere called le *Potager Extraordinaire* (the Amazing Vegetable Garden) at la Mothe-Achard, a small town a short way inland from our course. Driving through the town we spot a completely naked blonde trollop sprawled in a blatantly, lewdly suggestive pose in the doorway of a café. We drive back round the square for a closer look, which reveals that she is a life-sized plastic model; an equally realistic pirate clambers from an upstairs window with a swag bag over his shoulder. Seems like a town with a sense of humour.

What is it that makes the *Potager Extraordinaire* amazing? Where can I begin? Covering five acres is a collection of the most peculiar, intriguing and truly weird plants we've ever seen, felt, smelt or tasted, as the signs invite us to do. Gherkins explode when touched. There are plants that declare they smell of *crotte de chien* (dog poo). They do. We shan't be buying any seeds. There are tomatoes that look like sweet peppers; aubergines that look like tomatoes; other aubergines that looked like boiled eggs; mile-long beans; and gourds in the most astonishing variety of shapes and sizes, including one rather rude one used by Papuan males to shield Big Jim and the twins. Another is speckled, 7 ft. long and curled round like a coiled snake.

The colours of the vegetables and flowers are startlingly vibrant; purple stems and orange stems, hairy ones, smooth ones, shiny ones and spiky ones. Fruits are long and thin, round or flat. Chocolate cosmos smells like After Eight mints. There are plants with timid leaves that flinch and curl up tightly when touched, and two labyrinths, one of flowers, and one of corn. We all know the difference between a maze and a labyrinth, don't we? In a sunny patch pumpkins relax and grow in preparation for the National Largest Pumpkin competition that takes place in October – the record stands at 780 lbs. The *Potager Extraordinaire* is indisputably the most fascinating garden we've ever visited. There is something to surprise and delight children and adults, gardeners or not.

By lunchtime we are in la Tranche-sur-Mer at a pizza restaurant. The Monaco Formula 1 Grand Prix is just about to start on the television. Like us, the restaurant's two owners are great fans of the sport, and we're happy to sit and watch the start with them before we order. Once the race is under way Eric cooks us the most perfect pizza. He is an adorable person with a kind, gentle and rather sad face. He tells us he is sad because his girlfriend has to live in Mexico to look after her mother. Eric hopes to make enough money during the summer from his new pizza business to enable him to go to Mexico to visit her.

4

Poitou-Charentes

Charente-Maritime

<u>The Marais Poitevin</u> is France's answer to Venice, 375 square miles of flat marshlands laced by a network of tree-lined natural and man-made waterways. Cattle graze the fields, and are moved from place to place in flat-bottomed boats in the absence of roads. We spend the night there at a pleasant campsite at Marans. Tally manages to escape and disappears to chase rabbits with Terry in pursuit. While they are gone I find some fragments of plastic on the floor. I piece them together until they form a thermometer and hygrometer, which had been fixed to the wall of the campervan. They are completely destroyed. Dobby has been at work again. During the night a rattling sound outside wakes us, and we open the door to find a hedgehog helping himself to leftover dog biscuits. He ignores us and continues munching noisily.

Staying opposite us is a diminutive French couple in a caravan, on holiday with their dog and their canary. They come from the Cher *département*, right in the centre of France. He is eighty-two and she is eighty. They don't find travelling as easy as they used to, so they keep their caravan parked permanently on this site. It's easier to drive backwards and forwards without having to hitch up the caravan each time, and they particularly enjoy the Marais. Have we been out on the water yet? If not, we really should.

Leaving the dogs in the van parked in the shade, we walk down to the river and hire a small motor boat. Terry steers it through the thick green water, where moorhens and ducks feed amongst yellow irises growing around the wooden jetties. Pretty gardens filled with roses, small orchards and fishing cabins stretch down the banks. It is peaceful floating along amongst the duckweed for a couple of hours, and as we make our way back we are able to enjoy a small drama. The girl who we had paid to hire the boat is in earnest conversation with an anxious lady who is pointing upstream to where a boat similar to ours, with several people aboard, is stranded against the bank. The passengers look helpless, embarrassed and glum. The girl wrings her hands; she and the woman start walking towards the stranded boat, then turn back. The woman hurries away, calling something over her shoulder. Shortly a man in yellow rubber trousers appears. He glances at the marooned party and leaps down into a boat like a cowboy jumping on to his horse from the window of a saloon. Full throttle, he charges up the river, swirling to an abrupt halt like a downhill skier. He turns the stranded boat round, restarts the engine and guides it slowly back to the mooring, where the passengers disembark in silence. Hey ho.

The maize is already a foot high, the still green water in the canals is filled with chirruping frogs, and a strong easterly wind is buffeting plants and trees almost to the ground. In a fallow field we watch a buzzard flapping as it struggles to get airborne with a heavy load. Terry goes to investigate and finds a newly dead rabbit. The buzzard keeps trying to fly off with it, but can only lift it a few inches before it has to let go. Three crows sit calmly a few yards away, watching and waiting their moment.

On the map is somewhere called Pointe Saint-Clément, which looks as if it might be a wonderfully wide sandy beach, but when we arrive it's just a large expanse of muddy scrub littered with dead oysters, fish heads and assorted dirty debris. The dogs think it is wonderful.

We haven't had a chance to get on the Internet since we left home, and have no idea of what has been happening in the world outside Tinkerbelle, so we drive into la Rochelle to find a cybercafé. This turns out to be one of the most frustrating experiences of my life as I try without success to remember our latest password whilst wrestling with a French keyboard which is fundamentally different to an English one. Forty minutes and seven euros later, we've achieved nothing, so we console ourselves with coffee and hot chocolate and two gigantic toasted cheese sandwiches. Then we head to Rochefort to make an early landing for the night at the *'Le Bateau'* campsite.

Inside the sanitary block, which is designed to look like a huge boat, a man sits cross-legged on a washbasin with a blissful smile on his face, listening to a CD player through a headset. It seems an odd way to spend an afternoon, but *chacun à son goût*....

The site is next to the Charente estuary, and we spend several peaceful hours sitting in the sun watching boats and barges sailing past. On a small lake two handsome white geese stand on an upturned rowing boat studying with apparent interest some small children paddling around in canoes. As an ochre sunset splits the ice-blue of the sky from the silver-blue of the river, a bat swoops overhead. During the night another hedgehog raids the leftovers in the dogs' bowls.

In Rochefort we are spoilt for choice for entertainment, there is so

29

much to do and so many things to see. We begin by walking down to the *Corderie Royale*, the royal ropeworks, through an avenue lined with palms and tulip trees just coming into bloom. The classically elegant 17th century royal ropeworks looks more like a stately home than a factory. More than 1,200 ft. long, the whole structure is balanced on oak beams to support it on the marshy land. They stopped manufacturing rope here in 1967, and now the *Corderie* is a maritime museum and library, faithfully and entirely rebuilt after being burned down in 1944. Under construction a few steps away is a replica of the Hermione, the 18th century frigate in which Lafayette sailed to America to join the fight against the beastly English. One day, she'll sail to Boston.

When we go for lunch, there are some English people behind us with a little boy who repeatedly bangs the table loudly with his fork, sits on the ground and is generally being awkward. One of the four adults hoists him on to his shoulders and takes him for a walk. We order grilled squid, which comes in bleached rubbery sheets that are impossible to cut; they skid around the plate trying to outrun the knife. When we do succeed in hacking off a morsel, it is like chewing a piece of car tyre. It makes me gag, so we wrap it in a napkin for the dogs. Behind us I hear the English people asking the waitress in pidgin-French what calmar are.

"Fish," she responds unhelpfully.

"What kind of fish?" they ask.

"White fish."

"Oh, fine, that sounds OK." They all order it. I wonder whether to warn them. But perhaps they'll think I've been eavesdropping. By the time their order arrives we are just leaving, so we'll never know what they thought of the white fish.

In a quiet road a removal team is loading a truck with paintings and pots of geraniums, bringing out larger items of furniture down a ladder from a second floor window. We make our way to an unassuming side street and a very ordinary-looking front door. It was once the home of a retiring, diminutive naval officer named Julien Viaud, born in 1850. His name may not mean much to many people. However, as the writer Pierre Loti, a *nom de plume* derived from an exotic blushing flower, he would become the youngest ever member of the *Académie Française* and one of the great names in early 20th century French romantic literature.

His house is two adjacent buildings, and the astonishing interior remains as it was while he lived there. When Loti's father, a town clerk, was accused of theft, he brought disgrace on the family, who were reduced to living in two small rooms. Loti joined the navy, and from his travels around the world, mainly in the Middle and Far East countries he loved and wrote about, he collected hundreds of artefacts with which the house is crammed. The first rooms are conventional, with family portraits and red velvet wall hangings, a piano and several uncomfortable-looking chairs where Mrs Loti received and entertained her visitors. When selecting a wife, Loti had three criteria: she had to be rich, she had to be shorter than five foot four so that he didn't have to look up to her, and she had to be a Protestant like Loti's mother. From her portrait she looks amiable enough, if not exactly beautiful.

After the drawing room things start to become interesting. Loti never forgot his family's early humiliation by the Rochefortais, and as he became rich and famous he flaunted his wealth. A vast chimney piece dominates the Renaissance hall from which two grand staircases lead to the next floor; chandeliers hang from the ceiling, which reaches right up to the roof, and the walls are draped with heavy tapestries. This is the room where he held lavish parties to impress the locals who queued up outside to peer through the windows. At one party two hundred invited guests paraded through the streets in rickshaws, carrying a young boy dressed as the Empress of China on a palanquin to impress the onlookers, who were unaware that the last Chinese Empress had died two centuries previously. Flamboyant is an understatement when describing little Loti, who loved to dress like an Arab prince.

Climb another staircase to the second floor, past walls festooned with exotic hangings. The Turkish room is filled with silken cloths, Persian rugs and tasselled cushions, brass trays and hookahs, and the walls decorated with oriental weaponry. An adjacent small room has a glass ceiling where Loti could lie looking up at the stars and imagine himself in the desert. The pièce de résistance is an entire mosque brought from Damascus, with marble pillars, patterned tiles, stained-glass windows, a fountain, and five sarcophagi. Our passionate young guide tells us that when Loti entertained young ladies (no mention of what Mrs Loti was doing at the time) a servant would hide in one of the sarcophagi and start moaning, in order to frighten the damsel into the writer's arms. In the mosque room is the headstone from the tomb of a Turkish girl whom Loti loved for years, and promised to return to one day. But when he finally did, she was long dead and buried, so he had a replica made of her headstone, stole the original and secretly brought it back to Rochefort.

All these rooms glow with a kaleidoscope of brilliant colours from deepest red to brightest blue. In total contrast, Loti's bedroom is a small ascetic room with plain white walls hung with Hindu, Catholic, Buddhist and Protestant icons. Obsessed with death, the writer spent his life seeking a religion he could believe in. He was complex and intriguing man of many talents: naval captain, writer, collector. Also a skilled acrobat, as a photograph on a small table shows. Of all the museums and places of interest in Rochefort, if we had to choose just one to visit, it would be Loti's magical house.

31

On our way out of town we pass a sign to the *Conservatoire de la Bégonia*. I rather like begonias, and persuade Terry against his better judgment that we should go in to have a look round. We buy tickets to join a guided tour that is just starting. The giant greenhouse is crammed with begonias of all shapes and sizes and colours, but all begonias and all looking very much like the begonias all around them. The guide speaks French very fast, at great length and in unfathomable technical detail about the personal habits of begonias, and we hardly understand anything. Nothing, in fact. Standing in the humid and incredibly hot tunnel is like being in a rain forest during a heatwave. We decide to embark on an independent tour, but the guide tells us sharply we must stick with the group. Nobody is permitted to wander around alone.

Over the next five minutes we progress about six inches and are still in the cuttings area, a sea of very small stems with newborn leaves sprouting from them. We are hot, sticky and bored, beginning to feel a certain resentment towards begonias in general and the guide in particular. I attract his attention and apologize that we have to leave. He shrugs his shoulders and turns back to his more appreciative audience. As we escape from this humid hell I am sure I hear him make a disparaging remark about ignorant foreigners. This is probably somewhere that would most appeal to anybody who is totally passionate about begonias.

Our route takes us past Rochefort's *'transbordeur'* bridge across the river Charente, the last remaining one of its kind in France. It had to be high enough that ships could sail beneath it, but that would have required an unfeasibly long and steep incline for vehicles to access it. The answer was a tall metal framework spanning the river, supported by two metal pillars, from which a moving platform was suspended by steel cables. Vehicles drove on to the platform which moved over to the opposite bank with the stationary vehicles upon it. It's an historic monument now, and open only to pedestrians and cyclists.

In Moëze there is a sign pointing to '*la croix hosanniere.*' While Terry entertains the dogs I go to find out what a hosanniere cross is. Planted in the centre of the town's cemetery, it's a gigantic Renaissance tower perched upon 20 Corinthian columns, and was at one time an assembly point for religious processions. It's like a Greek temple and I estimate that it's nearly 50 ft. high. All around it the dead slumber peacefully in the sunshine, although a couple of headstones are tilted upwards as if their incumbents might climb out at any moment.

After driving through a rather bleak area of salt marshes, we arrive in the small, attractive medieval walled town of Brouage. The restaurants are doing a cracking trade at tables spilling over the pavements of the cobbled streets. In its heyday, before it became silted up, the town was the salt capital of Europe, as well as an important arsenal used by

32

Richelieu as a base for his merciless attack on la Rochelle. Samuel de Champlain, who sailed to Canada and established a trading post that would become the city of Quebec was born here. Quite an impressive pedigree for a little place in this backwater of flatlands and river courses, cattle, trees and bushes. We seldom know what to expect when we set off each morning. We don't know how far we'll go, nor what we'll find: that is the whole idea, and the joy of it. Discovering little jewels like Brouage is a bonus.

At 4.00 p.m. we're in Marennes where the temperature is 40°C (104 F); the millions of oysters in their beds must be close to cooking. Outside a butcher's shop is a happy, beaming wooden pig supporting a blackboard advertising a long list of gruesome pork products. It's mystifies me how French butchers came up with the concept of animals joyous at being killed and eaten.

We drift along the Atlantic coast, around the Bay of Biscay and down the Gironde estuary, until we reach Chenac-St-Seurin-d'Uzet, a delightfully unspoilt typically French small town. The campsite is next to a muddy, marshy inlet populated with sludgy-sided river boats and a decaying half-sunken catamaran. There is something indefinably pleasing about this place, as if we have roamed into a part of the world forgotten by time and immune to progress. It is France untouched by tourism. A herd of twenty horses are galloping around in the marshes in a choreographed equine ballet, twisting and turning like a shoal of fish. The church clock sounds the hour twice; if you miss the number of rings the first time you can catch them a minute later. The mechanism of the bell is a kind of metal lollipop that creates a rather feeble, tinny sound.

Dobby has turned green! His coat is entirely covered in large green mosquitoes. They swoop down upon us like wedding guests on the buffet, as if they've been waiting all year for a meal to arrive. Every smack kills dozens of them and leaves us smeared with green and red smudges. Dobby isn't bothered; his coat is thick, but he's confused as to why we are swatting him, albeit very gently, with a tea-towel.

Terry forgot to remove his slippers from the van this morning, and Dobby has eaten part of one of them. Terry feels it is unreasonable for Dobby to chew things that don't belong to him when he has at least half a dozen of his own things specifically designed to be chewed. He is clearly puzzled as to why he can chew some things but not everything, while Tally adopts his normal expression of "I'm a good boy, it wasn't me." He's always anxious not to be suspected of any wrongdoing.

Distracted by the battle of the mosquitoes, I turn on the gas cooker and forget to light it. Later, when I strike a match we narrowly escape being blown into orbit. Luckily no damage done except for part of my hair and my eyebrows being burned off.

33

Next morning we head towards Blaye. In the peaceful and productive backwaters of the Gironde, in villages ignored by the advance of time, the countryside is at its most beautiful: the gardens romantic jungles of roses and lilies, the sunflowers six inches high, the wheat starting its transformation from green to gold, the hallowed vines all of a uniform height and bushiness, and not a weed in sight. This is wine territory, and every few hundred yards there are signs offering *dégustations* of wine and Pineau de Charentes, the sweet fortified wine that is one of the region's most popular products.

It's mid-day when we reach Mortagne-sur-Gironde. A notice advises that ducks have priority, dogs must be kept on a lead and vehicles driven at walking pace. Sure enough, there are ducks waddling all over the road by the harbour. It's Wednesday, half-day for schoolchildren, and they trudge along in singles or small groups, weighed down with heavy satchels. Standing in the road defiantly, rather foolishly is a hoopoe, a bird of great charm and apparently no intelligence whatsoever. It bounces out of the way grudgingly when Terry hoots it.

In a region famed worldwide for its fish we anticipate a good lunch. I go in to enquire at a small rural restaurant whether they have fish on their menu. The man smiles and says, yes, we have roast pork, and beef, and chicken. I say we don't eat any kind of meat, but we do eat fish, and did they have any fish today? The man says they also have pork chops, and lamb, both of which are excellent. I give up, and we drive on. Everywhere we go the restaurants serving fish are either closed or full.

Driven by hunger and desperation we arrive at a large supermarket, and even there the restaurant is closing. The waitress is wiping the tables with a damp cloth as the leftover food disappears back into the kitchens. We plead for something to eat, and the manageress takes pity on us. We have a meal of something that can't really be described as food, but for which we are grateful.

5

Coastal Aquitaine

Gironde

Afterwards we drive in to <u>Blaye</u>, whose citadel and fortifications were built by France's greatest military engineer, Sébastien Le Prestre Vauban. We will see much more of Vauban's work, but it is with Blaye that he said he was most satisfied.

Charlemagne's nephew Roland was buried at Blaye after his legendary death at Roncesvalles. It is also the birthplace of Jaufré Rudel, 12th century troubadour and Prince of Blaye, who according to legend was in love with a lady he'd never met, the Countess of Tripoli. On his way to the Second Crusade he fell mortally ill and was taken to Tripoli, where he finally met his lady-love and fittingly died in her arms.

Not only is Blaye historically interesting and aesthetically delightful, it is absolutely crammed with enticing restaurants. They are all open, and all serving fresh fish. And we are now full of fast food that was past its best.

We queue for the ferry to cross the Gironde, waiting for the whistle to invite us to board, as instructed on the notice. Beside us an old lady sits on a bench in the sunshine with her beautifully groomed apricot poodle. She's watching a group of tanned men playing *boules* on a sandy patch of ground, waving their arms around and yelling, pointing and laughing.

The tariff for the ferry crossing is printed on a board: €7 for a horse, €58.50 for a harvesting machine, while combine harvesters pay €84. How a combine harvester will fit on the ferry isn't clear. It's a teeny-weeny little craft, and Terry isn't certain he can wrestle Tinkerbelle aboard and round the ninety-degree turn required at the bottom of the ramp. However, following a horse-box he makes the turn effortlessly, and the ferry chugs over the narrow estuary and delivers us to Lamarque on the opposite bank.

This is the muddiest place I've seen for years, and reminds me of the

35

Essex coast many years ago when I held our daughter's hand and jumped off a jetty straight into three feet of slimy unexpected mud. She was only two foot six at the time.

Vineyards and châteaux are ten a penny here – Lamarque, Cartillon, Vauban, Haut Moulin, Clos de Relais, Lacour Jacquet, Château Beychevelle with its Viking emblem. Every square inch not occupied with châteaux sprouts perfectly tended vines, each row ending with a rose, whose purpose we'll discover a little later. We settle for the night in Pauillac on a campsite where a young child emits an almost constant squeal like a whistling kettle. Our immediate neighbours are a Swiss couple, retired bakers who have sold their business and are spending their dough touring France in their luxury campervan.

After a shower I am standing at a basin applying face cream, when an elderly lady at the next basin nods approvingly.

"At our age it's so important to take care of our skin," she says. She tells me her age. She is six years older than me.

"Ah yes," she continues, "we're about the same age. And don't forget," she adds, "to pull back your fringe from your forehead sometimes during the day, otherwise you'll have a big white mark there." She toddles away, and her place is taken by the Swiss lady, who remarks that she and her husband are shocked and most disappointed with Pauillac.

"What a dreadfully scruffy place," she says. I say we've only driven round the outskirts on our way to the campsite. It doesn't seem a very inviting town, but maybe, I say hopefully, the centre is more attractive.

"No," she says, pulling a face, "it's all horrible." We set off in the morning to inspect Pauillac for ourselves. Sadly we have to agree with the Swiss lady. It is awful, the most run-down town we've seen since we set out. In fact, the only run-down town. The home of three premiers crus classés, Châteaux Latour, Mouton Rothschild and Lafite Rothschild is dirty, unkempt and entirely unappealing. The restaurants look insalubrious, the pizza parlours more so, and there are unsavoury-looking characters hanging around in grubby alleys. On the main drag is a funfair whose attractions include a giant purple octopus. The few elegant houses on the harbour front are shabby and in need of a fresh coat of paint, apart from the notaire's office which is spick and span. Occasional pots of geraniums are not sufficient to endow it with any charm. The Gironde is a murky sandy colour; across the estuary skulks a nuclear power station, and just outside Pauillac is a sprawling petrochemical complex. Ugh.

We drive round despondently searching for somewhere to eat that doesn't look like a botulism breeding plant, and end up in Saint-Estèphe at a heavenly restaurant named le Peyrat. Terry has a heap of oysters, while I opt for the vegetable soup, which tastes fine although it is strangely full of alphabet spaghetti. The main course of salmon, the cheese and dessert are all as impeccable as the service. The waiter suggests a Château Canet rosé, an organic wine of a rich pink colour and strong raspberry flavour, which is quite sublime. Interestingly, it is not a local wine, but comes from the Languedoc. It is also very reasonably priced.

While we are in the Médoc we decide to visit one of the châteaux open for tours. With many to choose from, at random we book a rendezvous at Château Pichon-Longueville, not to be confused with Château Pichon-Longueville Comtesse de Lalande, which is right next door and was once part of the same estate but isn't any more.

We find <u>Château Pichon-Longueville</u> beseiged by bulldozers and heavy earth-moving equipment rumbling all over the grounds. The château is an elegant building closed to the public. It's fronted by a large square lake embellished with water lilies and carp, and flanked by two modern neo-classical style buildings. It's the product of an American/French architectural collaboration to combine the old with the new. The reception area's terracotta floor tiles are expensive and squeaky. Through portholes in the curved white walls you can look down through on to stainless steel storage vats and python-like pipes running all over the place. Our guide is a stunningly pretty and adorable girl named Aurélie. She is quietly spoken and struggles valiantly with limited English and over the noise of pneumatic drills and heavy machinery. Every so often she turns to ask if I know the English for a particular word.

The tour starts amongst the vines, where Aurélie lists the grape varieties used to produce Pichon-Longueville's wines – Cabernet Sauvignon, Merlot, Cabernet Franc and Petit Verdot. She explains their method of pruning and harvesting by hand, and indicates small brown plastic capsules attached to the ends of the rows. These contain a chemical that deters a particular pest from breeding and harming the vines. The roses planted at the ends of each row fulfil a similar function by attracting diseases away from the vines. The vineyard manager, Aurélie explains, favours organic methods as far as possible.

On the tour with us is an Israeli family, mother, father, their son and his wife. They are on a two-day tour of the Bordeaux vineyards. This morning they 'did' Château Lafite Rothschild, and pronounce favourably upon it. The mother is charming and would like to talk to us. We want to know about life in Israel, but her son, a heavy-set and ferocious-looking man tells her to shut up and listen to the guide. He's a wine fanatic, his mother confides, and we can tell that by the way he stares obsessively at the vines, the barrels and the bottles. He clings fervently to every word Aurélie says, as if she is divulging the combination to the safe of Fort

37

Knox. Once inside the chai – where the wines are stored and aged – he poses in front of the stacks of barrels with his chest outthrust and one foot on the bottom barrel, like a great white hunter with a kill. He orders his quiet, pale wife to take photographs of him. Taking advantage of a brief moment when her son is out of sight, the mother tells us that he is a solicitor. He overhears and barges back into the room, bellowing: "**Barrister**, Mother, I'm a **barrister**." When noise and the language barrier overwhelm her, Aurélie takes a deep breath, blinks several times, smiles exquisitely and tries again. She explains something about corks: Pichon-Longueville use synthetic corks that are hygienic, she says, unlike Château Lafite Rothschild's traditional corks which harbour bacteria. She wrinkles her nose.

By the end of our tour of the production line the racket created by hammering and drilling machinery makes it impossible to hear a single word Aurélie is saying, although we can see her lips still moving determinedly. We finish with a tasting. Terry's the wine buff in our family. Most of them taste the same to me. Neither of us likes the Pichon-Longueville premier wine, grand cru or not. The second fiddle is an improvement, but more than we want to pay and certainly not nearly as good as our lunchtime Château Canet rosé. Aurélie happily confirms that the wines we are tasting are not their best vintage. Our Israeli companion agrees it isn't particularly good. He buys a magnum.

Our next destination is the northern tip of land at the Pointe de Grave on the opposite side to Royan on the Gironde estuary. When we reach Soulac, for some reason Terry decides to stop, and steers Tinkerbelle on to the edge of the road. We recognize instantly this is a mistake, as her front wheels sink down two feet into soft sand. No amount of revving or reversing or using the gears in ingenious ways achieves anything apart from digging us deeper. We hunt around for branches and twigs and ram them into the abyss beneath the tyres. This does not help. Very crossly Terry barks at me to go and find help.

Fifty yards away are several campervans in a small car park. I approach the only English-registered vehicle, next to which a gentleman is sitting peacefully reading his newspaper. I say: "Hello, we're stuck!" He looks up from his paper, rather surprised at this abrupt introduction, and I continue: "I'm really dreadfully sorry to bother you, but my husband has driven us into the sand, and we need some help." Up he jumps and climbs into his vehicle and drives to where Terry is still trying to dig Tinkerbelle out. Our new friend, whose name is Mick, produces a tow rope and hitches the two vehicles together. At this moment a French gentleman arrives, and stops to watch. As Mick climbs into his cab, the Frenchman, whose name is Thierry, takes my arm and pulls me away from the van. Mick starts his engine and nudges forward. The tow rope becomes longer and longer, and thinner and thinner, then starts to fray, and finally explodes. If Thierry hadn't moved me aside when he did, I could have been decapitated.

Thierry says people frequently get stuck here, and the best solution is to jack up the vehicle. But Terry and Mick are confident that towing it out is the answer, so Mick joins the two broken pieces of rope together and tries again. Thierry and I watch the rope repeating its lengthening, thinning and snapping act. After the third attempt the remaining pieces of rope are no longer long enough to be joined together, but another Frenchman stops. M. Miran has a stronger tow rope than Mick's, and it only breaks twice. The road is covered in pieces of rope that look like little fat plaited snakes. M. Miran and Thierry are entertained by our predicament, but determined by one means or another to get us out of the sand. Mick's wife Hilary joins us, and passing motorists park on the side of the road to enjoy the fun. Finally, with Mick towing, using the remaining lengths of rope all knotted together, and with Thierry and M. Miran both heaving, we are back on terra firma.

Montalivet is a pretty seaside town with a 1950s air about it, and has a splendid beach and an abundance of restaurants, bars, night-clubs and gift shops. Everything is closed because the holiday season hasn't really started. Terry says, wherever you look, there's nobody. Gusts of wind whip sand all over us. The dogs are ecstatic to have the beach to themselves, and when they have run until they are tired we drive further south until we arrive at le Pin Sec. It's a surfers' paradise of crashing Atlantic rollers hitting a vast sandy beach hidden behind steep dunes.

There is a simple rustic restaurant, not much more than a shack, adorned with African and South American hangings and masks, and a large photo of Che Guevara. Le Café du Soleil has an appetizing menu of tapas and snacks, all freshly cooked. While we wait for our meal we talk to the Spanish owner Sergio, who wears dreadlocks and has a deep tan and a soft voice. He plays haunting South American music on his sound system, and tells us how he and his girlfriend have taken the restaurant for the season. They don't know if it will be successful, because for some reason all the trees on the campsite have been chopped down so it will be very hot in the summer, with no shade for campers. During the winter they like to travel, usually to Africa, but last winter they'd been to Mexico for a change.

Le Café du Soleil offers a change from traditional French fare. Marie, Sergio's green-eyed girlfriend, serves home-made potato tortillas with a fresh green salad, and it's very pleasant sitting here with the peaceful background music and a glass of wine. Sergio's Old English sheepdog, a birthday present from his parents ten years ago, sprawls out in the shade of an umbrella on the terrace. We ask whether they think we can stay the night in Tinkerbelle. The campsite is officially still closed, but several other people are staying there and we'll be perfectly safe, says Sergio.

So far Terry has done all the driving, saying Tinkerbelle is too awkward for me. But I want to try, so I drive around the car park for a while and then head to the campsite and draw up under one of the few remaining trees. It seems to me a perfectly good place, but Terry directs me forward twenty yards. Obediently I move to where he is pointing, where Tinkerbelle sinks gently down until she is once again up to the tops of her wheels in the sand. I try to reverse, but sand showers everywhere and Tinkerbelle sinks deeper.

Like white rabbits from a magician's hat, four young Germans appear, laughing, and push us out.

During the afternoon Dobby has entirely destroyed the expensive mattress we bought for him. While I am clearing up chunks of foam rubber I find a mangled yellow plastic object of unidentifiable origin and purpose. It must belong to something, it looks as if it might be important, but I can't see any obvious place where it could have come from.

Our location here is idyllic. The dogs can wander at will. The site is almost empty, far from the road, and on the other side of the dunes is the beach where they can play for as long as they like.

After a peaceful night at we wake to the familiar sound of a revving engine and spinning wheels. Jochen and Silke, two of our German rescuers from the previous day are thoroughly bogged in the sand.

"We only went to buy a *baguette*," laughs Silke, "and we've been camping here for five days without getting stuck." Their vehicle is twice the size of Tinkerbelle. We tramp about collecting logs and stones to put under the tyres. Jochen tries to drive out, but only manages to bury our offerings beneath the wheels. We try using doormats, which the sand swallows. With Tinkerbelle's wooden chocks Terry and Jochen build a ramp for the van to drive up. More people come to help, until there is a jolly assembly of ten all heaving and digging and offering suggestions. Somebody else arrives with a powerful vehicle, and with everyone pushing, and the tug-van pulling, the sand lets go of the camper.

During this two-hour interval Dobby hasn't been idle. He has mangled a 2½ lb. Bag of tomatoes, leaving each one perforated with teeth marks and coated with sand; he has also knocked over half a cup of tea on our atlas. All 250 pages are stuck together in a soggy lump. And he's drowned the mobile phone with the tea, and ripped to shreds the remains of his mattress. Tally is sitting as far away from him as possible, distancing himself from any blame.

Once we've cleared up the mess we drive off with a wave to our German friends, quite forgetting Tinkerbelle's chocks, which are probably buried for all time beneath the sands of le Pin Sec.

This part of the Landes coast was planted as pine forest during the 19th century to stabilize the marshy land and keep the advancing dunes at bay. Mile upon unending mile of pine trees grow obediently in straight lines, bisected by long, arrow-straight roads. Tinkerbelle coasts along in the pancake-flat terrain.

We stroll around Arcachon's enchanting *Ville d'Hiver*. The architecture has changed abruptly from the white-painted, blue-shuttered houses of the Atlantic coast into wildly extravagant, over-the-top Belle Époque villas. Palaces, temples and pagodas, with ornate twisty columns, curlicued wrought-iron balconies and intricately carved wooden fascias sit in sumptuous landscaped gardens. The *Ville d'Hiver* was conceived by two wealthy industrialists in the late 19th century, to provide accommodation for the wealthy from all over the world who came to benefit from the Arcachon basin's mild winter climate. There's very much a 1920s feel to the town, and you expect to see bustle-bottomed, parasol-twirling ladies and gaitered, top-hatted gentlemen strolling around the elegant streets and through the exotic Mauresque public gardens.

Sooner or later we expect to reach the fabled *dune du Pilat*, but it takes us by surprise. I don't connect signs to 'Pyla' with Pilat. The different spelling, we later learn, is because Pilat, in which the final 't' is pronounced, means in French 'a heap of sand' – which is what the dune is. A very, very big heap of sand. Local estate agents didn't find it conducive to attracting house buyers, so the spelling was changed to Pyla. Maybe the estate agents hoped potential buyers would be fooled by the change in spelling and not notice the monster. Our first sight of this sandy leviathan is breathtaking. It's an amazing work of nature, a sinister creature that's stealthily growing and eating its way across country from its lair on the Atlantic shore. It's the biggest sand dune in Europe, nearly two miles long, more than a mile wide, approximately 400 feet high and composed of 70 million cubic yards of sand. Fed by the wind off the Arguin sandbank, it's estimated to be edging eastwards by some fifteen feet each year, munching up anything standing in its unstoppable path.

Somewhere in its belly are trees, tarmac roads, campsites and an entire hotel. It's a worrying thought that grains little bigger than ground pepper can be so invincible and beyond the control of any means known to man. We start trying to climb it, but our feet sink into the sand and we slip backwards faster than we can move forwards. We are exhausted after a few minutes and admit defeat, driving on to a beach further south, where the dogs disperse some of their infinite energy. There are still faint traces of oil from the spill on the Galician coast that has cost Rosa her job, but they are no more than dark shadows in small patches of sand. Three men are playing football, a game of which Tally appears instinctively to know the rules. He joins in enthusiastically, to the amusement of his new friends who pass him the ball backwards and forwards and cheer him as he leaps and pounces on it. Dobby doesn't understand at all, and annoys Tally by interfering. When Tally snaps a public warning he retires to sit and watch from a distance, his head tilted and black brow wrinkled in bewilderment.

For the last couple of days the weather has been uncomfortably hot and sticky, but by the time we reach Gastes the skies are gloomily grey. We find a municipal camping site beside the Biscarrosse lagoon, where a sharp energetic wind lashes the water into choppy waves. During our travels today the wardrobe door has come open, and I find all my clothes scattered around the van, one pair of knickers chewed beyond repair.

The campsite is basic, just toilets and no hot water, so I boil up a few kettles and wash our clothes and the dogs' spare blankets in a bucket. We hang everything to dry under Tinkerbelle's spacious awning.

I haven't slept well since we began our journey. I find the space in the van restrictive, and even with the two roof ventilators open there isn't enough air circulating. The privacy provided by Tinkerbelle's pastel-blue curtains mean I can't see the sky, something I'm used to at home. A green light from the refrigerator and a glowing red halo from the electric mosquito repellent are like a set of traffic lights in my face. I am either too hot or too cold, and thrash around until I end up sprawled out like a disorientated starfish, with no idea where I am. I wake almost every night in sweaty panic, yelling to be let out. Terry is very tolerant, always managing to get the light on quickly, and never complaining at being woken by a screaming wife.

During the night the heat is washed away by a monumental storm embellished with cracking thunder and sheet lightning. Next morning the awning has collapsed under the weight of the rain water, and its aluminium legs are crumpled like a dead spider's. The things I washed last night are a soggy, muddy mess trailing in the grass. What was our patio is now a paddling pool for a cocky little pied wagtail. The tents around us are almost afloat, the canvas sagging to a few inches above ground level. I sympathise, vividly remembering the misery of similar conditions during my hiking trip across France in 1998. Tinkerbelle may have problems, but we do keep dry and relatively comfortable.

Landes

There is no sign that the rain will stop, so we shovel the wet clothes into bin bags and cart them off to our next destination. It's still raining hard when we reach Mimizan, where the road is lined with exquisite pink and white dog roses growing from the sandy soil. There's a triathlon taking

42

place through the town. A tall, thin man with a damp moustache, wearing an ankle-length transparent plastic raincoat over his T-shirt and shorts holds up a paddle. We've seldom seen anybody looking quite so miserable and embarrassed. He snaps the paddle irritably, signalling us to the side of the road, next to a bundle of spectators gently steaming inside their anoraks and waterproof clothing.

Past Mimizan the landscape reverts to pine trees, an infinity of them in varying stages of growth, from babies to great-grandfathers, their foliage all at the top so that they look like a forest of big prickly lollipops. The roads are lined with marguerites and bracken, and signs offering *foie gras*. In Saint-Girons voluptuous groups of arum lilies cluster on the banks of the river, like a huddle of naked courtesans preparing for a swim. As the road becomes more undulating we break out of the pine forests into deciduous trees, glistening green and shiny in the rain. Beyond the sand dunes at Hossegor massive breakers hurl themselves on to the beach.

Hossegor, a corruption of Horseguards from when the good old Duke of Wellington was prancing about in the area, is one of France's finest surfing beaches. The waves along this stretch of coastline are the most powerful on the Atlantic seaboard. I find the water particularly sinister and menacing as it swishes around hungrily as if looking for its next meal. Hossegor is heavy on barrack-like holiday apartments, and every crack and crevice is covered in sand. It creeps over the pavements and into the roads, through gardens, along paths and up stairs. There's no doubt about it, sand is invincible.

Spanish restaurants and signs for paella and sangria indicate we are moving into the Basque country. Leaving behind sandy, windy Hossegor we drive inland to Saubusse to visit the ponies on the Barthes – marshy lands planted with oak trees and flooded by the river Adour when it fills with melt waters from the Pyrénées. There's a herd of about fifty of the stocky semi-wild ponies. They look sleek and well cared for, and are relaxed as we walk amongst them. A young foal with naïve eyes comes to investigate us, shadowed by a small stallion who has appointed himself as the youngster's guardian.

Two lads of about twelve arrive with bicycles which they load into a crude little boat on a narrow waterway running through the fields. They climb into the boat and propel themselves along the water, one punting with a stick and the other steering with a paddle, until they reach a low stone bridge. We watch in admiration as they struggle and eventually succeed in negotiating the boat beneath it, taking turns to curl up like dormice on the bottom of the boat and twisting their bikes into strange configurations. A few feet away a herd of ponies led by a grey stallion watch warily, ears pricked and tails high, necks stretched and nostrils flared, ready to flee. The stallion keeps the herd behind him until he's satisfied that the boys, their bicycles and the boat are no threat. Then he wheels round and leads the herd away. It's a scene straight out of Huckleberry Finn.

On our way to the campsite at Labenne-Océan we visit the nature reserve at Orx, a haven for herons, egrets, crested grebes, ducks, and coypus swimming around like giant water-borne guinea pigs in the weedy water. We arrive at the campsite early enough to spend a few hours relaxing in the sunshine while our laundry dries on rope stretched between two trees. The campsite showers are heavenly, with unlimited hot water. While I spend a blissful ten minutes under a cascade of steaming water, I can hear slithers, whispers and giggles from the adjacent cubicle. As I emerge the neighbouring door opens and out comes a wet, red-faced young man followed by a wet, chubby young girl. Neither of them have towels or soap.

In the morning we go to explore Labenne, following a sign to a breaker's yard where we hope to locate the exhaust system and mysterious *pignon baladeur* for Tinkerbelle. It's been two weeks since the original exhaust fell off, and although her gearbox seems to be under control it could die at any moment. Every place where we might have been able to find the necessary spare parts has been closed when we are there. Labenne is no exception, because today is the fourth French public holiday in May.

From Ondres we have our first view of the Pyrénées looming ahead. I feel a *petit frisson* of excitement knowing that soon we'll be exploring this region hitherto unknown to us. We are beginning to feel hungry when we see a roadside restaurant called the Roi de Gueux, where €6.50 buys a large grilled hake steak drowning in garlic and parsley, with potatoes and salad. As far as I can remember it was the best-value meal we had on our journey, and the tastiest fish. Our waiter exudes toothy charm, and except for a red Basque beret is becomingly dressed entirely in black to show off his svelte ballet dancer figure. He speaks English, learned when he used to travel to Dover and Folkestone from his birthplace in Boulogne. He assures us that we are going to simply adore the Basque region.

Oozing garlic from every pore and follicle, we stroll down to watch the surfers at Anglet. Young men with long hair and earrings, faultless bodies and seamless tans dress and undress uninhibitedly in the car park. Dogs are unwelcome on the beach, says a sign. This is a blow to Tally and Dobby, after the several hundred miles of unrestricted access to the beaches they have enjoyed so far. They don't highly rate walking on leads.

A short distance from the beach, amidst topless clubs, tattoo and body-piercing parlours and fast-food outlets, is the cave called the *Chambre d'Amour*, the room of love. According to legend a young orphan boy and the daughter of a wealthy disapproving father met here secretly to pledge their love. One day a freak wave flooded into the love room and swept them both away. The only sign of life we see is a group of three pigeons nesting over the entrance.

Pyrénées-Atlantiques

Glitzy Biarritz is a confection of turrets and castellations, majestic, wildly ornate buildings, glorious gardens, and the superb Hotel Palais, once the summer palace of the Empress Eugénie. Forget that the town started life as a nasty whaling port. When Napoléon III and Eugénie fell in love with it in the middle of the 19th century, Biarritz became the summer playground of the royal, the aristocratic, the super-rich and super-famous from around the globe. They left behind a legacy of elegance and grandeur. It is still a place of architectural extravagance in the best possible taste. At the same time there is an egalitarian and relaxed feel to the town, where blue-rinses and blazers sit side by side in the cafés with T-shirts and back-to-front baseball caps. Personally, I think that compulsory dress in Biarritz should be rustling taffeta gowns with bustled backsides, frivolous bonnets, top hats and tails, monocles and waxed moustaches.

There is nothing genteel or gentle about the sea. It is wild and furious, smashing angrily around in the bay, swirling into a brown scummy foam, and looking thoroughly bad-tempered, as if it hates Biarritz. We sit for half an hour watching it hurling itself on to the rocks, then crawl our way through traffic-jammy roads into Saint-Jean-de-Luz, and on to Hendaye, the last French town on the Atlantic coast before the Spanish frontier. The ocean here is calmer, the beach wide and golden, and the waves perfect for surfers.

Hendaye, meaning 'big bay' in Basque, is a town in two parts – the medieval Basque quarter and the more modern district around the beach and marina. With the Pyrenees in the background, it's right on the Spanish border, and has had a predictably turbulent history of war with that country. It was in Hendaye that General Franco gave Hitler his undertaking to keep Spain out of WWII. A little way down the road in the river Bidassoa is Pheasant Island, jointly owned by France and Spain. Traditionally a place for exchanging hostages and prisoners, it witnessed the signing by the two countries of the Treaty of the Pyrénées in 1659, and the marriage contract between the Infanta Maria Theresa and Louis XIV – Louis the Godgiven, also known as the Sun King who would so radiantly rule France for seventy-two years.

Pierre Loti came to Hendaye to die, so that his death wouldn't tarnish his wondrous house in Rochefort. From what we see, it did nothing to spoil Hendaye either.

Notices and signboards are in three languages now – French, Spanish of which we understand very little, and Basque of which neither of us knows a single word. Basque is not a helpful language; it's impossible to pick out even an odd word here and there to make some sense of it. There are no hints or clues as to its meaning. Unless the signs are also written in French, they might as well be in Japanese or hieroglyphics for all the use they are to us. It's said that after seven years of trying to learn the Basque language, the Devil had only mastered two words: "Yes, ma'am." Parked by the port and sipping sangria, we watch a female driver struggle to negotiate her car into a narrow parking space, mangling an adjacent car quite badly. She gets out of her car, locks it and walks away without a glance at the damage she has wreaked.

We walk the dogs around the harbour, then read in the sunshine for a few hours before nightfall, when the lights come on across the bay and in the hills.

6

Inland Aquitaine

Pyrénées-Atlantique

Soft rain fell through the night and is still falling this morning as we turn
left at the bottom of France and into the mountains of the Pyrénées. On a
pretty roundabout on the way out of Hendaye, a giant terracotta pitcher
lying on its side spills out a torrent of petunias and marigolds like a
stream of jewelled water.

After ten minutes we are lost on winding roads in wooded mountains.
A heavy mist parts momentarily to uncover valleys and vistas of rich
greenness. Good fortune guides us into the village of Biriatou, which sits
on a hill surrounded by similar hills and fields of hay bales. Everything is
closed apart from the Hotel Bakea. During our journey so far I have
drunk many cups of hot chocolate, but nothing yet has matched the
perfection of that served at the Hotel Bakea. Just sufficiently sweet, the
texture thick and velvety, as if hot naked chocolate languorously melted
into fresh cream. It's a rich mahogany colour with an indescribably
seductive aroma.

A framed photograph on the wall shows a bouquet garni of chefs
surrounding Queen Elizabeth II. The Hotel Bakea owner/chef's wife
points out her husband Eric, who was a chef at the Connaught in London
at the time the photograph was taken when the hotel celebrated its
centenary. I would be content to stay at the Bakea drinking hot chocolate
all day in front of the fire, but Terry reminds me that if we are to
accomplish our aim to encircle the entire country in six weeks, we must
push on. The size of the challenge we have given ourselves is beginning
to dawn on us, and we need to organise our time skilfully to make the
most of our journey without turning it into a whistle-stop tour.

Tatters of mist snag the surrounding hilltops as we drive away from
this beautiful village with its patches of evening primroses and balconies
crammed with geraniums. Grazing donkeys and cattle, their coats dark

with moisture, raise their heads as Tinkerbelle roars past. Dank hikers flatten themselves in the hedgerows when they hear us coming.

This is the mysterious Basque country, a land of people whose origins are unknown, who speak a language whose roots are unclear, and whose blood group frequencies differ from those found anywhere else in the world.

An elderly lady is walking to the *boulangerie* in a startling cerise-coloured woolly dressing gown in the lovely village of Ascain, where workmen are planting flower beds around an old lavoir and fountain. Wisteria engulfs a small hotel, and the banana palms are heavy with fruit. That colourful little man Pierre Loti stayed here while he wrote Ramuntcho, an adventure set in the local area. Despite its beauty, the village has a sinister history – the local priest was burned alive for sorcery in the 17th century.

We enjoy an excellent, good value lunch at the St Jacques, a typical Basque restaurant with a rose-pink wooden ceiling, smoky-blue painted beams and heavy strings of wrinkled, shiny dried peppers hanging on the walls.

Following a road with more twists and turns than a plate of spaghetti, we drive to the Col de St Ignace to take a ride on the little cog train up to la Rhune, the mountain straddling France and Spain. A notice at the ticket counter advises that the top of the mountain is shrouded in fog and visibility is *'nulle'*. But the sun is shining and it hasn't rained since we finished lunch; and who knows if we'll ever pass this way again? We wait as the train tiptoes down the track and stops politely alongside the platform. Between the rails that support the wheels is a third rail, notched, operating on a rack-and-pinion mechanism to help the train haul itself 3,000 feet up to the top of la Rhune.

Except for the brass door handles the carriages, renovated to their original 1924 design, are made entirely of wood: local pine and chestnut, and African iroko. The highly-polished slatted seats are supported by turned wooden legs. They remind me of trams and the time the buckle on my new school raincoat slipped between the seat slats and was lost forever, leaving me the only girl in school without a raincoat belt.

There are no glazed windows on the train, just open spaces with canvas curtains to draw over them. Our train driver is a plump, lugubrious gentleman wearing a black Basque beret with a little stalk on top. Once the two dozen passengers have climbed aboard and the doors are closed, he sounds a whistle and we lurch off at a dignified five miles an hour. It feels as if we might at any moment stall and slither backwards. The countryside is heavenly, young oak trees and bracken splashed with purple digitalis and flat, lichened rocks with blue alpine flowers growing upon them. A flock of red-faced Manech sheep graze beside the tracks until the train is within fifteen feet of them. Then they decide they must cross to the other side. Tail-end Charlie is within a fraction of an inch of being bowled over.

The little train crawls up the side of a steep ravine. Below are remote villages and green mountains; above is thick cloud. The driver switches on the headlights. Vaguely through the clouds we see white wraith-like cattle, and our first sight of the scraggy little pottoks, the wild ponies who live on the mountains. Generally grey at birth, the foals' coats darken as they mature, to camouflage them from their traditional enemies, wolves and bears. Their dark colouring also helps them store solar energy for protection from the cold damp of the mountain. These hardy little creatures, perfectly adapted to survive their harsh environment, were traditionally rounded up and sent to the butcher until they verged on the edge of extinction. Thanks to Michel Laforet who established a breeding and conservation programme in 1990, they are now flourishing.

The nearer we come to the top of la Rhune, the colder and cloudier it becomes. By the time we disembark it is raining and there is a bitter wind. We climb up to the cloud-shrouded summit, from where we can see nothing but cloud, and within moments we are blue with cold. We go back and sit in the little train as the carriages quickly refill with our fellow passengers: women with damp flat hair dragging small, grizzling, anoraked children by their arms, and men with their hands jammed into their arm-pits. The children don't seem to be enjoying themselves: "Boring, boring, boring," chants a fat boy. Clouds float in through the glassless windows during our descent, but through gaps we catch glimpses of spectacular scenery. The bellies of pottok mares with their gangly foals are already bulging with the next generation.

I think how pleasant it must be, driving the train up and down this wild place and watching the changing seasons hour by hour. Terry says he can't think of anything more boring. Funny how people see things differently.

Each winter the train goes for a rest and refit. Her woodwork is revarnished, her handles polished, her curtains cleaned, and her mechanisms stringently checked for safety. Then she waits for the coming of spring and a new season.

The cloud seems stuck to the train as she glides back down to the station, and we disembark into cold drizzle.

At Saint-Pée-sur-Nivelle we find a campsite, where we are the only residents. The dogs gallop around happily, oblivious to the rain that drips from the trees and plips rhythmically on to Tinkerbelle's roof all night.

By morning the rain has stopped and the cloud has lifted to reveal the landscape and large Basque houses with their ox-blood painted timbers.

Several notable historical events have taken place in pretty Saint-Pée-sur-Nivelle. The *chistéra*, the wickerwork glove used to play *pelota* (a ball game played on a court, against a wall) was invented here, and with *pelota* being the *raison d'étre* of the Basque population, this is probably regarded as Saint-Pée's greatest achievement. It was in Saint-Pée that Napoléon's elder brother Joseph learned he was no longer King of Spain. The town had the misfortune to be at the centre of the 17th century witch-hunt in the Basque region, and the château was the scene of the torture and trials of men, women and children accused of witchcraft.

Horses and blond Aquitaine cattle graze on curvy hills and buttercup meadows. Something struck me as strange yesterday, and I realize what it is. Amongst forests of coniferous and deciduous trees, lofty palms and banana plants look incongruous. I wonder how they arrived here. Did the Moors bring them? Maybe not. I don't think banana plants were introduced into Europe as early as that. It seems an unlikely place for them but they appear to be flourishing.

In quaint Ainhoa virtually every door, shutter and exposed timber is painted deep red, except for one green radical. During WWII this was a major crossing point for people escaping from the Nazis, and villagers and local mountain guides risked their lives to shelter and help them flee over the border to Spain.

We are going to Espelette, the village famed for its production of red peppers. Shiny scarlet strings of them hang from every building. There are shops selling nothing but red peppers in various forms – fresh, dried, powdered and pickled like Peter Piper's peck. It's all very colourful and picturesque and a bit touristy in a nice way. We look forward to another good Basque lunch, but in Espelette our luck is out. At the first restaurant we wait politely, patiently and in vain for the lady in charge to stop shuffling little pieces of paper around in a drawer at the bar. After several minutes I interrupt her and ask if there is a table free. She glances up momentarily and says: 'No, we're full.' Across the road the restaurant is only half full, but the manageress tells us rather triumphantly that we are too late. Maybe that's due to the long wait across the road.

We end up munching a toasted cheese *panini*, which is good as toasted cheese sandwiches go, but not exactly what we had hoped for. Leaving Espellete feeling a little disgruntled, we pass the <u>Antton Chocolaterie</u>. Outside, a group of elderly people are climbing out of a coach and trailing into the shop. On impulse we follow them and are invited to join a guided tour.

It's in French, and for many weeks Terry will remind me bitterly of the hour he spends not understanding a single word, but I am enraptured by what I am able to understand of the romance, history and cultivation of the chocolate tree. Our guide, Virginie is passionately enthusiastic about her subject. She relates how the Spanish, led by Cortés in his excursions into Mexico, were the first Europeans to taste chocolate when the Aztec king offered them the cup of friendship. Cortés and his men repaid this kindly gesture by slaughtering their hosts wholesale.

The Spanish took cocoa trees (whose Latin name *Theobroma Cacao* means 'food of the gods') back to Spain. The trees wouldn't grow there because they can only develop in humid equatorial regions where the temperature doesn't fall below 25°C. They're tender creatures, and need a protector tree, or 'cocoa mother' to shelter them from the sun. Their large cucumber-shaped pods grow directly from the tree trunks, and when they turn brown they're harvested by hand to avoid damage to their delicate parent. From the hard outer casing the precious cocoa beans and surrounding mucilage are scraped out, fermented and dried before being packed and shipped around the world for transformation into temptation. The sweeter South American chocolate goes best with delicate fillings, while chocolate from Africa marries better with stronger flavours. It was the chocolate-trading Jews fleeing the Spanish Inquisition who crossed the Pyrénées and established themselves in Bayonne, making it the chocolate trading centre of Europe.

Virginie has a captivated audience.

"Who eats white chocolate?" she asks. Several hands shoot up.

"Do you know how it's made?" Several heads shake.

"Well, during the processing of the beans, the contents are separated into two products: cocoa powder, and cocoa butter. The cocoa butter is all the grease from the bean. White chocolate is simply cocoa butter mixed with milk products, and isn't chocolate at all. It's very bad for you!"

The hand-shooting head-shakers gasp and moan in dismay. We follow Virginie down a mouth-wateringly fragrant corridor to a small laboratory where new flavours are developed and tested, and watch shreds of crystallized oranges being smothered in thick black chocolate. A girl dressed like a nurse in an operating theatre produces a tray of their most exotic chocolates – ganache de piment d'espelette – hot chilli pepper ganache. Some spectators are sceptical, but most are eager to experience a new taste. What we mustn't do, emphasizes Virginie, is bite into the chocolate. No, no. Place the chocolate in the mouth and wait. Let it melt slowly to enjoy successive waves of changing flavours and textures. We obediently stand there, unmoving, unspeaking, mouths full. After a few moments there are faint murmurs, raised eyebrows, nods, lip-smacks. Beneath alternating layers of sweetness and bitterness, the chilli filling is subtle, just sufficiently fiery without being overpowering, and an exquisite gastronomic experience.

We buy a box of these delicacies and sit eating them to compensate for the missed lunch, before setting off to our next destination. On our way we drive through Cambo-les-Bains, an elegant spa town, once home to Edmond Rostand, creator of big-nosed Cyrano de Bergerac. Itxassou is somewhere I've marked on our map to visit, because Ossau Iraty (ewe's milk cheese) is my favourite French cheese, and we are going to buy some direct from a producer. We follow a sign for *Ardi Gasna*, which means, in Basque, ewe's-milk cheese and is traditionally eaten with cherry jam. Tinkerbelle bounces and shudders down a stony track until we arrive at the farm of Nicolas and Mirestxu. While Nicolas, who has dark skin and hair and sharp bright-blue eyes, carves the cheese, he tells us he has a herd of 200 Manech sheep. He talks about the bears in the mountains. There are only about four left, he says, and it is virtually impossible to see them as they're very shy and highly intelligent. He talks of moonlit nights spent on the heights with his flocks. How the bears wait for cloud to slip across the moon, and then attack. How they circle patiently until they can slide up and strike from behind. Despite the threat to his sheep, Nicolas doesn't harbour any malice towards them, but has an admiration and deep regret that those still left in the mountains will die out quite soon – like we shepherds, he adds sadly. He is scornful of attempts to introduce bears from Eastern Europe into the area. Millions of francs were spent on the project, he says, and it has been a catastrophe. The imported bears don't stay where they are put, but wander all over the place, attacking herds. A total waste of time and effort, says Nicolas.

We say we'd like to buy some cherries, Itxassou's other specialty. He shakes his head. A wet and windy spring has spoiled the crop. They've only managed to harvest a handful so far.

I ask where we can watch a *pelota* game. Nicolas looks surprised that anybody can be so ignorant and not know that *pelota* is only played in the summer. It is far too early in the year.

Off we drive with a wave and our chunk of cheese. Shortly afterwards we see a sign leading to the Pas de Roland, and follow a ridiculously narrow twisty lane past pretty white farmhouses, meadows, palm trees and bamboo, and a swishy white-water river dashing along in the valley below. The lane isn't much more than a mule track with a low stone wall to prevent vehicles toppling into the river. The side of the road not next to the river is lined with boulders that don't look particularly firmly attached to the mother rock. What happens if a vehicle comes the other way? There is no room for two vehicles to pass without one either crashing into the rocks or going into the river.

The situation does not arise, and we reach a rocky formation where a plaque announces that here Charlemagne's army, led by his nephew Roland, found their passage blocked during their retreat from the Saracen army across the Pyrénées. Using his fabled sword Durandal, Roland walloped the rock and opened a breach allowing his soldiers to pass. From there he'd go on to be betrayed by Ganelon, and would die at Roncesvalles just over the Spanish border, because he was too proud to blow his horn to summon help. Roland may have had some satisfaction if he'd known how Ganelon would pay for his treachery. His arms and legs were tied to four horses, and he was torn apart. It didn't do to mess with Charlemagne's kin.

We drive around past fields splashed with pink Canterbury bells growing through cushions of moss and legions of digitalis in hues from white to purple. A herd of soft-eyed cattle, guided by a very little boy with cropped hair and a twig, stop every so often to help themselves to wild flowers from the roadsides. From 1,000 ft. we can see the vistas denied by the clouds yesterday, and the countryside is simply gorgeous. On one side the mountains, on the other the sea, and in the fields between herds of grazing cattle, sheep and horses.

Our sight-seeing detour leads back via a series of curvaceous hills to the rose- and honeysuckle-covered village of Itxassou where we bought the cheese from Nicolas a couple of hours ago. We drive on until we arrive at a peaceful farming hamlet called Saint-Martin, or Lantabat (it seems to have two names). An apple-cheeked old boy driving a van and herding a flock of sheep at the same time asks if he can help. We say we are looking for somewhere to stay for the night, and he indicates a fronton, the court where *pelota* is played. It's at the back of the local church, bordering the cemetery. He assures us we'll be '*très tranquille*' and nobody will disturb us. As we park in one corner, a steady trickle of villagers casually walk past to have a look at the strange English people. A mournful Basset hound waddles up and stares at Dobby and Tally, then turns in disgust at their rude barking and plods away. Our nearest neighbour is an old lady in a cottage opposite the church. She watches us suspiciously and doesn't return my wave.

When we let the dogs out of the back, we discover the purpose of the yellow plastic thing that Dobby had mutilated at le Pin Sec. It was the security pin for the fire extinguisher. By removing it, Dobby had empowered himself to activate the extinguisher. Every surface of the interior of the van is covered in white powder.

Night falls, silhouetting the mountains against the darkening blue of the sky. Lights from scattered houses sparkle on the hillsides, and the floodlit front of the white-painted church and bell tower is like a scene from a Western. Through the night the church bells ring hourly and half-hourly. The first few times Dobby hears them he throws back his head and howls like a wolf. Owls hoot, crickets chirrup and sheep bells tinkle a delicate, ethereal symphony. It's idyllic.

Next morning we are up early, wanting to be dressed before the population stir; you feel rather exposed sleeping in a tin box in the main square of a village. There's a lady watering flowers in the cemetery. I go to talk to her and say how grateful we are for being allowed to stay in such a beautiful place. Yes, she agrees, there's probably nowhere else in the world more lovely than Saint-Martin, where she was born and will die. But there is no work here, so people must travel to faraway towns, which means a driving licence and car are essential. She gives a little sigh.

I mention the church bells, and she says they are rung electrically, and that she never notices them because they've been there since she was born. "But," she laughs, "if ever something goes wrong and they don't ring the hour, then I notice their absence." She's surprised when I say they strike on the half-hour as well.

"I never realized that!"

She points to some heavy stone circular discs and crosses.

"Those are Basque steles," she says. "There are no bodies beneath them. They've been found over the years and brought here. But if you go over there a little way " she waves her hand towards to the west, "you can see the old Basque cemetery, where there are still bodies buried under the stones."

While we're talking, Tally and Dobby escape and run wildly around the square. Terry and I chase after them, and the old lady comes out of her house and shouts. I say we are trying to catch the dogs, and she shouldn't be afraid because they are friendly and harmless. She stares back silently with hard green eyes.

Once we've captured the dogs we set off to see the Basque cemetery. We wave at the old lady as we drive away. She stares back.

We drive through a small farming hamlet to a dead end (no pun intended) and find a little church that is locked up and falling down in places. A notice on the door requests donations for repairs. Cemeteries are by their nature not cheerful places, but this one is truly dismal. The ground is dry and cracked, covered in broken tiles, and devoid of any plant life. Not even a weed grows here. There are two dozen Basque headstones engraved on both sides with the person's name and date of death. Time has effaced most of them, except for one or two sheltered by the church. The oldest legible date is 1627. On most stones we can just make out the curly Basque swastika, the *lauburu*, or sometimes the Star of David.

It seems sad that there is nobody to remember these long-dead people; no relatives to place a single flower upon the neglected graves here in the middle of nowhere. I wonder where these dead people came from, and how they ended up here, and whether they ever feel resentful. And I also wonder what it is like for the residents of the hamlet to have this rather spooky place in their midst.

It's a bright June day and although out in the fields hay is being harvested the air is still rather chilly, and there is smoke curling from chimneys. We drive through oak forests fringed with bracken laced with dog roses. High in the trees are wooden platforms, covered with old fir branches. Hunters hide on them to spot and slaughter pigeons. That's why the place is called *'l'enfer des palombes'* – the wood pigeons' hell.

In a hay field a black-bereted old boy is scything by hand. The field is large, and we wonder how long it will take him to cut it all, and whether by the time he reaches the end it will be time to start again at the beginning.

The delectable Ossau Iraty cheese we bought from Nicolas hasn't lasted long, so when we see a sign for *Ardi Gasna* 'two minutes away' we follow a trail that leads into the wilderness. It becomes narrower and steeper by the inch, over a switchback of humps and bumps, round sharp blind bends, along a track that a goat might have difficulty negotiating. The enticing signs lead us further on for very much longer than two minutes, through a rural idyll, up the side of a mountain. Finally we reach the end of the road and drive into the immaculate farmyard of Maison Etxepareborda, at Béhorléguy, Unhassorbiscay. There's a fine example of the exuberance of the Basque language.

The views are breathtaking and wild: mountains and valleys and a clear blue sky in which several kites are circling, singing their joy. The lady who sells the cheese to us says that if we wrap it in a dry tea cloth and kept it in the warmest part of the fridge, it will last for several months. (This won't turn out to be true: it won't last very long at all because we just can't leave it alone.) We have writhed and wriggled a round trip of nearly five miles over almost impassable terrain to buy it. And it's worth every last inch.

With our precious cargo swaddled in the dry tea towel in the warmest part of the fridge, we continue through spectacular mountain landscape. The road winds and twists alongside precipices. There is nothing to prevent vehicles tumbling down to the valley below. As we drive over the unpronounceable Burdincurutcheta pass 4,000 ft. above sea level we overtake a grey-haired cyclist pedalling casually upwards. At the summit of the Bagargui pass we break through cloud into sunshine. Like the Pointe du Van, this is a place where the grandeur of nature makes speech superfluous. It is too majestic for words to describe.

The descent from the plateau at les Chalets d'Iraty is as convoluted as intestines. Always lurking in my mind is Terry's remark when we were in Morlaix about Tinkerbelle's brakes. Edging round tight narrow bends with nothing between us and the valley far below, my feet inadvertently operate imaginary brakes. There's an interesting moment when we meet a herd of cattle plodding up the steep road, neck bells tolling from wide leather collars painted with their names. They step politely to the side of the road (the side where the high banks are, not the long drops), and we creep past with a whisker between them on the one side, and the abyss on the other.

The landscape becomes more rugged as we come to the border between the Basque and Béarn regions. At the Gorges d'Holzarté we stop at the Auberge Logibar for an omelette with onions and potatoes. Assorted poultry strut around the patio, and a grey pigeon with a glittering iridescent purple neck carefully chooses twigs for its nest. It inspects them methodically, rejecting many until it finds one that passes its strict quality control criteria. A bantam hen strolls amongst the diners on the terrace, and jumps over the low fence into an adjoining garden. Shortly afterwards she returns leading a battalion of colleagues over the gate and into our midst, the cockerels growling and offering morsels of food to the hens, until they are chased away by a waitress with a tray. Unperturbed, sparrows bounce from chair to chair hoovering up crumbs. The Auberge is a starting point for hiking, and from there you can walk across a precarious Indiana Jones-type bridge of swaying planks spanning a gorge almost 500 ft. deep. We don't want to do that. Instead we follow the course of the river Saison towards Oloron-Sainte-Marie to buy a Basque beret.

Our route leads through the village of Aramits, from where Alexandre Dumas took the name for one of his three musketeers, Aramis, who kept a secret mistress and couldn't decide whether he wanted to be a priest or a musketeer. I wonder why they were called musketeers when they're always depicted as swordsmen? We don't find any Basque berets in Oloron-Sainte-Marie, but we do find a breakers' yard that is open. Alas, nobody there is interested in Tinkerbelle's plight, nor in suggesting anywhere else that might be. So, still farting and spluttering, roaring and rattling we arrive in the Béarn district.

The shadowy gorge of Lourdios in the Aspe valley is brilliant with blue aquilegias and golden buttercups, cooled by spray from the river's green pools and white cascades. Flocks of sheep graze alpine meadows against a backdrop of snow-crested mountains. On the hillsides farmhouses and stone cottages with steep slate roofs perch among deciduous forests. The only human being we see is a gentleman relieving himself onto some buttercups. A 50 yard tunnel hewn from the rocks leads into Lourdios-Ichère, the sort of sleepy, unspoilt village you dream of, tucked in a valley encircled by craggy mountains. Pastel-green shutters on the village restaurant make a perfect backdrop for boxes of brilliant geraniums, petunias and impatiens. At the village school we ask a young woman if there is a campsite where we can stay for the night. She says with a smile that there is no official site. However, she points, up there is the nearest thing they have to a flat parking area, where we are welcome to stay, but it isn't very flat.

In fact it's ideal, on a patch of grass beneath a willow tree, alongside a clump of yellow irises growing cheerfully on the banks of the river. We sit half reading and half dozing, soaking up the alpine air and listening to the chuckling water. Tally lies quietly soaking up the sun, while Dobby amuses himself hunting and digging up small rocks from the floor of the shallow river. Bubbles billow from his submerged nose and his tail wags furiously as he keeps emerging triumphantly until he's built up a pile of fist-sized rocks.

Tally makes his second social gaffe on the journey by mistaking Terry's leg for a lamp post. Terry washes his trainers and lays them to dry in the sun on the concrete beam that forms a crude bridge over the river. Comfortably trapped in our folding canvas chairs, we notice too late that Dobby has picked the shoes up and dropped them into the water. He watches in fascination as they bob downstream like little boats. Terry manages to catch them just before they are washed out of reach.

In the cool of late afternoon we walk through the village's single street, past the school where the children have set up a 'station bio-surveillance' to monitor ozone levels by means of a row of aubergine plants with pieces of red wool tied to them. I wonder how that works? Strolling down the hill we pass an old lady who looks at least a hundred and thirty and is bent over at ninety degrees from the waist. She is walking so slowly that only by watching her in relation to a fixed object can we see she is actually moving.

Towards the lower end of the village is a stone bridge where we watch the water tumbling over the rocks. A large adder with distinctive 'V' markings down its head and back is sunbathing on a rock, but it shoots into the water as our shadows fall on it. On our way back we stop at the *auberge* for a glass of wine, and I mention the adder to the *patronne*.

"Ah yes," she nods. "Adders. They bring them here in helicopters. "

I stare at her. Perhaps I've misheard.

"No," I say, "I mean a snake, a viper."

"Yes," she replies, "I know. They deliver them by helicopter."

"What did she say about helicopters?" Terry asks.

"She says they deliver adders in them."

"Either she is barmy, or you have misunderstood," he says.

Through the doorway into the kitchen we can see the slow old lady. She is preparing vegetables, propping herself up on ancient elbows on the table and methodically peeling potatoes and carrots. There is an enormous pile waiting to be done, and I can't help thinking she is being exceedingly optimistic.

Lourdios-Ichère is utterly peaceful. Back at Tinkerbelle we watch the sun fading. A melodic, clinking, drumlike noise signals the approach from round the corner of a little boy of about six, marching with his chest thrust out. Behind him, with wooden-clappered copper bells swinging from their necks, comes a herd of a dozen Béarnaise cattle and their calves, tails swishing, big limpid eyes turning to examine us. They are followed by a couple of men with sticks, murmuring to each other. The cattle plod quietly behind the small boy in a scene of rural life that must have been repeated through the centuries. With the mountains outlined against the deep blue of the night sky, and the faint tinkling sound of distant animals' bells, we go to bed that night feeling we've found a small paradise. Dobby sings when the church bells toll, and wakes us early next morning, groaning indignantly because a fat bay horse with feathery fetlocks is standing drinking from the shallow river.

Lourdios-Ichère is no longer peaceful. Cars and trucks appear from both ends of the village and park on the roadsides. There's an air of excitement – shouts, laughter, music blaring from loudspeakers. We go to the *auberge* to ask what is happening. The *patronne* is dashing about setting tables, and in the kitchen the old lady is still peeling vegetables. We ask for a coffee, and a cup of hot chocolate.

"*Oui, oui,*" says the *patronne* as she passes with her arms full of plates.

We wait ten minutes at the bar, next to a couple of old boys sipping red wine. As she darts in and out collecting cartons and crates from a van, I ask what is happening.

"*Mais, c'est la transhumance aujourd'hui!*" she exclaims.

Oh bingo! We've arrived at exactly the right time to witness the centuries-old ritual of moving the livestock from their winter grazing in the valleys up to the high summer pastures on the mountainsides. This gives the valleys time to grow fodder for the following winter while the animals fatten up on the flowery alpine grass.

We can see there isn't any chance the *patronne* can find time to make our drinks, so we join the chattering crowds making their way down the hill past the church from where Our Lady of the Shepherds watches over the village. A collection of donkeys and ponies stand beneath a tree, and two small self-important boys with sticks are marching about on some unknown mission. A little girl wearing a neat red headscarf waves another stick (everybody round here seems to carry a stick), as she drives a flock of sixty of the distinctive horned, Roman-nosed, Basco-Béarnaise sheep over a small stone bridge, their bells clanging rhythmically. Behind the flock comes a dog and two bereted men. Berets are the other thing that everybody seems to have in Lourdios-Ichère. Sticks, berets and sheep.

We follow the swelling crowd to the main square. Yesterday's emptiness has been transformed into a bustle of men setting up barriers, women carrying paper tablecloths, stacks of plastic cups and glasses, children selling drinks and packets of very sweet little cakes, and a few dogs grubbing around. Somebody is testing a sound system, and a dozen self-conscious hand-holding infants are shuffling round in a circle in some sort of Béarnaise folk dance. They shamble a few steps to the left, and a few steps back again to the right. The little boys are noticeably unenthusiastic except when they have to jump up and down, which they do with gusto. A couple of men appear carrying a long pole hung with cow bells of varying sizes, from big to enormous, attached to wide leather collars and beautifully painted with flowers, pastoral scenes and wildlife.

It's 10.00am, the sun is blazing, and the temperature hot enough to bake cakes. We are unique in being the only two people not wearing berets. Even a very young baby in a pram has one pulled down to where its eyebrows would have been if it had any.

Armed with the regulation sticks and berets (one black and one purple) two urchins run down the hill followed by a flock of woolly sheep, some marked blue on their backs, and some marked mossy green. The flocks trot down the road snatching mouthfuls of ivy and plants overhanging garden walls. As they reach the square bereted men in checked shirts and jeans corral them into enclosures with portable barriers. Men shout, the wooden bell clappers clang, the sheep bleat, the dance music thumps and the traffic hoots impatiently as it tries to circumnavigate the animals. As sheep pour into the square in a woolly torrent, shepherds direct them by gently tapping them with their sticks, crying, 'Ay ha!' Tightly-wedged into their pens the animals look like a sea of multi-coloured fleece with faces sticking up out of it. They are panting in the heat, and I ask one of the shepherds why they aren't shorn. He replies that they'll be shorn in the autumn. Up in the high pastures they will need their coats to protect them from the daytime sun and the cold night air.

By now there are several hundred creatures bleating and bellowing. The commentator says we shouldn't mistake this noise for distress: the sheep have been bleating in excitement for several days because they know the time has come to go up the mountains. We watch as the animals are marked in the traditional way to identify them. The equipment is a saucepan full of some sort of dye, and two stripped corn cobs. Somebody holds the sheep by its horns, which make useful handles, and somebody else dips the corn cobs into the saucepan and

59

then smears the dye on the shoulders, back or backside of the animals. Our shepherd explains that the main purpose of the sheep is to produce the rich sweet milk used in the manufacture of our favourite Ossau Iraty cheese. The wool is of an inferior quality, but they are hoping to find ways of using it as insulating material.

During the summer months the shepherds stay up on the mountains with their flocks, making cheese. Donkeys deliver provisions and newspapers to the shepherds, and bring the cheeses back down to the village. We watch a demonstration of the meticulous loading of the delivery donkeys. A wooden frame is strapped to their back, with various components attached to it. There are two things like gutters that carry the discs of cheese. It's essential for the donkey's comfort and the safety of the cargo that the load is attached in a specific way. We meet Nanette, a patient brown-haired girl with enormous ears, dozy eyes and a soft muzzle who stands happily being patted and stroked by a circle of admirers as more and more paraphernalia is piled on her back. She is so used to her journeys that she finds her own way up and down the mountain.

Next to arrive is a small herd of light golden Béarnaise cattle with their lyre-shaped horns, their calves trotting beside them. This is a breed, we are told, prized more for its beauty than its meagre milk yield, although it makes an excellent cheese either alone or mixed with sheep's milk. By now the square is jammed with livestock, but another herd of 200 sheep arrive, and the animals are crammed even more tightly in their pens.

Following a momentary hiatus, a loudspeaker announces the arrival of the mares. They are powerful glossy chestnut animals, with foals at foot, running loose and clattering into the village at a spanking pace, heads high, snorting as they make their way up the road, and their foals are proud beside them. Spectators should stand well back. An impatient fool in a car tries to push past, spooking one of the mares so she careers wildly across the bridge; one of the shepherds runs to head her off before she knocks anyone over. Unlike the sheep and cattle, the horses are not penned, but make their way straight to a field of belly-high buttercups.

Two hours after the first animals arrived in the square they take their next step towards their summer holiday. The shepherds remove the barriers and start encouraging the animals up the hill towards the square outside the church, escorted by a band of people playing bagpipes. The faces of the local folk all have the same contented, weathered, gentle, kindly expressions, as if they are totally happy with their life. And why shouldn't they be in this idyllic location of mountain and valley, where the air is clean and traffic rare? In the churchyard a group of shepherds chant in soft, high voices while the priest roams around in his white robes stopping for a word here and there. The deputy mayor is here too, marshalling animals into pens, where they stand panting. The cattle go straight past up a small path and out of sight, but the sheep still have a long wait as the deputy mayor, a handsome man, slim and tall in a purple shirt and black beret, begins talking. A good orator, he speaks at length. He talks of the time when life in the Aspe valley was hard. How it had been difficult for men to attract wives because life was so harsh. Some people had given up and moved away, but a few had persevered. Thanks to them and their hard work, and improved communications and technology, today life was good and people were happy once more. He praises those people who had the tenacity to stay.

He talks also of the need for communication, how the Internet makes it possible for people to keep in contact with others thousands of miles away, but how often people forget to say hello to their neighbours. He really does go on for a long time as we swelter along with the sheep, whose sides heave and heads hang down. A choir of shepherds sing hymns and blessings, and the priest prays for the flocks and their custodians. Local ladies and children circulate with baskets of wonderful bread, glasses of wine, and the incomparable Ossau Iraty cheese. Still the deputy mayor talks. The crowd grows restless. The sheepdogs abandon their posts and lie in the river, where small children sit keeping cool. Behind the square in a barn we find a herd of shaggy, horned goats. I ask a nearby shepherd whether they'll be joining the sheep in the climb up the mountain. No, he says no, not the goats. They'll go up by tractor and trailer, because if they're let loose in the village they'll devastate everything in their path.

At last the sheep are released to follow the cattle up to the high meadows. The chimes of neck bells mingle with their collective bleats as they jostle and barge each other. They stream across a small stone bridge, their painted backs forming a moving abstract canvas, followed by those people energetic enough to undertake the hike to the top of the mountain.

The mares and foals bring up the rear, and I ask another shepherd with vivid blue eyes and a gentle smile what the horses are used for. He grimaces slightly, and says: "They're bred for meat. The foals go to the butcher." Seeing the look on my face, he goes on: "Ah yes, it's a shame. I don't like it myself, but if they weren't bred for meat the race would die out." I've always found that a strange argument. I can no longer look at the carefree, frisky foals bucking and prancing so merrily beside their mothers.

In the afternoon we sit by the river in the welcome shade of the willow tree. Tally sleeps quietly on the grass, while Dobby, active as ever, walks backwards and forwards over the narrow concrete bridge until he manages to fall in, landing hard on his side on a flat rock. Twice.

61

We watch a toad scrabbling around in the water, its elbows bent like a fishwife with hands on hips. The bay horse that had disturbed Dobby early this morning comes back again to drink. It takes no notice of Dobby's indignant growls. We are almost asleep when his high-pitched bark announces a visitor. Down from the hillside opposite comes a lady in carpet slippers and a flowery apron. She makes her way over the narrow bridge, and calls out to ask whether the baker has been. I say I haven't seen him, but she keeps on coming and looks into a box on the wall next to us, and extracts two *baguettes*.

Then she starts talking. She talks without taking breath for over a quarter of an hour. She talks about the terrible floods of 1992. How she'd been visiting her daughter when the floods came, and how she couldn't get back to her house. She'd tried to phone her husband, but the phone line was down. He'd been dreadfully worried. She'd never seen rain like it before. The terror of seeing the valley turned into a lake was indescribable. The mayor's car was washed away. How frightening it was that a small stream could grow so fast into a rushing torrent. Of course, it was because people didn't look after the land as the old-timers had done. They didn't clean out the ditches, or dig channels for the water to run away. In the old days people understood the importance of husbanding the land, but they don't bother any more. No wonder all these dreadful things happen. She heard Dobby singing the previous night – just like the poodle she used to have; how they laughed when it tilted back its head and sang like an opera singer! He was a fine dog, and so was the other one under the tree. She hasn't been to watch the transhumance. She did the first year, about nine years ago, but once you've seen it once, there's no point in watching it again. She doesn't think there are as many visitors this year. It goes on too long – there's far too much talking.

With her *baguettes* under her arm, she looks as if she will be happy to stand and talk for ever. I would like to ask this warm and friendly soul about her life in the valley, but she is unstoppable. And what about the heatwave last year, she wants to know. The temperature of the water in the stream reached 31°C, and the trout leapt out of the water and died. My head is spinning, and in desperation I yell: *"Serpents! Vipères!"*

That brings her to a halt for long enough for me to tell her about the adder we saw in the river yesterday, and to ask if there are many in the area.

"No, they're rare. The ecologists used to bring them in helicopters, because they were a disappearing species. But whenever we see them, any snakes, we hit them with a stick." She raises her arm above her head and brings it down with a swish.

"Piff! Or we shoot them. All snakes are bad, so we kill them!" she trills merrily.

I wonder how much it cost to bring the poor adders to this place by helicopter to be killed by old ladies with sticks.

Finally she excuses herself and trots back over the bridge and up the path to her house. A light breeze stirs, and up the mountain we see the miniature figures of the people who'd climbed up earlier making their way back down.

We go for dinner in the *Auberge*. The *patronne* bustles around in controlled panic, delivering bowls of soup here, snatching up empty plates there. There's a lot of laughter at a table of six ladies who'd been involved in organizing today's festivities, and they are joined by a gentleman almost incapable of standing up. He slumps into a chair and mumbles at them, and starts stroking one lady's thigh. They chastise him good-naturedly, the *patronne* has words with him, and out he wobbles.

Two couples arrive and sit at a table between us and the fireplace. They speak English. One couple comes from Paris, where they have a business cleaning out tankers, and their friends from Marseille are in the paper business. The wobbly man keeps coming in and out, ordering drinks and leaving them half finished on the bar, and each time he appears the tanker-cleaning man ducks under the table.

Then the wobbly man arrives with a huge piece of steak in a plastic bag and asks the *patronne* to cook it for him. She gives him a big hug and sits him at a table in an adjoining part of the restaurant. He settles down noisily with another group of diners, and she takes the steak away to the kitchen. Periodically he staggers back into our room, and each time he does so the tanker man hides beneath the table.

Throughout the evening this strange behaviour continues; it is pure French farce. The people at the table behind us tease us for being English, and for a couple of hours we are the butt of their friendly humour. Innocently we make some comment about how lucky they are to live in such a lovely part of the world, and they look quite shocked.

"But we're not Béamaise! We're Basques! We are from Biarritz." They don't look any different from the Béarnaise people to me.

When he is not hiding under the table the Parisian gentleman is lively and out-going. He insists on paying for coffee for all the other twenty-two diners in the room. After our meal we walk round the village, stopping to look in at the church which is packed with chandeliers, cherubs, lilies, carved painted statues and an ornate altar. Coming out we meet the Parisian couple who explain the odd goings-on in the *auberge*.

The husband had visited the Paris Agricultural Salon earlier in the year, where he had been very much taken with the charms of one of the beautiful Béarnaise lyre-horned cattle, named Paroquet (Parakeet). Her owner had invited him to Lourdios-Ichère for the transhumance, and he'd brought his wife and their friends from Marseille. This morning he had met up with Paroquet's owner and invited him to join them for a drink at the *auberge* that evening. However, he had not expected his new friend to turn up legless and potentially ruin the evening for him and his friends. Hence the disappearing act.

Before leaving next day we visit the Ecomusée de Lourdios-Ichère, a presentation of life in the Aspe valley in the days when local government was led by a clan chief who considered himself independent from France. There are video presentations of life through the seasons, and the manufacture of the *sonnailles* – the bells worn by the sheep. The bells are chosen with care to distinguish not only herds from each other, but individual sheep too, so that the notes of each flock harmonize with each other.

We stop for coffee at the *auberge*, and mention the melodrama of the previous evening.

"It's a shame," says our hostess. "He's a lovely man, but he has a problem with the drink, and he lost his driving licence and his job as a truck driver. He can't get work, so he has to live with his parents. Now all he has is his cattle, which he loves. *Le pauvre.*" I feel I'm leaving a little of my heart here in Lourdios-Ichère. If somebody waved a magic wand I think we'd be happy to stay, although we are seeing it at its best, in summer and during the year's biggest event. I console myself with the thought that in the depths of winter it will certainly be bitterly cold, bleak and isolated. And we'd probably never see snakes there twined together or basking innocently in the sunshine. So we drive away from the stream and the cascades of water coming down from the mountains, and the tunnel cut from the rocks, and the winding roads, the wild flower meadows, and the small moving dots of cattle and sheep high up on the side of the mountain.

Beside the river by a clump of banana plants a herd of cattle stroll along unaccompanied, like a group of elderly ladies taking a riverside constitutional. It is a perfect Sunday morning, the trees silver in the early sunlight, the sky stretched out like a blue sheet between the mountains below a thin slice of white cloud.

We head to Aste-Béon in the Ossau valley, a lovely area of twisting streets and medieval cottages sheltering between the mountains and rivers. There we find a fine black woollen beret complete with the little stalk on top. I'm not sure it suits me.

Following a sign to the *Falaise aux Vautours* (Vulture Cliff) we arrive there in time to join fifty young schoolchildren in the six to eight age group, who have come to learn about the griffon vultures living on the limestone cliffs. The Ossau Nature Reserve was established in 1974 to help the dwindling griffon vulture population multiply. At the time there were just 10 nesting pairs and 7 surviving young. By 2002 their ranks had grown to 117 nesting pairs and 70 surviving young. To breed successfully griffon vultures need plentiful food and undisturbed peace and quiet, which is what they find at the Falaise aux Vautours. Throughout the winter and spring they're supplied with meat, and during the nesting period their realm is out of bounds to hikers and airborne traffic. Through discreet webcams viewers can watch the creatures without disturbing them. We sit with the children in a small theatre while a guide talks about the birds and points out what they are getting up to on the cliffs. Our small companions are so excited and interested that they are a joy to see. However, for the poor girl trying to give her talk, their fervour is a handicap. She tries to make herself overheard over fifty shrill young voices simultaneously blurting out questions like "What sex is it?" or "How can you tell?" Many times she threatens that unless *les enfants* keep quiet and save their questions until later, she will stop telling them any more about the birds. This wins her a brief reprieve.

Until our eyes adjust to the screen it is hard to pick out the cliff's inhabitants until the girl points with a cane at nesting chicks. Once we've focused on them and on the large white splashes of the vultures' toilet areas, we begin to see more and more birds hopping around on the cliff's edges. Each time one of them moves, it's like a Punch and Judy show, as children shout out excitedly, "It moved, Miss! Look, it's moving!" We are delighted that such young children are being taught the importance and wonder of their heritage and to care about wildlife.

Griffon vultures can live for forty years in ideal conditions. Carrion feeders weighing about 16 lbs, their 8 ft. wingspan can carry them up to thirty miles in their search for food, and they can hold over 12 lbs. Of meat in their crop and gizzard. They're fastidious birds who bathe in pools of water to wash off the sticky remains of their food, then stand with their wings outstretched to dry. Their naked necks prevent food remains becoming trapped in feathers and causing disease. To keep cool, because they cannot sweat, some vultures pant like dogs. Others urinate on their legs. They must be skilled contortionists. Because their beaks are not particularly strong, they rely on other birds or animals to break open carcasses before they can eat them.

The *Falaise aux Vautours* is proud that each year the white-feathered, yellow-headed Egyptian vultures (so named because they were worshipped by the ancient Egyptians) return here, as well as bearded vultures and lammergeyers. The latter both eat almost exclusively bones, which they break by dropping on to rocks – a lammergeyer is said to have killed a bald man by dropping a bone on his head, mistaking it for a rock.

We spend the night at a pretty campsite just outside Louvie-Juzon. A Dutch camping car arrives and parks beside us. The driver, a short, moustached gentleman wearing a headband, collars the gnome-like campsite owner and marches him about. He swings a small hand-held machine and points it wildly in every direction. Round and round they stride, directing the machine at trees and mountains. I simply have to ask the Dutchman's wife what he is doing. She explains that the machine is a compass, and her husband has to locate a position where their television can receive the satellite signal. Looking at the mountains encircling us, and the trees all over the place, we think it unlikely that he'll succeed, and that in a place of such extraordinary natural beauty and with so many wonders to explore it is strange that anybody could place that much importance on watching television. But chacun a son goût.

The campsite is regulated by a mob of bantam cockerels who act as alarm clocks. At first light they surround Tinkerbelle and roar until we get up and chase them off towards the Dutch people.

In colourful, geranium-decked Louvie-Juzon somebody has been experimenting, not entirely successfully, with topiary, leaving their hedge looking like a collection of decapitated heads. There are beehives in a field, and a sign for goat's cheese – a renegade in this almost entirely sheepy area. It is a gloriously hot, sunny day, hovering in a blue smoky heat haze. On snake-like roads constantly winding back upon themselves we drive through forests and fields just enjoying the lovely Béarnaise landscape.

Hautes-Pyrénées

The forests give way to golden wheat fields, people raking up hay with wooden forks, and in one large field an old man holds a scythe, looking as if he doesn't know where to begin. The outskirts of Lourdes are industrial, devoid of charm and teeming with traffic. We drive onwards, and into a wall of onion-scented air.

Trébons, south of Tarbes, is in the midst of a three day celebration of its onions. We wander into the town centre across a rustic bridge to find out why. We find a marquee filled with several dozen diners being entertained by a lively jazz band fetchingly dressed in white trousers, turquoise shirts and jaunty boaters.

The Trébons onions, of which we buy two bunches, are like very large spring onions (green onions) with a fiery taste and an overwhelming aroma that permeates Tinkerbelle and makes the dogs sneeze.

It is Sunday afternoon, and apart from Trébons every village we pass is dormant, shutters closed against the heat. Every living thing is asleep except the sunbathing roses, and one suicidal red squirrel that dashes in front of us quite unnecessarily, bringing us to a violent halt and nearly putting us through the windscreen.

In the graceful town of Bagnères-de-Bigorre we stop for cake and coffee at a pavement table on a wide avenue. Elegant two- and three-storey buildings with arched windows and pretty balconies are framed against a backdrop of snowy mountains. We are both conscious that we smell strongly of onions.

We've heard of a restaurant in Valcabrère serving 'authentic Roman meals', and Terry suggests we head there for dinner. En route we pay a brief visit to the 12th century cathedral of Saint-Bertrand-de-Comminges. It's a huge buttressed church perched upon a small mountain and surrounded by narrow streets cluttered with restaurants and gifte shoppes. Inside it's cold and dank, and smells of damp and suffering.

Valcabrère is a pretty village but the restaurant is out of our price range, so we dine on a bagful of sugary buns we had bought in Trébons.

Haute-Garonne

Crossing the silky green waters of the river Garonne into Haute-Garonne leads into a sparsely inhabited wild countryside of hills and trees. The forêt dominiale de la vallée du Gers is a fairyland of young trees, mosses, ferns and fallen bronze leaves. Tinkerbelle struggles with the haul up the Col de Portet d'Aspet. Her temperature gauge sticks in the red, and here we are almost in the middle of nowhere. What will we do if she gives up the ghost? Roll backwards all the way down to the bottom? But brave old lady, she keeps crawling upward, and just when we think she won't make it, we reach the top and see a welcome sign to a campsite.

On a scale of one to ten, this campsite scores eleven. Standing on a plateau surrounded by peaks, with nothing above us except white-headed mountain tops and a pair of birds circling lazily. We walk in the cool of the beech trees with the dogs, letting them run off their pent-up energy of the last few days. It is 10.30pm and where two mountains meet on the valley floor the sky fades from aquamarine to baby blue. The golden sun settles down for the night. Utterly heavenly.

We wake to an early-morning chorus unequalled by anything we've ever heard before. It sounds as if all the songbirds in the world have gathered in the trees around us and are singing their very best solely for our pleasure. This is another of those places we could have happily stayed forever. As our host is nowhere to be found, we leave the campsite fees with a young German couple in a tent. I always feel you can trust Germans with things like that.

Ariège

The Hansel and Gretel village of Portet-d'Aspet has probably the most sinuous high street in France. We wriggle through on our way to Bethmale, home of the splendid legend of the spiky-toed clogs. When the

Saracens invaded the south of France and the Pyrénées in the 9th century, during their occupation of the village of Bethmale the son of the invaders' chief fell in love with a local maiden named Esclarlys, which means 'luminous white lily'. Despite being engaged to a local boy named Danert, the girl welcomed the attentions of her new suitor. The young men of the village took to the mountains plotting revenge on the invaders. But while they fashioned weapons, Darnert carved clogs with long thin spiky toes. The other men mocked him, but Darnert just kept whittling away.

One night the villagers swooped down and attacked the sleeping Saracens. Next morning Darnert was walking around in his strange footwear. Each spike was embellished with something red and shiny wet. On his left clog dripped the heart of the faithless luminous white lily, and on the right the heart of the chief's son.

It's been a custom ever since for Bethmale's young men to give their lady loves at Christmas a pair of spiky-toed clogs decorated with a heart made from golden nail-heads, as well as a spindle and a red distaff. The girls give their men an embroidered wool cardigan and a decorated pouch. I find something rather sinister about a custom that seems to contain a veiled threat to the fiancée.

I am particularly looking forward to meeting the Bethmale *sabotier* – clog-maker, not only because of the legend of the clogs, but because I've never met a *sabotier* before. I'd love to learn how he became one in the first place. Was his father one before him? How many other *sabotiers* make similar clogs? How many pairs of the famed long-toed clogs does he make, and how long does it take? A series of the spindly lanes characteristic of this part of the world lead to an exquisite row of cottages, bordered by pink snapdragons and hollyhocks just on the point of opening. Roses clamber down the railings and around a trough whose pump handle has a frog sitting on it. We pull up outside a stone cottage almost suffocated with hanging baskets, flower boxes, roses, Californian poppies and lilies. A beaming lady emerges from this flowery address and says that yes, the *sabotier's* premises are right next door. But today being Monday he's at his workshop in Audressein, where we were just half an hour ago. So we re-wend our way there and find the workshop down a side street.

The place is crammed with clogs in various stages of evolution from crude blocks of wood to almost finished footwear. A man wearing earphones is working at a screeching bandsaw, slicing corners off the blocks of wood. He glances at us and returns to his task. An elderly man at the back of the workshop smiles encouragingly, so we ask if he is the famous *sabotier*. No, he laughs, that's the boss there, indicating the bandsaw man. We stand politely for a long time, waiting for a convenient

68

moment for him to stop. We move from one foot to another, look around the room, and smile at him. He ignores us and keeps slicing at the bits of wood. I take out a card with my name on it and offer it to him. He takes it without looking at it, puts it on a bench, and continues with his task.

I ask the older gentleman whether we can see some long-toed clogs, and he says we are welcome to look round a room at the back of the workshop. This place is stacked from floor to ceiling with racks of half-made clogs, all with disappointingly short toes, apart from one small model that is the sort of clog we've come to see, long-toed and decorated with copper studs. We leave the *sabotier* still bent over his bandsaw. He's what our neighbour would call a *drôle de coco* (shady customer).

We stop at the Auberge d'Audressein for hot chocolate. It arrives in a large jug, with a plate of delicate little cakes, and is very nearly as excellent as the chocolate at Biriatou. The waiter is wearing a striped waistcoat and an Hercule Poirot moustache, and says the forecast is for rain on Wednesday, Thursday and Friday, although he isn't certain if that is locally, or everywhere. Under the table is a gigantic ginger-biscuit-coloured dog called Princesse. She's a Neapolitan mastiff, even bigger than Dobby. When I sneeze she runs and hides behind the bar.

Between Saint-Girons and Foix the countryside flattens out into wider, more open space and gentle hills. A little grey-haired old lady in a straw hat and checked apron drives a flock of sheep through the village of Rimont, a pretty place perched upon a hillside. The air is scented with freshly-cut hay, and puffy clouds are building over the mountains.

The Château de Foix looks down protectively over the pretty town snuggled against the mountainside. This vast castle was the realm of the powerful 14th century Count of Foix, golden-haired Gaston 'Phoebus', named after the Greek god Apollo. One of the most dazzling, cultured and clever men of his time, he was also politically skilful, and successfully trod the thin line of divided allegiance to both France and England. Awarding himself the title of Prince of Béarn, he asserted his power as a ruler under the swashbuckling motto 'Touch if you dare'. A lover of and authority on music and literature, he was also a passionate huntsman, author of the classic *Livre de la Chasse*. Fittingly, he died returning from a bear hunt.

Until 1620 the Béarn province belonged to the kingdom of Navarre. Almost two centuries after Phoebus' death, a son was born to the Queen of Navarre. When she died her eighteen-year old son Henri, a Protestant, became King Henri III of Navarre. He married Marguerite de Valois, the daughter of Catherine de Medici and Henri II of France. A week after Henri of Navarre's wedding in Paris, his mother-in-law Catherine launched the St Bartholomew's Day massacre of Protestants. The new bridegroom only escaped death by rapidly converting to Catholicism.

Once he was safely back in Navarre, he reverted to Protestantism. After Catherine de Medici's death seventeen years later, her son François became king of France. He died of a brain abscess after a paltry year on the throne, having married Mary Queen of Scots and laying the foundations for a claim to the throne of Scotland. François' brother Charles took up the reins as Charles IX of France until he died of tuberculosis. Charles was succeeded by his brother Henri, who liked dressing up in ladies' frocks and became the new King of France, Henri III.

King Henri III of France and King Henri III of Navarre fought each other in the War of Religion. Another powerful Henri – the Catholic Duke of Guise, appeared on the scene, supporting the French King Henri in his fight against King Henri of Navarre. But the Duke of Guise became too powerful and so Henri of France had him assassinated. The two remaining Henris then formed an alliance, and when French Henri was fatally wounded by a mad monk, he named Navarre Henri as his heir. Thus Henri III of Navarre became also Henri IV of France.

He'd have to re-become a Catholic, though, to avoid strife, but as he is supposed to have said, "Paris is well worth a Mass." His see-saw religious convictions upset the Protestants, but he pacified them by the creation of the Edict of Nantes, which gave them the freedom to worship in their own way.

He wasn't entirely satisfied with his existing wife Marguerite. He got rid of her and took on a new one, Marie de Medici, his ex-mother-in-law's cousin. Marie is credited with introducing into France the recipe for puff pastry, which would lead to the birth of the croissant, and Henri is remembered for saying there should be a chicken in every peasant's pot on Sundays.

Marie was crowned Queen of France on 13th May, 1610. The following day Henri was stabbed to death by a religious maniac, and Marie became Regent of France for their eight-year-old son Louis. He would become Louis XIII and would unite France and the Béarn. It was of those enthralling and blood-thirsty periods in French history which tend to sidetrack me every so often.

We are trundling along contentedly through the small towns of Tarascon-sur-Ariège and Ax-les-Thermes close to the Andorran border, past rocky crags capped by small churches with conical roofs, when I make a horrible discovery. Ahead of us is the 6,000 ft. Puymorens pass. Tinkerbelle cannot haul herself and us up the pass. She is simply not strong enough. We have to drive through the four-mile tunnel cut through the mountain. It takes twelve minutes. Terry tries heroically to take my mind off where we are. But by the time we emerge into fresh air at Porta I am clinging to the remnants of my limited sanity, struggling for breath, and clammy with sweat.

7

Languedoc Roussillon and Mediterranean

Pyrénées Orientales

We hug the Spanish frontier down to Bourg-Madame, and then just for fun drive into the town of Llivia, a Spanish enclave entirely surrounded by France. Under a 17th century treaty between Spain and France, thirty-three villages in the area were to belong to France. Due to a clerical error, because Llivia was classified as a town, not a village, it was omitted from the treaty. So it remained, and still remains, a Spanish territory. It solemnly maintains its Spanish identity, language, food and police force. There's a small museum there housing Europe's oldest pharmacy established in 1416, that had survived until 1926. It is closed when we arrive.

It takes twenty-two seconds to drive into, through and out of Llivia. The road becomes impossibly wiggly, wigglier than any other road we've met so far. It takes all Terry's concentration and cool to negotiate Tinkerbelle round the tight bends perched on the rim of bottomless drops. My right foot is almost through the floor in a futile attempt to provide a secondary braking system. It is a nerve-racking drive through most dramatic scenery. Frequently we catch glimpses of the yellow toy-like train that runs from Latour-de-Carol a few miles west of Llivia to Villefranche-de-Conflent. The cute yellow train is not only a tourist attraction; it's an important means of transport for the isolated villages along its track.

We follow signs to a campsite along a lane several inches deep in what looks like snow, but is actually pollen from the poplar trees. Terry feels the camping fees are unreasonably high and says so to the proprietor, who replies "Goodbye", and walks away. That leaves us in a quandary because we are extremely tired and have no idea where or when we might next find somewhere to stay. We have to keep driving.

Villefranche-de-Conflent is dominated by the great fortified wall built by Vauban, and the noise of the rushing waters of the river Têt. Tired as we are it is too good a sight to miss, so we go to explore the town. We take the dogs with us because they've been in Tinkerbelle for hours. The entrance to the town is through the Port de France, past the giant mechanism that operated the drawbridge, through a colossal wooden door pierced with studs and hung with bolts. It's an immensely picturesque and very touristy place. Water runs down the sides of the narrow alleys and geraniums burst from window boxes.

Historically Villefranche-de·Conflent was like a bone fought over by packs of dogs, owned successively by the Counts of Barcelona, the kingdoms of Majorca, Aragon, France, Castile and back to France. Under French ownership it hosted an internal rebellion when some inhabitants conspired to bring the town back into the Spanish fold. While an early version of Mata Hari attempted to seduce the military commander, the garrison was massacred. The French regained control and the rebels were put to death, their bodies chopped up and displayed in iron cages on the walls of the town. The Spanish retook the town at the end of the 18th century, and the French took it back soon after. They've managed to hang on to it ever since, and the last French soldiers marched away from the Fort in 1918.

Dobby is looking in shop windows and yelling angrily at the large black dog staring back at him. We roam around for an hour and then stand outside the walls watching the golden pink colour of the sunset on the rock behind the town. Night is approaching and we are really very tired.

We drive on in search of a campsite. Ria is full of signs supporting José Bové, the French farmers' and ecologists' moustachioed and pipe-smoking militant little hero leading the fight against globalization. The road is lined with orchards of peaches and cherries and fields of melons. At dusk the lights are coming on in the hillside town of Eus, as the rays of the dying sun pick out the strange conical rock formations of les Orgues.

On and on we drive, through a whole load of nothingness. There are no houses, no campsites. We drive through Perpignan towards the vivid pink-striped sunset, until we eventually reach the Mediterranean coast at Saint-Cyprien. In a scruffy car park beside a large harbour where yachts are rubbing fenders, we creep in amongst half a dozen campervans. It is almost midnight. Quietly swapping places with the dogs, we all fall asleep in seconds.

When we wake at 8.00am Saint-Cyprien is mostly still asleep apart from a couple of joggers, some dog walkers, and a camel from the circus, standing in a field and looking at the sea. After the restriction of their freedom during our trans-Pyrenean interlude the dogs race madly around the beach under the disdainful eye of the camel. We stand in the

73

sunshine, on the sand, beside the sea, looking at the snowy mountains of Spain. While Dobby plunges unhesitatingly into the Mediterranean, Tally trots demurely about on the sands. The harbour is a jungle of jingling masts overlooked by low-rise apartment blocks that glow pink and terracotta in the rising sunshine amongst oleander bushes and palm trees.

Tinkerbelle is noticeably more relaxed as we begin our voyage up the Mediterranean coast. She's earned a rest after bringing us so far despite her sorry state. We drive through Canet-en-Roussillon, I think this is where the delicious organic wine comes from that we drank at Saint Estèphe.

l'Aude

At Leucate-Plage campsite the *gardien* invites us to install ourselves wherever we like, and then return to the office with our passports to check in. We find a parking area in a grove of tamarisk trees. I walk 300 yards to the toilets. I can't get in, though, because I don't yet have the requisite badge that unlocks the door. However, I find an obliging campsite worker who lets me in. Then I walk 300 yards back to Tinkerbelle to get our passports that I had forgotten, and take them 400 yards to the office. The *gardien* needs to know the number of our plot, which I haven't noted. So I trudge 400 yards back to Tinkerbelle, make a note of the number and return the 400 yards to the office. Then I buy a token for the washing machine, walk 400 yards back to Tinkerbelle, collect our mountain of dirty laundry, walk 300 yards to the laundry room, load the machines, walk 300 yards back to Tinkerbelle and sit down to wait for the machines to finish their cycles before the 600-yard round trip to unload them.

"You've been gone a long time," says Terry, who is sitting reading. "What have you been doing?" We share the campsite with brigades of sparrows that bounce along the sandy paths like clockwork toys. Only a few yards away is a perfect beach and the weather is pleasantly warm without being uncomfortably hot. Washing hanging from the trees all around flaps in a brisk, mellow wind.

The *gardien* has given me some papers to read about the campsite, including what to do in the event of earthquakes, which apparently are prevalent in this area. There are three things to remember: not to panic; to evacuate buildings, and to return to our tent or van. We settle down to read and wait to see whether we'll be caught by an earthquake. Under the tamarisk trees the dogs are relaxed and happy lying in the sand. Above in the bright blue sky the gulls circle, crying like babies. An elderly gentleman walks past laden with shopping; he nods and stops to talk. His name is André and he comes from Quebec. Currently he is touring

Europe visiting members of his family and having medical treatment in France for cancer.

His shopping bags are full of cat food. He tells that while he is staying here he is trying to rescue as many stray cats as possible. Those he can catch he takes to the local vet, who finds homes for them. All around his campervan there are neatly stacked cat baskets, beds, bowls, and boxes and tins of cat food. He's worried what will happen to the cats when he has to move on. André is a charming man, well into his eighties and still fit and handsome. He talks about his life in France during the war when he'd been a young man working for a French company building airfields for the Germans. He said refugees from Paris and the provinces had been refused any help from the French living in the countryside, even a glass of water. And despite stories of how the Germans would cut off the hands of French children to prevent their being able to fight, when the Germans entered Paris it was they who fed the starving Parisians. It's always interesting to hear a different perspective on historical events from somebody who witnessed them at first hand.

We also meet an English couple and spend an entertaining evening drinking too much wine with them. They regale us with tales of their life in Papua New Guinea, where his job was setting up cattle ranches, and he describes how he found suitable land by using the services of a CIA satellite in return for supplying them with certain information. He also tells a frightful tale of an English lady 'pack-raped' – a strange term that we've never heard before – by a gang of Papuans who'd been arrested and imprisoned. They took their revenge on their victim by getting their friends to go and pack-rape her, too. We crossed Papua New Guinea off the list of places we'd like to visit.

It's a pretty drive next morning, through the Fitou vineyards shrouded in morning mist, and past a large flock of flamingos. Standing with their long necks curled up they look like an illustration of the croquet mallets in Alice's Adventures in Wonderland.

There's a sign in Gruissan pointing to 'Cimetiére marin', (marine cemetery). We follow a dusty bumpy track to a peaceful grove of trees and vines overlooking the Mediterranean. All around are headstones, poignant memorials to those who lost their lives at sea. Somewhat bizarrely in this barely accessible place a large piece of cardboard propped up against a tree displays the telephone number of somebody who is interested in buying violins.

Drifting along, we end up in a time-warped little village called les Cabanes de Fleury, where we join several other campervans parked in the village square. We buy an inflatable football to amuse the dogs. In less than two minutes Tally has punctured it, but they enjoy playing with it in its deflated state.

75

I collect some brochures from the campsite, which warn of dangers we could encounter while staying here. Not earthquakes as at Leucate, but floods from high tides on the Aude; forest fires due to the resinous vegetation, and poisoning caused by the transportation of dangerous materials on the nearby autoroute. In case of flood – get to high ground, close doors and windows, disconnect gas and electricity, and do not collect our children from school – the schools will take care of them. Listen to the radio for information. Better make sure we have a battery-operated radio, then, if we've disconnected the electricity. Ah, no, forget that – in the event of flood we'll be gone! In case of fire, close the shutters and water the walls, open our gates and lock ourselves in a building. Nope, we'll be gone, unless the fire is in Tinkerbelle, in which case we'll be out.

If attacked by dangerous chemicals, do all these things, but don't smoke or light a flame. We shouldn't use the telephone, but leave the lines free for the emergency services. We'll just leave.

The roads in Fleury are lined with fruiting mulberry trees. For Dobby, a natural scavenger, the beaches are paradise, submerged under layers of dried flotsam and jetsam, driftwood and detritus. He gallops around with unspeakable things hanging from his jaws. Tally concentrates on trying to destroy the football.

Along the banks of the inlet shoals of fishermen sit with rod and line, while stretched across the river is what we are told is the last globe fishing net in France. It's like an enormous trampoline spanning the inlet. Every five minutes the net is raised and lowered by an electric winch, and the catch is loaded into a small boat and despatched to a teeny little shop on the quayside. You won't find fresher fish anywhere.

The couple who do the fishing and selling are M. and Mme Affre. Mme Affre's great-grandfather had fished there in 1902, at a time when several dozen fishermen took turns to have the fishing rights for one week at a time. Mme Affre shows us the brick oven where, before the days of nylon, the old-fashioned cotton fishing nets were cured, rinsed and draped outside to dry in the sun to make them last. She is a friendly lady with very green eyes, and tells us that one of her relatives has a headstone marker at the marine cemetery at Gruissan.

Les Cabanes de Fleury doesn't look as if it has changed much over the last hundred years. It is a really unspoilt little backwater, forgotten by time and only used by local fishermen. Some neat houses, a small shop, a bakery and a couple of restaurants. We have a particularly fine dinner at the Globe restaurant: fish soup, mussels in garlic cream, and *rascasse en papillote* (a member of the scorpion fish family, baked in a paper parcel.) Very early next morning we go to the beach, expecting to have it to ourselves, but already local fishermen are arriving on scooters and bicycles. It is an intensely fishy place: everywhere there are fishing lines, fishing nets, fishing men, and a smell that is not at all unpleasant, of fish. A fisherman's paradise.

From sleepy Fleury we drive through the busy centre of Valras-Plage with its casino and apartment blocks called Hollywood and Kansas City with carved Red Indians and totem poles all over the place. We carry on to Sérignan to buy the most excellent *turron noire*, a sort of nougat made from dark honey, pistachios and almonds, which we eat for breakfast.

There are times when we are irritable and not speaking to each other, generally due to being tired, hungry, lost or a combination of all three. Terry is driving long hours every day over difficult roads, in temperamental Tinkerbelle. I'm responsible for navigation, which is not my forte, so quite often we find ourselves driving backwards and forwards over the same difficult roads. Terry tends to drive too fast for me to catch the signs in time. I tell him to slow down; he tells me to read the maps and anticipate. Today we have had words, and are driving along in silence. We stop to silently admire a flock of flamingos in the marshes between Sète and Frontignan, and only when we are sitting down later to a meal of *pot au feu de poisson* (a fish stew) and a Greek salad do we start talking.

From Montpellier we divert briefly from our perimeter route. We drive through scrubby grass and woodlands, the ground glaring bright and white in the sun, to the picturesque medieval town of Sauve, where pitchforks grow on trees.

Gard

In the old cobble-floored barracks at Sauve we meet Dominique Sevajol, who takes us on a fascinating tour of the <u>*Conservatoire de la Fourche*</u>. The tour traces the development of traditional three-pronged wooden pitchforks from trees to the finished article. The micocoulier tree, also known as the hackberry tree, is a member of the elm family and naturally grows very straight. In Sauve the trees are lovingly cultivated by hand in a technique going back twelve centuries.

When it's still young the tree is pruned to encourage it to grow in the shape of a trident until it attains the desired height. Then it's cut and placed on a rack in the left-hand side of a deep brick oven, and smoked at 100°C. The tree 'whistles' to indicate when it's ready to come out. At this stage it is still supple enough to feed through metal rollers that bend and shape the tines into their classic curves. The bark is stripped off, and a narrow strip wound round the neck of the pitchfork in a figure-eight pattern.

The fork goes back into the oven again, but this time on the right-hand side, over embers made from the redundant bark. After the oven door is sealed with a mixture of ash and water, the fork is smoked again for eighteen hours. During this time the wood will harden and become a deep golden brown, resistant to pests.

When it comes out of the oven it's a perfect wooden pitchfork, and once the figure-eight of bark is peeled from the neck it leaves the exclusive Sauve 'necktie' design.

"*Très snob!*" laughs Dominique.

Next the tines are trimmed and the fork is polished except for a length at the end. The unpolished end of the haft makes it non-slip for sweaty hands. Now the new pitchfork is left to mature for a year.

Dominique tells us her grandfather used the same pitchfork for forty years. But who buys the finished article these days, we ask.

"Well," she explains. "They're very good for working with feathers, because they're antistatic. People working close to livestock like them because their blunt tines won't hurt the animals. And many people buy them simply as decoration." If you're near Sauve, do visit the Conservatoire. It is not a commercial enterprise, it's a fascinating testament to an ingenious ancient tradition.

Unfortunately we can't think of any way we can keep a lengthy wooden fork in Tinkerbelle and out of Dobby's jaws until we get back home.

Making our way back towards the coast we follow the road towards Clarensac. There is a stunning panorama over the plains in the misty blue heat. In peaceful medieval villages old men play boules in the shade of the plane trees, and water spurts from fountains guarded by life-sized stone lions.

People stare as we negotiate the narrow lanes, as if they'd never seen a foreign-registered campervan with two large dogs looking out of the windows, or heard one making quite such a noise. We meet that rarity, a rude French person. A young woman drives a car the wrong way down a one-way street. Arriving nose to nose with Tinkerbelle she flicks an imperious hand indicating that we should reverse. Terry switches off Tinkerbelle's engine. The woman becomes satisfyingly irate. Her face contorts into all kinds of unflattering designs. As she is clearly incapable of reversing her vehicle we eventually back up. She accelerates past with a ferocious scowl. Because I usually find French people to be almost excessively courteous, it always comes as a surprise to meet one who isn't.

Our next destination is Robert Jouval's shop in Vauvert. M. Jouval makes glorious, delicate little cakes, and chocolates flavoured with Camarguais *fleurs de sel*. The slightly salty chocolate is a sophisticated and refreshing taste. Madame Jouval wraps our purchases so lovingly that I don't like to tell her we're going to rip them open and eat them the moment we get back into Tinkerbelle.

The delicious fragrance of horse-sweat rises from the white horses tethered along the roadsides. We're in the Camargue now, at the shambolic Grau-du-Roi campsite where we squeeze into a small parking space. There's a fence to keep intruders out, as well as a bouncer at the gate to repel them. It's quite a hike on foot, 500-yards of dark-brown, coarse salty sand, then some sandy dunes, before we reach the beach itself. A string of tractor-towed wooden carriages ferry campers to and fro, but we enjoy the walk across the hot sands as Dobby and Tally rush around deliriously. Dobby plunges into the sea, and when Terry calls him into deep water, he swims, for the first time, unhesitatingly and fearlessly. Tally watches with mild interest but won't be tempted out of his depth.

A couple of elderly French people are foraging amongst the webbed footprints in the damp sand, chucking *tellines* – small clams, into yellow plastic pails. Terry digs up handfuls, too, and drops them in the pails. The last time we were in the Camargue was nearly twenty years ago. It had been a torture of blistering heat and voracious mosquitoes, but this time it's as perfect as you could wish. We sit outside until midnight in warm air stirred by a flutter of breeze.

This morning a flock of flamingos fly overhead as we set off. They're so ungainly in flight with their large heads stuck out in front of them on skinny outstretched necks, and their legs dangling behind. Why don't they fold themselves up into neat parcels like herons? Aigues-Mortes is a perfectly preserved 13th century fortified town, originally built as a launching pad for the Crusades. Pyramids of salt in hues from bright white to murky grey lie heaped outside the plant at les Salins du Midi. The barren landscape is dominated by the Listel vineyards. Their "*vins des sables*" (sandy wines) owe their distinctive flavour to the sandy soil, which also gives the vines immunity to their deadly enemy, phylloxera. Once the vines have dropped their leaves in early autumn, cereal crops are planted to prevent the soil being blown away by the wind. During the winter sheep graze on the crops, which they convert into organic fertilizer which will in turn nourish the vines the following season.

During WWII the Germans planted 35,000 landmines here to thwart any attempted Allied invasion. These all had to be harvested before the vineyards could be revived.

8

Provence – Alpes – Côtes D'Azur

Bouches-du-Rhône

We drive through rice fields and desolate, scrubby landscape where the livestock glow with good health and seem to thrive on the sparse vegetation. It takes just a few minutes on the tiny Bac de Sauvage cable ferry to cross the narrow Petit Rhône lined with boats and fishing platforms. Herds of black bulls, white horses and pink flamingos make a colourful splash on the Etang de Vaccarès. We climb onto a raised viewing platform at Mas Neuf to look down onto the marshes at horses with their foals, glowing clouds of flamingos, and a coypu with outsize yellow teeth munching its way through a sea of floating weed.

Our arrival in Arles doesn't start well. We are lost in the town centre and trapped in dense traffic. Even being rude to each other doesn't help. By the time we reach the campsite it's raining and we are barely speaking. During the night there's a violent thunderstorm.

But by morning the rain has cleared and it's a beautiful sunny day. I'm off to explore Arles, and Terry is going to an air show. I love meandering at leisure through the streets of strange towns, which Terry doesn't. We arrange to rendezvous later in the day by mobile phone.

At the Tourist Office Isabelle tells me that this afternoon we must see the *courses Camarguaises* – men playing with cows, she explains. She assures me that in this most popular local sport no harm comes to the cattle. She draws a small map so that we can find our way there.

I thread my way through the market, a typically French affair which is at the same time tremendously cosmopolitan. Mingling with chic, tanned and fashionable locals are groups of veiled Middle Eastern and North African ladies in their voluminous clothing. Amongst stalls of cheeses, olives, spit-roasted chickens, dried sausages, breads, rice, garlic and honey, the Catholic Aid Society is selling used clothes. There are colourful ceramics, bunches and sachets of aromatic herbs, glistening fruits and vegetables, gorgeous linens, and in the middle of it all a musical merry-go-round. Racks of jeans hang next to pots of olive trees, bougainvillaeas and vivid, exotic plants; there are oil paintings, sun glasses, natural cotton clothing, hammocks. At a leatherware stall a colossally fat man is trying to buy a belt. It is obvious that even the very largest belt on the stall won't go round him. A crowd collects and people rummage through the belts looking for one that might fit. Somebody joins two together, but they still aren't nearly long enough. There's a great deal of laughter and merriment. The stallholder produces a tape measure and suggests he will make a belt for the fat man – but the tape measure is far too short.

A minor traffic incident develops. One driver threatens to punch another. I watch hopefully for a couple of minutes, but after a loud exchange of words they both drive away. A truck is trying to tow another with a thin piece of string, which breaks repeatedly and reminds me of something.

The streets are filled with stalls selling straw hats and espadrilles, lawn mowers, saddlery and cages of livestock, dried flowers and incense, and soap in a hundred different perfumes. I get lost in the back streets and emerge into the square in front of the Hôtel de Ville where four men with violins, a cello and an accordion are playing 'Hava Nagila'. There's a striking sculpture of a group of naked men, a monument to the Resistance. A passing bicycle trailer flies a luminous flag saying 'Dog Taxi'.

I like looking at roofs and chimneys and shutters, and Arles is a great place for that. There are wrought-iron balconies hosting pots of bright flowers, and a fine collection of shutters that aren't new or pretty but picturesque and intriguing. In a little side street flaking grey wooden shutters frame a second-floor window sill decorated with golden suns and hanging plants, and a family of grinning ceramic cats. The houses are colourful: pink and green, cream and blue, yellow and pink. No wonder poor tortured Van Gogh chose to live in this town of 'blue tones and gay colours'.

One thing I don't want to see is the Roman arena. I've always disliked these arenas with their history of death and suffering, the atmosphere of centuries of cruelty clinging to them, the sound of voices baying for blood and screams of pain still echoing round the old stones. It's still used today for the abhorrent activity of bull-fighting. I pass it by.

A grey-bearded man sits on the pavement playing a tom-tom drum. Beside him his dog lies on her back with her legs in the air offering admirers the opportunity to tickle her voluptuous belly; nearby another man is playing a violin.

I enjoy the vitality of Arles enormously. I love imagining Caesar's legions stamping around here, and seeing the vestiges of buildings

81

they've left behind. I love the noise and smell of the place, and the vibrant Provençal colours. If I was going to live in a town, Arles would be high up on my list if it wasn't for the city's passion for bullfighting. Stamp collecting, cricket, trainspotting, macramé or Morris dancing I could live with. Bullfighting, no.

I've been roaming for less than two hours when my phone rings. Terry asks how I'm enjoying myself.

"Fabulous. I love it here. What about the air show. How is it? Are you having a great time?"

"Not really," he says. "It's model aeroplanes. I've been sitting in a car park for the last hour."

I can't expect him to sit all day in a car park in Tinkerbelle with the dogs. We arrange to meet in twenty minutes. In the meantime I'm in urgent need of a pee. The public toilets are windowless steel cylinders and I'm terrified of getting into one and not being able to get out. I approach a woman and ask if she'd be kind enough to stand outside for a couple of minutes and help me if the thing won't open. She looks at me strangely and quickly runs away. I go into a bar and buy a Coke so I can use their toilet.

One of the market stalls is selling fragrant bread in a range of shapes, sizes and colours. I ask the owner to cut me half of a gigantic rustic cottage loaf. Then I realize I don't have any money left. I rummage about in my bag and pockets, and find a few worthless little coins. He laughs, takes my purse and shakes it, keeping the coins which amount to almost nothing, plus an English sixpence, and insists I take the great hunk of bread.

I spot Tinkerbelle working her way through manic traffic as the market starts packing up for the day. We decide to have a picnic before the *courses Camarguaises*, and find a place to park in a quiet residential street looking down onto the Rhône. We tie the dogs to a rail on the wall while we are in Tinkerbelle assembling our meal.

Suddenly there's a loud panic-stricken yelp. Dobby has gone over the wall and is dangling from his collar over a 20 ft. near-perpendicular drop. His paws scrabble desperately for purchase. Terry starts to haul him back up. It's terrifying: if his head slips through his collar, Dobby will fall. Inch by slow inch, Terry moves him upwards, until he arrives back on the pavement with a toothy smile. He's wagging his tail, unfazed by his misadventure.

After lunch we set off to watch the *courses Camarguaises*. Two slim and tanned men wearing red bandanas and check shirts direct Tinkerbelle into a shaded area. Both speak English and say they'll keep an eye on the dogs to make sure that they are all right. One of them asks if we are fans of the *corrida*.

"No," I say vehemently. "We're absolutely against it."

He shrugs. "It's a pity. We have one tomorrow."

"This afternoon, you aren't going to kill the bulls, are you? Because if so, we won't stay."

"But no! This afternoon we just play with them. It's a game – you'll see that they enjoy it as much as we do."

"You don't hurt them at all?"

"No. Absolutely not. Not today. But tomorrow," his eyes light up, "we'll kill them."

I can't reconcile these pleasant men with the degrading activity of bullfighting. Don't misunderstand me. I could thoroughly enjoy it as a spectator just as long as both sides were on equal terms: one to one and each armed only with a pair of horns.

The arena is made up of two concentric circles of maroon-painted wooden boards propped up by scaffolding. The inner circle is where the action takes place, and the outer circle an area for the players to take refuge if they need to. A man waters the sandy ground with a hose to dampen the dust, while another plays a guitar and sings lustily. A dozen teenage lads – *raseteurs* – dressed in white trousers and shirts, with red belts, leap over the boards, bouncing from the ground to the scaffolding with the skill and zest of a bunch of monkeys. Sometimes the hosing man sprays them playfully. As fast as he dampens the sand it dries under the blistering heat. A truck parked near the arena is rocking and rolling and emitting bangs and crashes. On its roof two men prod a pole into the back, trying to attach rosettes to the heads of cattle inside. Judging by the commotion the cattle are putting up a spirited defence. We sit melting in the heat while the cattle crash, the boys leap, the music blares, and the hosing man sprays the sand.

Eventually the young *raseteurs* and several adults position themselves round the arena. With a great crash a young heifer leaps from the truck into the alleyway leading into the ring. She stands looking very small and utterly bewildered. Then she turns tail and scrambles clumsily over the boards into the outer circle. An official chases her back into the ring. She shows no pleasure in being there. All she wants is to get back to the relative security of the truck. A second little heifer is much the same. She trots half-heartedly towards the lads who race in front of her raking at the rosette tied between her horns, until one waves it triumphantly aloft.

The third heifer isn't having fun either, continually clambering over the boards and at one point falling and hurting herself. Her flank is stained with blood and foam from her mouth. Terry and I are not enjoying the afternoon. Although admiring the speed and acrobatic skills of the humans the animals really don't show any signs of pleasure in the event.

Number four into the arena is a not-very-large black bull, who trots proudly into the centre of the ring and stands pawing the ground, swinging his head around. The boys easily leap to safety from the bull's feeble attempts to reach them. As soon as one target runs he turns his attention to another. One of the adult *raseteurs* racing close to the bull's horns misses his footing as he leaps for the scaffolding and falls, landing heavily. Officials gather round him and the activity in the arena stops for five minutes until he limps away; his injuries aren't serious. The men and boys resumed their game with the bull. It isn't a very exciting spectacle, and doesn't convince us that the cattle are enthusiastic participants. It certainly has to be a better alternative to bullfighting, though, and maybe we aren't seeing the game at its best.

We continue our journey to Saint-Martin-de-Crau, searching for a campsite featured in our little bible of camping grounds, which says it is easy to find. We drive round and round, up and down, backwards and forwards. We follow miniature hand-painted signs that stop at critical junctions. We ask local drivers who shake their heads, cyclists who shake their heads, pedestrians who shake their heads and a lady in a garden picking flowers who shakes her head. Nobody has heard of the address we are looking for. Terry is never one to give up, and after bumping down a track through some vineyards, we emerge into a ghastly scene of desolation and neglect. There are decaying vehicles lying all over the place, and a large barking Rottweiler. It is a cul-de-sac. I ask Terry to turn round and get us out of here, because I'm not staying the night in what looks like a setting for The Texas Chainsaw Massacre. As Terry reverses in the narrow lane a pleasant-looking young woman comes to the gate, smiling, and asking if she can help us.

"No, thank you," I reply idiotically. "We just came down here to turn round." She looks a little disappointed and I feel embarrassed. Then I console myself by deciding she is probably a decoy for a bunch of murderous French rednecks playing banjos on the back patio.

We find another campsite in the village. During the night a violent wind develops. It thrashes the plane trees, and the constant moving of the leaf shadows and noise like crashing waves on a beach is hypnotic.

Next morning we leave for Marseille.

Beautifully situated against a backcloth of rugged wooded hills and with its toes in the deep blue sea, Marseille claims to be France's oldest town. When Greek sailors arrived there 600 years before Christ, it was love at first sight for their leader and the local king's daughter, and they married the same day. Greek marketing expertise transformed the town into a major Mediterranean trading post. Over the centuries it has had a turbulent history of invasion and disease, punctuated by interludes of prosperity.

It's Sunday. The streets are busy but the freight port is deserted except for a mountain of orange fishing floats. There are cranes everywhere, and raucous arm-waving men playing boules in small parks. The harbour front heaves with pedestrians and diners lunching at seafood restaurants and pizza parlours. Signs invite drivers to 'se *garer au cheval*' – park horse-style – a French way of saying cars may park on the pavement.

In 1977 Marseille saw the final execution by guillotine in France, of a murderer named Hamida Djandoubi. The guillotine, designed by a doctor as a quick, humane method of despatch was not initially popular with the French, who were used to methods of execution that offered a lengthy spectacle. A robber called Jacques Nicolas Pelletier was the first person to enjoy the fruit of the doctor's compassion in 1792. We will never know his verdict.

We drive up to Allauch, a pretty Provençal village and favourite setting for Pagnol's stories. Allauch sits on Marseille's shoulder, perched on a hillside coloured by the flowers of prickly pears. It looks down onto the Mediterranean over the extravaganza of green and gold tiles of the church spire. Trying to reach the summit to view the panorama stretching from Aix-en-Provence to Aubagne, we are trapped on the narrowest imaginable hairpin bend. It seems impossible that Terry can negotiate Tinkerbelle round and out of the place. Interested and amused pedestrians watch, and to their astonishment – and mine – he clears the walls with nothing more than a coat of paint between them and Tinkerbelle's bodywork. Somebody applauds. A Pagnolesque character, fat, bristly-faced and belligerent in a string vest and braces glares at us as he waddles across the road.

Climbing towards Sainte-Baume from Gémenos, the lush green landscape transforms into stunted little trees. Wire nets are pinned to the sides of the hills to keep them in place. We pass the remains of the Cistercian abbey where legend says virtuous nun Blanche de Simiane hurled herself to her death on the rocks, rather than participating in an orgy proposed by some horsemen sheltering from a storm. Five centuries later the rocks are still stained with Blanche's blood. The marks could be due to red algae, of course, but that wouldn't make a good Provençal story.

The skies turn black and purple. Clouds open and empty themselves with a huge sigh. Tinkerbelle's wipers slosh backwards and forwards in a losing battle. Following the road back down towards the coast, we are in a pleasant forest populated by merry little pine trees, deliciously fragrant in the soggy wet air. There are no houses and no traffic, just open spaces, woods and rocks. Thunder cracks and lightning flashes as we head round sharp bends down to the palm trees and pretty apartment blocks and houses of La Ciotat, where abruptly the rain stops and the sun comes out.

The town is busy with ice-cream lickers and kids on bikes weaving through hooting traffic, and the sea fades away from turquoise to dark, deep blue.

La Ciotat is a small town with two claims to fame. In 1895 the Lumières brothers pioneered the moving picture industry, featuring a one-minute film of a train arriving at the railway station in La Ciotat. And it was in the town early in the 20th century that a less strenuous version of *boules* was invented, for the benefit of players handicapped by age or infirmity. The new rules stipulated that both feet are firmly are planted on the ground – '*pieds tanqués*' which became known as *pétanque*.

We can't find a municipal campsite in la Ciotat, so we stay at an extraordinarily expensive place. The luxurious offices have leather sofas and potted palms, but campervans and tents are jammed together like a refugee camp. To access what is described as the beach, we are given a code to tap into a heavy metal gate. This leads to a barren narrow strip of lumpy rock growing out of a swirling sea. We take the dogs for a walk and naturally Dobby manages to fall off the rocks and into the sea. He bobs around looking confused, and only with considerable difficulty Terry manages to fish him out.

Next morning we leave the refugee camp early in a grey curtain of drizzle. Terry has ingeniously made a temporary repair to Tinkerbelle's gearbox with a baked-bean tin. He has also discovered a way of adjusting the driver's seat to reach the clutch without having to extend his leg to its full length. After a month of struggling, driving is suddenly less of an ordeal.

Var

Mist floats halfway up the hills of the Var. It is warm and humid, the vegetation is tropical, and there's little traffic. By mid-morning we are hungry, but every boulangerie we pass is closed or impossible to park near. At a roadside stall selling fruit I join the end of a modest queue of two old ladies. Old lady No. 1 talks and talks to the stallholder, who talks back to her. While talking No. 1 picks up pieces of fruit, turns them round, strokes or prods them, sniffs them, and puts them back on the pile. After ten minutes she is still talking, but hasn't selected a single piece of fruit. Old lady No. 2 has her arm in a splint. It doesn't seem as if there is any urgency attached to buying fruit, and I can foresee standing here while these dear old ladies chat and poke pieces of fruit until I collapse from hunger. Terry is gesticulating impatiently. I give up.

We skirt north of Toulon, following a rubble-laden municipal vehicle at snail's pace up a long, winding, wooded road leading to Mont Faron.

Eventually we find a bakery that is open and where we can park. Next door is a large shop selling all types of fresh and dried fruits and vegetables, spices and herbs. In a frenzy of hunger we fill a trolley with crystallized ginger and halva, sun-dried tomatoes, apricots, melons, nuts, strawberries and grapes. We also buy a warm *baguette* and half a dozen florentines, and sit munching madly for ten minutes. Then we set off again for coffee in flowery Hyères.

It has been raining since Toulon and is still raining when we reach le Lavandou. It's busy, trafficky and pretty with sprawling bougainvillaea, acacias, eucalyptus and coniferous trees. Boats bob cheerfully in the harbour, and everybody is wearing clinging nylon raincoats.

The rain continues until we reach Cavalaire, where the sun emerges timidly. Flat and silvery-grey in the weak sunlight, the sea looks like a slightly creased sheet of aluminium. There's a splendid view of the tree-smothered hilltops on the Corniche des Maures. We wriggle over little green hills and through pine forests on this pleasantly wild stretch of coastline until we arrive in Saint-Tropez, where it's raining again. Overlooking the gulf of St Tropez while we lunch, watching yachts racing in the rain, we agree that in relentless drizzle the French Riviera is as uninviting as anywhere else. The sky is light grey, and the sea dark grey, the gutters run with grey water, and women tug soggy little children by their arms. Bobbing umbrellas reflect colourfully from puddles on the pavement. We may not be stylish in modest Tinkerbelle, but we are smugly warm and dry.

We drive round the gulf to Sainte-Maxime, and the les Éléphants beach. This is where elephants come from all over the world for their annual holidays, to frolic on the sands and splash around in the shallows. No, it isn't really. I'm being silly. It's named after Belgian author Jean de Brunhoff, creator of the Babar books, who lived in the area for many years. The dogs have a brief run on the beach before jumping back into Tinkerbelle and shaking damp sand all over the bed.

Even in the rain it is a pretty drive along the coast to Fréjus, where a group of grim *gendarmes* are taking measurements around a mangled motorbike at a road junction. To avoid the tumultuous traffic we bypass the Corniche d'Or. Instead we follow the N7 through the Forét de l'Esterel, past Mont Vinaigre and the village of les Adrets, where Gaspard de Besse, the legendary 18th century French Robin Hood used to meet one of his lady-loves.

Alpes-Maritimes

The rain fizzles out and the air is fresh and clean as we make our way into the Alpes-Maritimes and down to la Napoule and the Côte d'Azur.

In Cannes a giant earth-moving machine is scooping up the dirty beach and replacing it with clean imported sand, leaving it neatly brushed and combed like a small boy's hair. Some kind of eatery on a seedy stretch between Cannes and Antibes is advertising the 'New 100 per cent Vegetable Chicken'. What on earth is a vegetable chicken? While Cannes was blessed with sunshine, it's raining again in Antibes. We head for a campsite located on the other side of a bridge whose height limit is three inches less than Tinkerbelle's declared height. She manages to scrape through. At the campsite a Charles Aznavour lookalike meets us at the gate and escorts us to an emplacement, after peering at the dogs and joking: "Ah, what handsome pit bulls!" He rides around the site on an electric scooter, explaining that he has a bad heart. The dogs don't enjoy their walk in the rain; they can't wait to get back into the warmth of Tinkerbelle. All through the night rain beats on the roof, aeroplanes growl overhead, and cars, trucks and trains rumble and rattle nearby. The campsite's showers compensate for the wet, noisy night with endless floods of lovely hot water.

Next morning after coffee in cloudy Antibes, we follow the Baie des Anges towards Nice, where the beach is disappointingly stony, and the sea-front lined with rather soulless apartment blocks. Tucked between them are ancient, flaking buildings where we imagine old people living, who have lived there for decades and have no intention of moving aside for property developers. Stubborn little old ladies who won't go away. We find in these old buildings, and a fantastic, wildly decorated little house with a cupola and statue of a nude in the courtyard, a charm which is otherwise rather lacking.

The flags of the world's nations flap slowly on the Promenade des Anglais. Few people are about, and there's little traffic, so it is a good time to view the flamboyant Negresco. The harbour with its collection of old Provençal buildings in ochres and yellows, reds, creams and green is an unspoilt oasis on a coastline I find largely to be unsympathetically overdeveloped.

We are depressed to see how urbanized the French Riviera has become since we were last here. There seems so little natural beauty left. It is as if exquisite Brigitte Bardot has been transformed into a grotesque Barbie doll. This part of the Mediterranean coast, to me, is the least attractive, when I think back to the beach at Leucate, or the lovely little town of Sanary-sur-Mer to the west of Toulon.

Tinkerbelle chugs past the aristocratic houses that live up the hill, and into pretty, tropical Villefranche with its glorious views down into the harbour. Ever-so-slightly downmarket Beaulieu-sur-Mer is set off by craggy hills and cliffs leaning out as if they are straining to reach the sea. On past Eze's hillside houses and flowery cliffs, through scruffy Cap d'Ail, and into the toy-town kingdom of Monaco.

It's a Legoland teeming with people, vehicles and policemen; everybody is scurrying around laden with shopping parcels and talking into mobile phones. There is a pervasive 'Eat, drink and be merry for tomorrow we die' atmosphere. The traffic is a frenzy of prestige cars and nippy little scooters. Construction cranes are busy here too, cramming in more blocks between existing modern and rococo buildings already jammed against each other. Tinkerbelle farts her way through the bedlam, attracting looks of appalled disbelief from Monaco's glitterati. For fun we drive to the starting grid for the Formula One Grand Prix, line Tinkerbelle up in pole position, and make vrrrmming sounds to match her roaring exhaust, which makes more noise than an entire field of Formula One cars. We roar off the grid through Monte Carlo and Roquebrune and arrive in Menton. Genteel and beautiful, it isn't trying nearly as hard as its neighbours to be 'in'. Just for fun we drive up to and across the Italian border, then back to Menton.

Now we're on our way up the Alps.

9

The Alps

Alpes-Maritime

The Route des Grandes Alpes is 450 miles of daunting mountain passes and breathtaking alpine scenery. We start to climb, passing a house in the little hamlet of Monti, which sits on a narrow corner on the edge of an abyss looking down to Menton. Parked outside the house is a large boat. There are several more boats a little further. How do they manage to bring them up here along the weeny, twisty little road?

Houses lean precariously against mountains optimistically secured with flimsy-looking chicken wire. Falling boulders and shale have left scars where they have escaped. Sharp-peaked mountains smothered in trees and wild flowers create a breathtaking landscape, and the road through the Gorges de Piaon is a tribute to the skill of the engineers who managed to drive it through the strata of rocks twisted, contorted and sandwiched together by millennia.

It's a hair-raising drive. Small rocks jump down onto the road. Sharp bends are only the width of a single car. On the left boulders that may dislodge at any moment, and to the right a plunge into nothingness. If a vehicle appears from the opposite direction, there is no way of turning back and no room for manoeuvre or error. One patch of road has completely collapsed, leaving a gaping hole surrounded by a few scaffolding poles and a strip of red-and-white plastic tape strung across them. It isn't a drive for the faint-hearted or lily-livered. I find myself holding my breath and digging my fingernails into the palm of my hand. Terry is rather quiet, too, as he does a fantastic job of driving the awkward vehicle round the difficult roads.

At 2,500 ft. the air in Moulinet is pure and the craggy scenery more open, dramatically wild, with beautiful alpine flowers sprouting from the rocks. In between Moulinet and la Bollene-Vésubie we cross the Turini pass, one of the most exciting and demanding stages of the Monte Carlo rally. Coiling back upon itself like a three-mile snake, it's a challenge for

Tinkerbelle even at a sedate pace; hurtling around at anything more than snail's speed is unimaginable.

We stop at the medieval village of <u>Saint-Martin-Vésubie</u>, an idyllic Provençal collection of intriguing courtyards and ancient doorways saturated in atmosphere. It was the first French village to benefit from electricity, in 1893. From the pleasant farm campsite it takes just a few minutes to walk up into the village. We amble around alleyways so narrow that overhead wooden balconies almost touch. An open stream known as a *gargouille* burbles down the street. Running through the village centre they enabled inhabitants to deal with any fires that broke out.

We allow ourselves to be lured into a bar for a *petit apéritif*. Later, walking back to Tinkerbelle at sunset we stop to talk to a chic lady shaking a bowl of cat biscuits to summon cats from all directions. She tells us she cares for all the feline strays in the village. We rate Saint-Martin-Vésubie as one of the most beautiful and unspoilt places we've visited so far.

Apart from the noise created by Tinkerbelle's exhaust, her interior is slowly becoming covered in a fine layer of black dust. Still having found nowhere to buy a replacement that we can afford, Terry decides to operate with a repair kit from a local garage, a hammered out empty tuna tin and two jubilee clips. When we leave next morning, Tinkerbelle emits a contented purr.

As we drive over the St Martin pass and the Colmiane summit in the distance we can see scatterings of snow on the peaks. A sign warns we are approaching six consecutive hairpin bends. We don't meet anybody on the turns, but in the short distances between each bend a stream of suicidal drivers pass at breakneck speed regardless of precipices and unforgiving rock face. One driver is talking on a mobile phone, his wheels dangling in space.

We're driving through the wild Mercantour National Park on the Route de la Bonette, which, at 9,000 ft, claims to be the highest road in Europe. Following the course of the river Tinée through the Gorges de Valabres, we stop to allow a herd of cattle with bulging udders and clunking bells to squeeze past. It's close to the Italian border; the mountain scenery is both spectacular and menacing. The mountainside is bare of vegetation. Huddles of deserted, derelict cottages look as if they simply became too tired of the struggle to exist. The devastated and abandoned little village of le Pra with its caved-in rusty tin roofs is surrounded by wide sweeps of fallen rocks and shale. A sad, ugly place, victim of floods and the perpetual threat of avalanche. It is a powerful illustration of the supremacy of nature, and the fact that when a mountain has something in its heart that it wants to do, there's nothing that man can do to stop it. A great ditch beside the road is filled with fallen rocks, and a series of vigorous waterfalls pounce unexpectedly from the side of the mountain on to the tarmac. In this bleak place clumps of alpine flowers spring from the stony surface, fragile and beautiful works of nature flourishing where man cannot. Either the road here has collapsed or is being dug up, because most of it is just a large hole.

Tinkerbelle throbs her way upward, past lovely flowery meadows and tussocky fields punctuated by areas of loose rocks and scree. Across the valley the snow is below us. Impossibly the road becomes even more hair-raising than it was yesterday, narrower still, barely the width of the vehicle, with no edges. At least the terrain is momentarily level and we aren't in danger of toppling into an abyss. All around are patches of snow, brown and grimy where dust has blown over it, still frozen and clinging tenaciously to life. Here we first see marmots, funny fat little brown animals that pop up from behind rocks, stare at us and vanish. With vast open space all around it, and 360 compass degrees from which to select a direction, one chooses to run right in front of Tinkerbelle, leaving us to suspect that marmots are not blessed with a particularly awesome intellect. As Terry jams on the brakes the dogs fly off their bed, their water slops over the floor, and the food and crockery in the lockers crashes and rattles. The marmot bounces safely to the other side of the road and into the snow.

The higher we climb the worse the road becomes until it is almost impassable. Snow is all around, either side of a few inches of ragged tarmac. National Forest Office engineers abseil on the rock face, chopping down trees and hammering safety netting onto the rocks to hold them in place. With a final bump we reach the Bonette pass, altitude 8,000 ft. The dusty brown snow is blown into waves and ripples by the wind. Where it picks up the sun, it glistens copper.

Alpes-de-Haute-Provence

Since leaving the Camargue the dogs haven't been able to run freely. They had to stay on leads on the Riviera beaches. If let off the lead they disappear into the great blue yonder regardless of traffic, sheep and any other hazards. At home Tally is a well-trained dog who comes when called; on the loose with Dobby he does what he wants. This works against them here in the Alps, because of grazing animals in the pastures and the danger of traffic. They spend hours wrestling on the bed while we drive. Each time we've let them off their leads where we think they'll be safe we've regretted it. They've always got into trouble of some sort. However, they don't show any sign of suffering, and when we stop each evening we take them for a walk, then they play happily on their chains, chasing a football or digging holes.

Now we've reached the snowline proper, the marmots – or Marmites as Terry calls them – pop up everywhere. Tally is beside himself with excitement, yelping and trying to climb through the window every time he sees one, or sees what he thinks might be one. Often it's just a small boulder, but he howls and wails at them until he's hoarse. Dobby is puzzled and looks at Tally trying to understand what the fuss is about. Terry stops to scoop up handfuls of snow for the dogs: Tally isn't impressed, but Dobby enjoys holding it in his mouth and letting it leak out of the side of his lips.

The scenery is majestic, awe-inspiring. At the Restefond pass a snow-topped mountain worships its reflection in a clear mountain lake of icy meltwaters. We drive through the high valleys of the Ubaye, past the fortifications of the Fort de Tournoux which occupy a whole mountain. It's a strange place with grilled windows peering out of the rocks. The Redoute de Berwick, last survivor of a chain of seven defensive citadels built by Vauban, owes its name to James Fitzpatrick, the Marshal Duke of Berwick, an illegitimate son of James II and his mistress Arabella Stuart. He joined the French army in 1691 and later became a naturalized Frenchman and a Marshal of France. Because of his military exploits and his relationship to the English king, he probably held more titles than any other person before or since. But he continued adding to the list for his services to the French crown, until a cannon ball knocked his head off during a battle between France and Austria.

It wasn't unusual during those turbulent times for people of one nationality to fight on the side of another, and to change their allegiances quite frequently. During the Spanish War of Succession, English-born Berwick commanded the French army, and German-born General Schomberg, who'd taken French nationality, led the English army. In the course of his military career General Schomberg served Sweden, Holland and France. Because of his Protestant convictions he was eventually forced to leave France, and died heroically at the Battle of the Boyne, at the age of eighty, fighting for William of Orange against the Jacobites.

The wind cranks itself up to gale force at the Vars pass. I think this is the coldest place I've ever been. Terry braves the elements to stand and photograph the scenery, whilst I rummage in a wardrobe for a jumper before making a cup of tea. A moment before striking the match I notice a strange smell, and remember that I forgot to turn off the gas bottle this morning. Dobby has obviously learned a new talent, because the cooker and both gas rings are turned on. He's almost succeeded in blowing us up.

Hautes-Alpes

We set off again, and the scenery becomes gentler. Sheep and cattle graze shallow slopes in weak sunshine. By the time we arrive at Guillestre campsite, surrounded by misty blue mountains and overlooked by Vauban's Mont Dauphin, the blue of the sky is only marked by a distant con-trail. We share the campsite with uncountable millions of winged insects.

Had we known before we set off the size of task we are asking of Tinkerbelle, we would probably not have attempted the trip. But we'd deliberately not researched our route in advance, as this was meant to be an adventure, and they're no good at all unless there's plenty of unexpectedness. We are demanding a good deal of her and she has risen to the challenge. Maybe she has a few aches and pains, and she does grunt and grumble sometimes, but her heart is stout. Beside the younger generation of campervans with their mod cons and high-tech fittings she looks small and humble, and also rather homely with her pastel-blue curtains neatly held in place with Velcro. The fabulous experience we are having, seeing the most beautiful scenery that France can offer, we owe to Tinkerbelle's gallant efforts and Vivien's generosity caring for our home and animals.

From Guillestre we go to Réotier to see the petrifying fountain. It's a natural phenomenon created by incessant trickling of mineral-laden water from a spring. It forms a rocky outcrop that has shaped itself into a long nose that drips constantly (reminding me of one of our previous neighbours) into a clear turquoise lake. For the dogs it's an opportunity to stretch their legs. Tally shoots away like an arrow from a bow. Long before we reach the fountain we see him standing at the tip of the 'nose', looking down on to the opalescent waters of the lake. Dobby, heavier, less athletic and by nature more cautious, stays close to us, puffing and panting his way up the steps to the viewpoint above the fountain.

The rocks beside the winding mountain road in the Queyras Regional Natural Park look as if they are tired of clinging to the mountainside and would like to let go and tumble down to the bottom. A little way past Fort Queyras one of the strange columns known as a *demoiselle coiffée* pokes up from the ground. It's an odd sight, a tall pillar carved from the rock by wind and erosion, tapering up to a point on which is balanced, as if by a giant hand, a heavy rock, the entire structure held up by its own compressed weight.

Although the Mediterranean seems faraway and long ago, we are still in the Provence region, surrounded by mountains topped with snow instead of lavender fields and olive trees. Over a mile above sea level, Saint-Véran is the highest village in France, beautifully set amongst

94

spacious meadows. You need a strong pair of legs and lungs to visit it, as the car park is at the bottom of a long hill. The village is divided into five separate quarters, so that if fire should break out, it can be contained to one part. The houses are quaint and ancient, the stone-built ground floors topped by higgledy-piggledy sagging wooden floors that look ready to fall down. Whole families live in them, and during the winter their livestock share the house, and provide 'central heating'. A sign outside one old house announces that it was 'a rough but happy life', and so it must have been, with no mod cons but also no traffic, stress or pollution.

Dobby hasn't been idle while we've been exploring. He's dug out the printer from its storage box beneath the bed, and begun eating his way through my typed notes. He's also disconnected a wire from the car alarm, rendering it useless. His toys, currently four different-sized plastic bottles, three tennis balls, a wooden log, a rubber bone and a football are all unscathed.

In the hamlet of le Roux we find a shop called la Plantiflore, which sells exquisite artisan-made plant and fruit syrups and liqueurs. We buy a large bottle of a raspberry liqueur called *'Amour de Framboise'* – Raspberry Love.

At the top of the Col d'Izoard coloured jumpers are painted on the road surface, a reminder of the Tour de France celebrating its centenary. Watching cyclists struggling up the climb. I can't ever imagine doing that for fun. It looks exhausting.

Seven foot high snowdrifts line the side of the road at La Casse Déserte, where baby trees and clumps of tiny purple flowers grow among sweeps of fallen shale. Russet-coated goats graze the meagre vegetation among the snow patches, and the barren rocks flush a soft golden beige, almost apricot, in the afternoon sunlight. Little waterfalls of glistening ice-melt run down the rocks, and the road narrows even further between crumbly edges and sheer sides. There's a couple sitting in the sunshine, stark naked in a field of wild flowers just a few yards from the road, as if it was the most natural thing in the world.

Surrounded by mountain tops ahead, behind and all around, for as far as we can see, we trundle on towards the Col du Lautaret, past swathes of pink and purple flowers. An unsuccessful acrobatic juggernaut has overturned and demolished itself just outside le Monétiers-les-Bains.

With a final effort Tinkerbelle writhes her way along the serpentine road, and crests the Col du Galibier. From there a brief tunnel leads into the Rhône-Alpes region and the *département* of Savoie.

10

Rhône-Alpes

Savoie

The campsite at Valloire nestles in a wild-flower meadow crowned by a small chapel. According to the *gardienne*, the town has a variety of excellent restaurants and we'll be spoilt for choice. This is true: there are auberges, pizza parlours, brasseries, créperies, restaurants and hotels everywhere, but they are all closed for the in-between winter-and-summer season. After we've tramped around for half an hour we find a table in the dining room of a hotel. It has a peculiar atmosphere. I have the impression that everybody in here feels guilty about something. Our fellow diners are muted and slithery-eyed, eat quickly and exit stealthily. The *maitre d'* is a tall, angular and handsome woman, a Martina Navratilova look-alike. She's wearing a strange, ill-fitting outfit that rustles, in a fabric that I think used to be called bombazine in Queen Victoria's day. The food is welcome and not unpleasant, if unspectacular. When we have eaten we leave in the same silent way as the other diners. The night air is suddenly cold.

We awaken to a glorious morning, wild flowers jostling for space in the meadows around us. In the shade, though, the air is still crisply cool. Terry finds a tiny black butterfly whose wings are heavy with moisture. He puts it on a sheet of paper to dry, and then on to a leaf in the sun until it flies away. A small golden beetle carelessly plunges into the washing-up bowl, and we have to dry that out too and see it safely away.

While we're organising ourselves Dobby and Tally escape. We find them running out of a neighbouring tent with a carrier bag of food. The inhabitants of the tent are a rather surly couple of young men with bulging muscles and a bull terrier. Fortunately they're not around at the time. We rescue the bag and put it back in the tent, and leave quickly.

After coffee at the Télégraphe pass we give Tinkerbelle a rest and take the level main road from Saint-Martin-d'Arc for a few miles, passing through Modane and the historic terraced forts at Aussois. There are some quite unpleasant areas between here and Bramans in the Val d'Ambin. Hotel-sized chunks of rock have detached themselves from their mother and slid down to the road, part of the Route des Grandes Alpes which is called the Chemin de Baroque.

Sunlight bounces from the stone roofs in Lanslebourg, which has a fine Baroque church with a distinctive jester's hat spire. In the 11th century a local curate by the name of Landry was sent to Lanslebourg to whip the locals into Christian shape after years of Saracen occupation. He was a popular priest. One day the church bells began to ring by themselves, and his flock noticed a processional cross moving by itself. They followed it to the river Arc at l'Ecot, where they found the body of Landry. Whether he died by accident or design was unknown. But just in case he'd been murdered, in an act of Divine vengeance an avalanche wiped out the neighbouring hamlet of Fausan. In the Haute-Maurienne area, Landry's the man to talk to if you need rain.

The cows in the meadows are fat and glossy, the beehives painted blue and yellow. Waterfalls gush from beneath sheets of snow clinging to the mountainsides, and a huge boulder of snow has rolled down on to the road. This is the rockiest place we've yet been to, thousands of tons of boulders balanced on and around each other, held only by gravity. If they decide to move nothing will be able to stop them. I am starting to become obsessed with the dangers of rock-falls.

In snowdrifts 10 ft. high people have carved their names. It's too bitterly cold for us though. We drive on to the 8,500 ft. Iseran pass and feel as if we are standing on the very top of the world. It's a marmot paradise. Gangs of the little creatures bound about in the deep snow, and Tally rushes frantically from one side of the van to the other, squealing and yelping. Dobby still hasn't worked out what the fuss is all about.

After some nasty little tunnels we arrive at the lac du Chevril, the dam under whose waters lies the old village of Tignes.

While still recovering from WWII, the farming community in the Tignes valley could not believe it when they heard in 1946 that the French government planned to submerge their little village to create a hydroelectric dam. Despite all their protests, on 10 March 1952 a child wrote on the blackboard of the village school: 'Last class.'

A fortnight later the villagers removed the bodies of their relatives from the cemetery to rebury them elsewhere. Two days later the village was gone, flooded out of existence. Although they received generous financial settlements, and the new Tignes became a prosperous resort, the villagers of old Tignes had lost their heritage. Beside the lake is a beautiful tall bronze figure of a slender girl in a long skirt, erected on the fiftieth anniversary of the flooding of Tignes, and a haunting poem called 'Larmes et Lumieres' (Tears and Lights): *Tears and lights, just two powerful words.*

Tears:

Tears at our last meal in our lost family home.

Tears on our last day at school – on the blackboard the words: *'We won't let Tignes die.'*

Tears during this last Mass as the hymns die in our throats.

Lights:

Lights in the windows at 2100 metres.

Lights shining bright in happy villages.

Lights of projects shared to enrich our lives.

Yes, after the tears of suffering, the lights of hope.

Every ten years the dam is drained for an inspection. In May 2000 the survivors from the original village returned to the remains of their drowned homes and celebrated Mass in their drowned church.

It's the hay-making season in Bourg-Saint-Maurice. Two men, a young woman and a very small child are gathering cut hay with old-fashioned wooden rakes. Behind them an ancient tractor is towing a baling machine. On a hairpin bend there is a huge pile of hay blocking the road. A bent elderly lady is forking it into a first-floor loft. I have to repress the urge to leap out of Tinkerbelle, snatch the fork from her, sit her down and stack the hay. But I don't think she'd appreciate that, so we sit patiently while she clears a passageway round the side of her hay mountain.

From the valley of Chapieux we chug up to the Cormet de Roselend, a broad plateau of mountain meadowland bathed in sunshine, where two women are marshalling a herd of copper-coloured cattle in and out of a mobile milking parlour towed by a tractor. This is one of the loveliest places we've seen since we started our journey through the Alps.

Except for Tally finding his way into a field of cattle and being chased by them, our overnight stay in Beaufort is unremarkable. When we leave next morning, parascenders are floating down over hills that are alive with the sound of motorbikes. From the start of the alpine leg of our safari we've met numerous herds of bikers roaring along the hair-raising roads at breakneck speed. As they whoosh past we can feel their exhilaration. But do they notice the wild flowers so tightly packed into the ground that there is no room for grass, or the wooden chalets sagging under the weight of geraniums dangling from their balconies? Haute-Savoie

Haute-Savoie is blanketed by a sky in various shades of grey when we reach the Chamonix valley. With impeccable timing and a despairing squeal, Tinkerbelle's brakes give out.

Our very special friends Pete and Marianne are waiting for us in Chamonix. Dobby and Tally speed away to investigate the house, and

98

Dobby returns in a few moments proudly waving a pair of lady's knickers. We dine on delicious whole bass, followed by *crème brûlée* with strawberries. Then we sleep in a comfortable bed that doesn't smell of dogs, have a bath and proper breakfast, and wash our clothes in a washing machine. Sheer luxury. Thank you, Pete and Marianne.

After the dogs have enjoyed a long wet walk in a boulder-strewn pine forest, we make a slight detour to the remains of the village of Montroc. During the first week of February 1999 an unusually high quantity of snow fell on the mountainside a little north of Argentière. As much as would normally fall in a month fell in two days, and a slab 5 ft. thick and covering an area of 75 acres detached itself from the mountain and descended towards the valley. Gathering speed until it reached 90 miles an hour it charged down the mountainside and leapt the river Arve. Its impetus carried it uphill and over the villages of le Tour and Montroc. Twenty-three houses and their inhabitants were buried 15 ft. beneath 100,000 tonnes of snow. Twelve people died. All that remain are the overgrown foundations, and one large house knocked on its side. Across the river the bare mountainside still shows the path of the avalanche. If you would like to see what a mountain can do when it sets its mind to it, have a look here.

The mayor of Chamonix was prosecuted for failing to evacuate Montroc's inhabitants when the risk of avalanche was evident. Only a month after the avalanche the Mont Blanc Tunnel fire claimed the lives of 39 people. The same mayor was prosecuted for his failure to properly deal with the situation. He was given a suspended prison sentence for manslaughter for each incident.

Seeing the result of this avalanche underlines my personal feelings towards mountains and their invincibility. Man can climb them, cycle up them or reach their summits in various ways. But how can anybody claim to conquer them? Conquering implies subjugating, and how does something as comparatively insignificant as a man subjugate something as comparatively indestructible as a mountain? I am starting to look forward to leaving the Alps. Beautiful and majestic as they are, I'm not at ease amongst them. My belief is that they don't really like people and only allow humans to live amongst them for as long as it suits them. Apart from their scenery and clean air, I don't much like them, nor their aura of melancholy. Around the Chamonix valley the glaciers that hold the mountains together are beginning to melt due to global warming. Maybe man will eventually destroy the mountains, but what will the mountains do to man in the process? As the glaciers melt they form lakes and release trapped boulders and rocks to threaten the ecological balance. Like a mountain, a glacier is a powerful creature, and unless it remains frozen, it's a threat. During the mid-17th century the Sea of Ice glacier on

Mont Blanc was creeping towards the valley, raising fear amongst the local inhabitants. It had already engulfed farms and villages when the Bishop of Geneva exorcized its satanic evil. It took several years for the bishop's magic to work and stop the glacier's advance. For now.

We drive on to the pink azalea-covered hills of Vallorcine, where the 19th century outlaw and counterfeiter Joseph Farinet used to hide. The son of a blacksmith in the French-speaking part of the Aosta valley in Italy, he used his father's techniques to manufacture currency in small denomination coins that he gave to the poor. Farinet is believed to have produced 100,000 counterfeit twenty-cent pieces, which at the time were the most common coins. For fifteen years he evaded the Swiss and Italian forces of law. Sometimes they captured and imprisoned him, but he usually managed to escape. He met a mysterious death at the age of thirty-five, shot in the back of the head and thrown into a mountain gorge near Saillon, in the Swiss canton of Valais. There was a large bounty on his head, presumably because no crime is more likely to outrage the Swiss than producing false money. The reward was never claimed, and the killer never discovered.

In 1980 a memorial to the values of love, freedom and understanding which he embodied, was created at Saillon to mark the anniversary of Farinet's death. Known as the Vine of Peace, the world's tiniest vineyard covers less than four square yards. Just three vines are planted there in soil brought from all parts of the world, and beyond: fragments of volcanoes and pyramids, the Acropolis and the Matterhorn, and even a sample of soil from Mars. Each year the grapes are pruned and harvested by celebrities and mixed with local wine which is auctioned to raise money for deserving causes.

A pathway lined with stained-glass windows leads to the vineyard, and a statue of Farinet. Traditionally the people who come to tend the vineyard, who include film stars and sportsmen, fire a gun and shout, 'Long live Freedom!' The Dalai Lama declined to fire the gun, choosing instead to simply touch it symbolically.

It's a damp, mild day. Clouds roll down from the mountain and float into the valley, which is densely crammed with houses of elaborately carved timbers and exterior walls decorated with agricultural implements. Even in the drizzle the road between les Gets, world capital of mechanical music – music played by machines like hurdy-gurdies – and Montriond is very lovely, wooded and green and punctuated by waterfalls.

No longer rumbling and farting, Tinkerbelle now draws attention to herself with a tooth-cracking screeching noise as steel grinds against steel when Terry brakes.

Just after le Biot, at the village unfortunately named Urine, there is grim evidence of a recent rockslide. Wrenched up trees stand with their heads buried in the ground, their roots pointing defiantly to the sky. We clock up the 4,000th mile of our journey at the spectacular cracked and split rock formations of les Gorges du Pont du Diable.

Our guide book takes us to a campsite at Saint-Paul-en-Chablais, beautifully situated on a green almost-plateau overlooking Lake Geneva. The owners are absent when we arrive, but a helpful lady scampers from her camper before we stop rolling. She tells us to install ourselves; the owners will be back within half an hour, and if we need any information, she has it. We thank her and start driving around trying to find somewhere that is (a) level, and (b) not a quagmire. The land has clearly been recently reclaimed and laid to grass. It's very squidgy after two days of rain. All the suitably firm places are occupied. We try here, there and everywhere, watched complacently by the other residents peering through their steamy windows. Finally we give up. Terry is certain that if we do put down our roots tonight, we'll be stuck in the morning.

Driving gingerly across what is quickly becoming swamp, we head off through thickening rain towards banana-shaped Lake Geneva, central Europe's largest freshwater lake. For an hour we drive around aimlessly, barely able to see through the windscreen, until we find a campsite. I've no idea where it is. Everything is shrouded in grey rain. The office is closed, and a notice advises that interested parties should enquire at the house, which is up a very steep pathway. I bang on the door for several minutes, increasingly loudly, until a grumpy teenage boy appears. He suggests we park wherever we like and wait for his parents to come back.

Terry reverses Tinkerbelle into a level space, and switches off the engine. We unwind the awning, and get the dogs out on their leads. Before their paws have touched the grass, a distraught old lady in a nightie (it is 6.00pm) scrambles from an adjacent campervan and shuffles towards us, babbling and waving her hands, pointing at the dogs. It isn't easy to understand her, because she sobs at the same time as she babbles, but it appears she is frightened of dogs, their noise will keep her awake, and at her age it isn't right for foreigners to upset her.

We move further away. As we set up again, irritated sounds come from the terrace above us. An old couple are sitting in chairs under the awning of their caravan, huddled in rugs, and tutting because we are blocking the view of the lake they would have if it wasn't obscured by driving rain. The man waves his hand to indicate we should move elsewhere. As soon as we let the dogs out and attach them to their chains, yet another protester appears. He points out that the dogs may obstruct the passageway to the sanitary block. Through gritted teeth I reply that as it is pouring with rain and they are lying peacefully beneath the awning, they are not obstructing anything or anybody. It is unlikely that they will decide to do so. I add that we will be leaving early the next morning (the earlier the better, I feel). He shambles away grumbling about foreigners and threatening to complain to the management if the dogs so much as look at the sanitary block.

During our stay with Pete and Marianne we had washed two loads of clothes – almost all our clothes, in fact. They have been festering, damp, in bin bags all day. The clothes we are wearing are soaking from all the tramping around and setting up of Tinkerbelle, and we face the prospect of having to put on wet clothes tomorrow. It's pointless hanging anything under the awning. Even if the rain stops – which doesn't look likely, there is no wind and the air is damp.

The dogs are unhappy under the awning and demand to go to their bed in the cab. We light the heater and string everything up inside the van. All the washing is draped over a network of lines tied to door handles and cupboard doors. We can't use the cooker because there are several pairs of shorts and socks dangling inches from the gas rings. For supper we share the last morsel of Ossau Iraty cheese and a couple of croissants we find in one of the cupboards, and wash it down with the bottle of Raspberry Love.

Being trapped in a clammy campervan in the rain is only slightly less miserable than being trapped in a clammy tent in the rain. If we stand up the wet laundry swipes us. The heat from the radiator coupled with the moisture from the clothes transforms Tinkerbelle into a steamy capsule. We sit huddled with our books, wiping condensation from our glasses every few minutes. When we take off our wet shoes and socks our feet are white and crinkly. The air smells of wet dogs and damp trainers, and the rain lashes the awning so that Terry has to go outside and wind it back in. Through the steamy window we can just see the grey choppy waters of Lake Geneva as the rain dwindles to drizzle.

Aided by the Raspberry Love we sleep deeply, and awake damp and early to bright sunshine. Across the now calm waters of the lake we can see the city of Lausanne. We string up our still-wet clothing under the awning to catch the sun, release the dogs from the cab and put them on their chains, watched by our vigilant next-door neighbour. On the terrace above us the gentleman pointedly moves his chair about to underline the fact that we are interfering with his view. The only cheerful person we see is a lady washing her clothing outside the sanitary block. By 10.00.m. Our clothes are nearly dry and the dogs still haven't crossed the sanitary block line. I go and pay our fees to the friendly site owner who hopes we have enjoyed our stay despite the weather. He hopes to see us again. I think it's most unlikely.

We are on our way now to breakfast in the eccentric town of Saint-Gingolph at the eastern end of the lake. There's a large empty car park behind an apartment block in a shaded area where we can leave the dogs in comfort. Nothing is likely to disturb them. Terry carefully parks Tinkerbelle and we draw the curtains. We've walked two paces when a voice shouts from a balcony above.

"You can't park there; it's only for residents." "But it's empty – there's nobody here, and we're only going to be an hour," I call back. "Would you mind very much ....." "No, no, you have to move straight away. It's only for residents." Another balcony-woman raps on her window and waves us away. There's room for at least a dozen cars, and we are the only vehicle in sight.

"I'm going to phone the *gendarme*s," threatens woman No. 1.

We move Tinkerbelle across the road and park in a legitimate space beside a small tree, watched by the two harpies. A man fishing on the lake glares at us, as if he is trying to think of a reason why we shouldn't be there. We've been to friendlier places.

A Customs/border post bisects Saint-Gingolph's main street. The post office, railway station and sports stadium are in Switzerland, the church and cemetery in France. Each half-town has had its own school and town hall since the 16th century, when Saint-Gingolph was divided by treaty between France and Switzerland.

We post a letter in France, and walk 50 yards to cross the frontier to have breakfast beside the harbour in Switzerland. Boats roll gently on the slapping waters, and we share our croissants with a flotilla of ducks and a couple of sparrows jumping around the table.

It's a pleasant spot, and on such a peaceful day difficult to imagine anything disagreeable happening here. But during WWII the local French Resistance attacked the German-manned Customs post. In the inevitable reprisals the French part of the town was burned, and several people, including the local priest, were executed. Luckier French inhabitants escaped to safety in the neutral Swiss zone. A painted borderline on the road meant the difference between life and death.

When we return to Tinkerbelle, where the dogs are sleeping and cool, the fisherman responds to our "*Bonjour*" with a frosty glance. Perhaps we won't come back to this part of the world again.

Meillerie, where Shelly nearly drowned, is a quaint and pretty village on the banks of the lake. We think about stopping for a cold drink, but failing to find a convenient parking place, fortunately, as it turns out, decide to press on a little further. Le Matin newspaper will report, a few weeks later, that the tap water in Meillerie has been found to contain '*matière fécale*' or, as we might put it more succinctly, shit. The news of this distasteful fact was slow in reaching Meillerie's inhabitants, and there were no warnings for tourists like us. Residents had noticed that the mayor was buying unusually large quantities of bottled water quite some time before the news became public. There was a suggestion that he knew about the situation before the local inhabitants.

The southern side of the lake between Saint-Gingolph and Thonon-les-Bains is one of those blessedly unspoiled places that seems to have been bypassed by developers. Instead of drinking the sewage-rich water of Meillerie, we stop in Evian-les-Bains where they produce four million bottles of clean water each day. The promenade is filled with roses and trees; crested grebes float between moored boats and sparrows mop up crumbs from snackers seated on waterside benches. A trimaran bears a sticker boasting that it is 'proudly made in France by Virusboats, a successful builder of sailing boats'. You have to admire the optimism of a manufacturer who chooses such a name.

We spend an enjoyable hour ambling around, admiring Evian's copper-tiled roofs, the fancy wrought-iron balconies of the Savoy Hotel, the flowery roundabouts and air of elegance and unrushed prosperity.

To the east of Thonon-les-Bains is the Réserve Naturelle de la Dranse, a marshy area of 150 acres at the delta of the Dranse river where it pours into Lake Geneva. The reserve is home to a wide diversity of plant and wildlife, including beavers. A notice says that if we are patient and lucky, we might see them. Although we are very patient, it is not our lucky day. We wade and slide around on muddy jungular paths, our faces scratched by elephant grass, looking as hard as we can. We see a grebe with a clutch of fluffy babies, a large flock of screaming gulls with small black heads, and some very pretty ducks, but no beavers.

Tinkerbelle screeches her way to Annemasse where we have found a place to buy her some new brake pads. I am mesmerized by the head of the first man who serves us: he seems to have two foreheads. His lower forehead is unusually high, and balanced upon it is a further high forehead, all topped with a shiny pink hairless dome. The distance from his eyebrows up is twice the distance from his eyebrows down, and I simply cannot take my eyes off him. I don't think he notices, though, as he is talking to a friend at the counter while he attends to us. He writes down the number of the part we need, which he doesn't have in stock. Without interrupting his conversation with his friend, he directs us to a shop where he assures us we'll find what we need.

At the next shop I thrust the piece of paper with the part number on it at a helpful youth, who sells us a heavy box. We go to find somewhere Terry can change the pads. Skirting the Swiss border we follow the road through peacefully agricultural countryside, turning northwards at the Fort de l'Ecluse, a 19th century stronghold fortified by that busy man Vauban. Gex is familiar to me as the final campsite where I'd stayed on my hike across France in 1998, so we head there. It's a spacious comfortable site at the foot of the Jura mountains.

In Tinkerbelle's living area Terry finds a glistening sliver of something blue and metallic. He recognizes the remains of one of the arms of his reading glasses. Dobby has been busy again. We find the lenses intact, but the frame is quite past saving. Dobby is puzzled by Terry's shouting. He sits with his head cocked sideways, staring at Terry as if he is conducting a psychological study of a raving lunatic.

The miserable grey wet weather returns and forms an impenetrable curtain of heavy rain shrouding the lake and the Jura mountains behind us. Terry struggles soggily to get Tinkerbelle's wheels off to change the brake pads. I hear him cursing and grunting while I am cooking, then there is a sudden roar of frustration. The brake pads don't fit Tinkerbelle. Terry replaces the wheels and climbs back inside, dripping from head to foot and very cross indeed.

When the rain stops we take the dogs with a new football to play on an open space that looks securely fenced. As soon as they are off their leads they vanish from sight. Tally reappears after a few minutes, but there is no sign of Dobby. We hunt everywhere, whistling, calling and shouting 'Biscuits!' and 'Dinner!' We walk round the site and ask everybody if they have seen a huge black dog, to no avail. After fifteen frantic minutes we go back to Tinkerbelle to decide what to do next. There we find Dobby sprawled on the bed, happily working his way through a packet of dog biscuits he's found. He glances at us briefly and then gulps down the remains of the packet as fast as he can.

The following morning when I go for a shower, as I switch on the water something quite large and grey flops to the floor. It's a young sparrow, which must have been perching on the tap. It hops under the wall into the adjacent cubicle, so I wrap myself in a towel and try to catch it. But I'm clumsy and miss. It panics and flies away, crashing into a window on the other side of the room. I find it on its back in a basin, its tiny claws clenched, its eyes closed and its neck limp. I am heartbroken, sure it's dead. I hold it in my hand against my shoulder, crying. Then I feel a faint heartbeat. After ten minutes the heartbeat seems stronger, but the head is still limp and the eyes closed. I can't walk back to Tinkerbelle in the rain dressed only in a small towel, and I daren't put the chick down. I struggle into my clothes, which isn't easy clutching a fragile body in one hand.

Terry finds a small plastic box and a large wad of cotton wool with which we made a sandwich of the little bird.

"It isn't going to recover, you know that, don't you?" he asks.

I nod. I know it doesn't stand much of a chance, but we have to try. We leave it in the cotton-wool sandwich for an hour. When we peel back the top layer, the bird's eyes have partly opened. It's time for us to leave, and we can't take the bird with us. If it survives where will we put it?

And how can we keep it safe from the dogs while we are driving? I go to the campsite office to see if anybody there will help. A kindly, professory-looking man is worried about keeping it in the office, because they have a cat. But he agrees to keep it on a shelf, and release it if it recovers. While we are trying to feed the bird into a yoghurt pot it begins struggling strongly. We take it behind to the shower block and place it on the ground beneath a thick hedge housing a mob of sparrows. As I release it from my hand, it erupts skywards and disappears into the branches delighting the professor and me. We hug each other. It's funny how such a small incident can create a bond so quickly between strangers.

On our way again, Tinkerbelle screeches her banshee wail to the nearest Citroën garage. There we find the correct brake pads, and taking no chances this time, Terry fits them in the garage forecourt. At last we can drive around without alarming people, and I can stop worrying.

We head for Geneva to visit Terry's good friend Herman, from Mexico. Herman works at the International Labour Organization, founded in 1919 primarily to protect the rights of workers and abolish child labour. In an imposing building decorated with works of art from countries all over the world, people of all nationalities wander around in corridors or pop out of lifts. You see men and women of every colour and creed, in different costumes, speaking different languages, united in their efforts. It's an inspirational place to visit. We sit drinking coffee with Herman, a quietly spoken law professor who tells us how worried he is about the population explosion in Mexico City. The populace has grown from five million to twenty million over the last two decades, largely due to improved health care and infant vaccination programmes. However, there's no work for all these people, so by the eradication of one problem, another has been created.

A 40 ft. high wooden sculpture of a chair with a broken leg stands on the roundabout in front of the United Nations building. It's the work of Swiss sculptor Daniel Berset, erected by Handicap International in 1997 to symbolize the horror of landmines. Called Broken Chair (a double-entendre here, as 'chair' means 'flesh' in French), it's a simple design conveying a poignant message. Every fifteen minutes somebody is killed or maimed by a landmine in this, the 21st century.

11

Franche-Comté

Doubs

From Gex we climb up to the Col de la Faucille for a fine lunch before setting off towards Pontarlier. Terry has set his heart on staying the night at the airfield there which we'd visited many years ago.

I find the Jura mountains gentler, more curvaceous and hospitable than the jagged and menacing peaks of the Alps. Here I don't feel melancholy or trapped.

Tinkerbelle purrs through Morez, home of the national school of *lunetterie* (spectacle trade). In 1796 a gentleman with the glorious name of Pierre-Hyacinthe Cazeaux bent a nail into the shape of a pair of glasses. From this he developed the idea of manufacturing metal spectacle frames, an industry that grew until today Morez is the French capital of spectacle frame manufacture. Terry isn't amused by my suggestion that we try to find a replacement frame for the one Dobby mangled yesterday.

Not far from Morez is the town of Morbier, where the cheese of the same name comes from. It's a cheese I've never particularly enjoyed. In fact, I haven't enjoyed it at all. It's probably most appreciated by people living in Morbier, like sago worms are relished in Papua New Guinea, whale blubber in Iceland, or witchetty grubs in the Outback. This is how Morbier is described by online source Wikipedia: 'Morbier is a semi-soft cows' milk cheese. It is ivory coloured soft and slightly elastic, and is formed in two layers separated by a thin layer of ash. It has a rind that is yellowish, moist, and leathery. The bottom layer consists of the morning milk and the upper layer is made of the evening milk. The aroma of Morbier is somewhat obnoxious, though the flavour is rich and creamy, with a slightly bitter aftertaste. The ash has no flavour. It is added between steps to prevent a rind from forming during the molding process. This cheese dates back to the dark ages, from the monastery of Morbier.' If you're on the lookout for an obnoxious-smelling, bouncy, elastic medieval cheese in a leathery rind with a slightly bitter aftertaste, in two layers encompassing some tasteless ash, consider Morbier.

We drive quietly through the Regional Natural Park of the Haut-Jura over gentle hills, along roads splattered with cow dung, and past fishermen standing chest-deep in streams. The unhurried atmosphere is accentuated by the fact that several villages are still displaying their Christmas decorations, and it is now mid-June, five weeks since we left home.

The afternoon sun reflects from south-facing walls of the houses, metal-clad to protect the wall during the winter months when snow accumulates on the roof and melts beneath the sun. A practical idea, but it doesn't greatly add to the aesthetics of the houses.

Terry is delighted to be back at the Aero Club in Pontarlier. We'd enjoyed their hospitality many years ago when we'd landed in a small light aircraft during a fierce storm just as the members were going home for lunch. "Make yourselves at home," one of them had said, "you'll be comfortable and dry in here. We'll leave the clubhouse open, so you can help yourself to anything from the bar. See you later." The current president of the club, Christian, says we are most welcome to stay on the airfield that night. After setting up Tinkerbelle on the tarmac outside a hangar, we cook a meal and go to spend an hour with Christian and Opale, his faultlessly mannered large white poodle, his friend Louis – call him Lou-Lou – and Philippe, a pilot with Air France who speaks faultless English. Terry's French is improving daily, but it is a nice change for me not to have to act as interpreter. The men talk flying, while I drink a little too much Baileys.

There is no indication that we should expect a thunderstorm during the night. Accordingly we haven't put away the awning. When flashes of lightning and drum rolls of thunder shake Tinkerbelle, and a deluge rushes in through the open roof vents and on to the bed, Terry braves the weather to go out and dismantle the awning to stop it collapsing beneath the weight of water.

By morning it is drizzling sullenly. It doesn't matter, because we are going to visit the Espera Sbarro concept-car exhibition just a couple of hundred yards from the airfield. But when we wander over there it's locked up, and won't be open until 2.00 p.m. Four hours of hanging around on the airfield in grey weather doesn't appeal, so we start to organize ourselves to leave. Terry opens the cab to move the dogs into the back.

As he jumps from the cab, Dobby gives a loud yelp. He does this quite frequently and dramatically if he suspects something frightful may happen to him. For example, if Tally looks at his bone prior to snatching it away, that is cause for an anguished squeal, so we don't take much notice. He bounces cheerfully into the back of the van and up on to his rug, while I put everything away and out of his reach. This takes three or four minutes, and when I turn round I am horrified to see blood everywhere. It's all over the floor, the door, the front of the fridge and the rug. Dobby is sitting on the rug, licking his foot from which a thick red stream is flowing. Tally is trying to help. Although he is wagging his tail Dobby will not let us examine the wound. He snarls and bares his teeth, and it is impossible to see what damage he's done. Despite searching every square inch of the tarmac around Tinkerbelle, we find no sign of anything that could have injured him. It remains a mystery to this day.

He's lying peacefully licking his foot, so we decide to wait a while until the bleeding stops so that we can get a look at the damage. As best we can we clean up the mess all over the van.

The sky is heavy with dark grey clouds for as far as we can see, which is a long way because Pontarlier is France's second highest town after Briançon. After we've had breakfast in Pontarlier Dobby's paw has stopped bleeding and he is chewing on a plastic bottle. But he's still resistant to having his foot touched. We decide to visit the sinister Château de Joux, which squats menacingly on top of a crag surrounded by a mournful pine forest. Almost a thousand years old (and updated by the indefatigable Vauban), on this gloomy day its desolate appearance is an indication of its unhappy history.

During the long absence of Lord Amauri III of Joux at the Crusades, his wife Berthe fell in love with a handsome young knight named Amey de Montfaucon. The inevitable happened – why hadn't Amauri locked her in a chastity belt before he went off gallivanting, I wonder? When Amauri returned unexpectedly he caught Berthe and Amey in flagrante. Filled with justifiable Christian indignation, he killed Amey, whose body was suspended from a gibbet. Berthe he imprisoned in a cell sufficiently high to enable her to kneel. From the tiny window she could enjoy the sight of the swinging and diminishing remains of her lover. After Amauri died, Berthe's son released her from imprisonment, and she retired to spend what was left of her life in a convent.

Loïse de Joux's fiancé Thiébaud also went crusading in the Holy Land. Many years after his departure, a visored knight arrived to tell Loïse that her fiancé was alive and happy, surrounded by beautiful women, and that he'd quite forgotten her. She replied that as long as her beloved was alive, that was all that mattered. The visored knight then revealed himself to be none other than, yes, you've guessed it, mischievous Thiébaud. Overcome with joy, Loïse fell down stone dead.

Maybe the most tragic of all stories connected with the Château de Joux is that of heroic little General Toussaint Louverture, leader of the Haitian slave revolt. Tricked and betrayed by the French, he was

109

deported to France and imprisoned in this awful castle. Standing here in mid-June, cold and wet waiting for the guided tour to begin, it wasn't difficult to imagine what it was like for a sixty-year-old man, a child of the sunny Caribbean, to find himself locked in a small bare cell in the coldest region of France, where the temperature has fallen as low as minus 41°C (minus 40°F). The poor man was dead within a year, nine months before Haiti achieved the independence from France for which he had fought so hard and given his life.

As if all this wasn't enough, a few weeks before our arrival at its creepy doorstep, a chunk of the château weighing several tons had fallen off due to the action of ice in a crack in the rockbed. It was only because the event happened at lunchtime, when there was no one standing beneath the walls, that nobody was killed.

There are municipal vehicles and barriers all over the place, and worried-looking people in hard hats walking round measuring. A coach load of French ladies queuing ahead of us become impatient as we stand waiting for the ominous wooden door to open. From time to time a harassed guide appears and apologizes for the delay. She reassures us that the tour will begin very shortly.

Standing at the doorway of this monumentally depressing place, I begin having serious doubts about our visit. I think of dungeons and cellars, and dark passages, so next time the guide pops up I collar her and ask whether visitors are free to roam at will around the château. No, she says, unfortunately it's too dangerous following the recent accident. We must follow the guided visit. Is it suitable for claustrophobics? I ask. She pulls a face, and says that some people find the narrow staircases uncomfortable. I've heard enough.

Terry declines to go on the visit without me, so we return to Pontarlier in search of something more uplifting. Our quest leads to the <u>absinthe Distillerie Guy</u>. Pontarlier was the birthplace of the first absinthe distillery and is the world capital of absinthe production. The original recipe was an adaptation of an 18th century herbal cure-all, based on wormwood, and developed over the years into a notorious liqueur. Cheaper than wine, and with a staggering alcoholic content of 72 per cent, it was favoured by the poor and the bohemian. In 1901, during a fire a quick-witted workman opened the storage tanks of the Pernod distillery allowing the spirit to flow into the river Doubs. It saved the buildings from exploding and burning Pontarlier to the ground. The local inhabitants, Pontissaliens as they are known, could drink to their hearts' content directly from the river, the soldiers using their helmets to scoop up its potent waters.

Absinthe's popularity was a challenge to France's wine producers, and its effect upon consumers didn't find favour with the National

League against Alcoholism, or the Croix Bleue as it was otherwise called. They campaigned energetically for the drink to be banned. Known familiarly as the Green Fairy, absinthe was credited with 'making you crazy and criminal, provoking epilepsy and tuberculosis, and killing thousands of French people . . . making a ferocious beast of man, a martyr of woman, and a degenerate of the infant, it disorganizes and ruins the family and menaces the future of the country.' It was, claimed a leading antagonist, 246 times more likely to cause insanity than wine, and furthermore 'the real characteristic of absinthe is that it leads straight to the madhouse or the courthouse. It is truly "madness in a bottle" and no habitual drinker can claim that he will not become a criminal.' The death knell tolled for absinthe production when in 1905 a Swiss farmer shot his pregnant wife and two children before trying to kill himself. His actions were attributed to the two glasses of absinthe he'd drunk prior to the event. No account was taken of the six glasses of wine, glass of cognac, glass of crème de menthe, brandy-laced cup of coffee, another litre of wine and then a further shot of coffee laced with marc that he'd drunk the same day. It was indisputably obvious that it was the absinthe that had caused his behaviour. This added the necessary fuel to the campaign to ban the stuff. Shortly thereafter, in Geneva an absinthe-bingeing man killed his wife with a hatchet and a revolver. Inexorably the garrotte tightened round the Green Fairy. It was banned in Switzerland, Belgium, the United States, and, in 1915, in France.

Eighty-six years later France legalized production, and in April 2001 the Distillerie Guy planted fifty-five thousand wormwood plants. Harvested by the end of September and dried during October, on 15 December 2001 the first bottles of absinthe were sold, with a reduced alcohol content of 45 per cent.

Today the distillery is buzzing with enthusiasm, laughter and the rattle of glasses. An exuberant employee asks whether we'd like to taste any of their products, and yes, we say, could we have a sip of absinthe? A young girl beckons. Absinthe, we learn, isn't something you glug into a glass, top up with water, and knock back. There's a time-honoured traditional way to drink it. We have a lesson in absinthe etiquette. You need first of all a bottle of absinthe and an absinthe fountain, a fancy glass container filled with cold water, with a varying number of spigots growing out of it. Then you need for each person a tall glass, a perforated silver spoon and a sugar lump. Fill your tall glass with the required level of absinthe; balance across the glass the perforated silver spoon, and place upon it half a sugar lump. Place the glass, the spoon and the sugar lump beneath one of the spigots, and allow the cold water to drip slowly, slowly, drop by drop, through the sugar lump and into the absinthe, which will 'louche' – turn cloudy. Your absinthe is now ready to drink.

"Et voila!" chirps the girl, handing each of us a cloudy glass, and taking one for herself.

"A votre santé!"

"A la vôtre!"

The word 'absinthe' comes from the Greek meaning undrinkable, because wormwood is so bitter. As clever as the Greeks may have been, they obviously didn't know about the sugar lump. Just as a matter of interest, the Russian name for wormwood is '*chernobyl.*' As we stand at the table sipping, workers come up and help themselves to tots, and local people pop in to say hello and have a little drink. The place is heady with fumes from the various concoctions being brewed and bottled. If we close our eyes we can imagine we are sitting with Van Gogh in a decadent Parisian bar.

Our first friend, the gentleman who'd offered us the tasting, comes to ask if it has pleased us.

"Very much indeed," we say.

He reaches for another bottle, and pours a slug of yellow syrup for each of us.

"Try this. It's made from pine. Very good for sore throats." It slides down nicely.

"Now you'll like this. It's anis, not as strong as absinthe."

He is pouring generous glassfuls. A selection of fruit liqueurs follows, and our host becomes increasingly enthusiastic. "I only speak very little English," he confides. "Except when I have some drink, then I'm fluent!" He roars with laughter and sloshes a pink liquid into our glasses. Terry abstains, because he's driving. But I'm not.

"How many different drinks do you produce?" I ask.

"Twenty-two," he replies proudly. "What would you like to taste next?" I decline because by now I've had six glasses of various liqueurs. I'm starting to feel light-headed, and the room seems to be tilting.

Beaming at our fellow shoppers and the staff, we order a large bottle of absinthe, and one of pine syrup, as well as a couple of posters. We skip happily back to Tinkerbelle, where Dobby is sleeping. He still will not let us examine his paw, tucking it out of reach, and growling quietly but firmly. For half an hour we sit laughing, hiccuping and feeling ridiculously pleased with ourselves, despite the fact that it is still pouring with rain. Any lingering depression from the Château de Joux has evaporated, and we continue on our way following the Doubs, a gentle and orderly sort of river today. A pair of swans proudly escort their clutch of grubby cygnets across the still surface; beside the river several herons stalk, and a large bird of prey struts around in a field looking important.

While we were in the Aero Club at Pontarlier, Christian said that we should visit the Republic of the Saugeais. Ask them to stamp your passports, he said.

The Saugeais Republic covers an area of approximately 40 square miles, and encompasses a dozen villages. This little-known democracy originated in the 12th century when, to atone for the sins of his ancestors, the lord of Joux gave a parcel of land to the Archbishop of Besançon. The minuscule state maintained a low profile until 1947, when a local hotel owner, M. Georges Pourchet, jokingly told a visiting dignitary that he needed a passport to enter the Saugeais. Entering into the spirit of the occasion, the *préfet* pulled some strings and M. Pourchet found himself named as the first President of the Republic. When he died, his wife Gabrielle stepped into the presidential shoes. The Republic has its own anthem, postage stamps and Customs officer. The French governmental hierarchy looks it on benevolently, and the Saugeais President receives invitations to State functions at the Elysée. When M. Pourchet met the so-very-patrician Valéry Giscard d'Estaing, he told him that he looked forward to discussing matters "as one President to another." We have our passports ready when we reach Montbenoît just before noon, but there is a decided air of nothing happening. I ask a pedestrian where we should deliver our passports, and he looks at me as if I am armed and dangerous. I go to the post office and ask the lady behind the counter, who is startled but wants to be helpful. She knows nothing about the regulations regarding foreign visitors, but takes me into the office of the supreme head of the Saugeais post office. He is very charming and suggests I try the tourist office. As I reach the door the incumbent is coming out, and says it won't be possible to entertain any requests until 3.00pm. If we go back then, they will issue us a *laisser passer*. They don't stamp passports.

A little exasperated with trying to fulfill these lax immigration requirements, we drive off and spend an hour exploring the rustic and unspoilt lands making up the Republic. Time and weather have carved caves in the limestone so perfectly that they look man-made. One cave houses the chapel of Our Lady of Remonot, which is a place of pilgrimage. Legend tells that a hermit placed a statue of the Blessed Virgin in the cave, and the local people came there to pray. Water trickling from a spring and flowing over the Madonna's feet cured eye diseases. When the hermit died, the monks of Montbenoît removed the statue to their monastery and the miracles stopped. One night the statue escaped, walked back to the cave and reinstalled herself, whereupon the water regained its magical properties.

Whilst we are on our tour of the Saugeais the sun comes out and shines down on the realm. We follow the Route Courbet towards Ornans, where Gustave Courbet, the first of the realist painters was born. It is a rather perilous road coming up to Mouthier-Haute-Pierre. A sign indicates where a M. Tompierre had fallen over a precipice 'a victim of his own zeal,' and a little further along a whole busload of travellers had gone over the parapet.

Just after Ornans it begins to really rain. It's like driving through a tsunami. We find our way to a campsite in <u>Besançon</u>, and I scamper from the van to the office up to my ankles in water. There's thunder and lightning and two little dogs in the office are frantic with excitement. Anybody who sets foot outside is drenched to the skin in seconds. It rains so torrentially that it becomes funny. A group of us stand dripping in the office, laughing hysterically.

Half an hour later it's a warm summer day. We are parked next to a German-registered camping car in a beautiful location beside the river Doubs. As we finish erecting Tinkerbelle's awning a freak gust of wind swoops off the river. It lifts the awning into the air, twisting it backwards over Tinkerbelle's roof, wrenching the metal frame half off its moorings, and breaking a small window.

Seconds later a blond giant appears from the German vehicle. He reaches over Tinkerbelle's roof and lifts the crumpled awning down as if it were a paper napkin. He says something we can't understand. I ask whether he speaks any French or English.

"*Nein, Deutsch,*" he responds, pointing at the number plate on his vehicle.

I only know six words of German – *kleiner, grösser, danke Sie, bitte* and *dungemittelfabrik.*

"*Danke Sie,*" I say.

He straightens the twisted metal frame with his bare hands and takes Terry by the arm with a huge paw. He starts explaining in German how to repair the frame. He mimes unscrewing the rails from Tinkerbelle, taking the thing apart, bending the rails into a straight line, drilling holes and remounting the awning. They seem to understand each other perfectly well. His wife comes over to join us, and they chatter happily. Every so often we catch a word we recognize, like Alsace, or Hanover. We nod and smile, and point at the sky which is changing from clear blue to heavy cloud, and grimace.

While Terry walks to a nearby hardware store to buy some screws to mend the awning, I persuade Dobby to show me his injured foot. I can see a deep jagged cut right through one of his pads. He runs around happily, holding his paw off the ground, and although it doesn't seem to be bothering him we decide to take him to the vet tomorrow.

Through the night rain drums on to the roof, but by morning the day is bright and sunny. I am excited about our visit to Besançon, because we are going to explore the town on Segways: electrically driven, self-balancing pairs of wheels with a handle, steered and driven by body weight. I telephone the tourist office to ask what we need to do to get our hands and feet on to the Segways.

"There are no Segways in Besançon," they say. I explain we've come to Besançon specifically because of an article in the glossy Doubs magazine, summer edition, produced by the Economic and Tourist Development Agency for the Doubs. It clearly features, over two pages complete with photographs, the delights of exploring the town by Segway. The tourist office is unmoved, and suggests I telephone the town hall. The town hall is apologetic for the absence of Segways for reasons they are unwilling to explain. They suggest that as we are here we might as well have a look at the town. They hope our visit won't be spoiled, because the town is crammed with interest and beauty.

Before setting off to find out whether this is true, Terry has to reattach the awning to Tinkerbelle. There is no room for it inside: it has to go back on. So he drills the holes and fits the new screws, which entails quite a lot of messing around, and our blond giant neighbour arrives at precisely the right moment to help lift the thing into place and hold it while Terry fixes it back on.

We drive into the city centre and find a vet for Dobby. It closes for lunch just as we arrive, and won't reopen until 2.30pm. Even if we have been lured here by a false promise, Besançon is a beautiful town of parks and riverside walks, with a lively, friendly atmosphere that reminds us of 'our' home town, Poitiers. And it's the birthplace of two French notables who have enriched our world, writer Victor Hugo and chef Raymond Blanc.

In the historic and colourful Battant quartier we find a simple restaurant decorated with ethnic carvings and hangings. There is no printed menu or wine list; you have whatever is chalked on a blackboard. I explain to the Middle Eastern waiter that we are vegetarians.

"*Pas de problème!*" He indicates the blackboard: cheese tart, tortilla, boiled eggs, tuna, stuffed tomatoes, all served with piles of salad and a cheerful rosé wine. Unlike the usual reverent hush and muted talk of a lunchtime French restaurant, the conversation is animated and the reggae music at the right volume so that it isn't intrusive. The clientele is bohemian: two guys in black leather jackets, sleeves pushed up their forearms, with wild standing-up hair and designer stubble; a woman in mustard-coloured trousers and a plastic lilac-coloured coat; another with violent pink hair; and an elderly professorish fellow wearing a crumpled linen jacket with the sleeves rolled back, accompanied by a sullen girl dressed entirely in black. He is stroking her leg under the table. She stares at the wall behind him and blows smoke from surly nostrils.

It is an agreeable change to eat food not typically French, and to be part of the relaxed lunchtime bustle in the pedestrian street. The meal itself is very reasonably priced; the anonymous wine shockingly expensive.

We pass half an hour roaming round the wide pedestrianized streets, admiring the pretty pale blue, beige and pink colours of the local stone. A pigeon is taking its bath in a fountain, sitting in the water and lifting its wings to wash fastidiously beneath them.

Ahead of us at the door outside the vet's surgery is a handsome young man with a friendly smile. He looks pointedly at his watch. It is 2.40pm, ten minutes after the stated opening time. Fifteen minutes later a harried-looking man turns up, with a younger woman rattling some keys. She opens the door and sits behind a desk in the entrance, the harried man disappears, the young man and we stand waiting. The harried man keeps coming and going, appearing in a white jacket, disappearing. He beckons the young man, and gestures that we should sit in the waiting room, which we obediently do. He holds up a finger that seems to indicate he will see us in one minute.

While we sit looking at posters of different breeds of cats and dogs, an advertisement for worming products and the lifecycles of fleas and ticks, we can hear a conversation between the receptionist and the young man becoming louder and more excited. We sit for ten minutes, thankful that Dobby isn't haemorrhaging. Finally the receptionist shows us into a small surgery. She smiles and says the doctor will be with us *"tout de suite."* A moment later he comes in, shakes our hands, and goes out. Shortly he is back again, and asks what our problem is. Before we can reply, he disappears out of the door once more. There is a lot of shouting coming from the lobby. I don't know how long we've waited by now.

At last he returns and drapes a stethoscope round his neck. He pulls a card from his desk and begins writing down our details, and then puts his pen down and sighs.

"That man hasn't paid his bill," he explains. "He owes me money. He brings his animals for treatment, and doesn't pay. The whole family are dishonest. Dreadful. Scandalous." We tut tut.

"Now, your dog. How old is he?"

"Eight months, approximately."

His eyebrows shoot upwards as he looks at enormous Dobby. I explain about the mysterious injury to Dobby's foot, and the vet examines it, squatting on the floor while Dobby licks the back of his head.

"Yes, it's a bad injury. I can't stitch it, though. The texture of a dog's paw is like cork – it won't hold stitches. What I'll do is clean it and put some staples in; they might hold." But amiable, easy-going Dobby has no intention of letting his foot be cleaned or stapled. He puts up a tremendous, although very good-natured fight that he wins. He slouches triumphantly against the wall, his long pink tongue dangling, while three

116

of us pant and heave.

"I'll have to sedate him."

The vet calls the receptionist and between all of us we manage to hold Dobby still long enough for the vet to give him a sedative injection. Slowly he subsides from standing to sitting, to slumping, and by the time we've lifted him on to the table he is unconscious. The vet works away cleaning the wound, and punches some staples through it while I grit my teeth and look out of the window. Then he winds a length of bandage round the paw and secures it thoroughly with adhesive tape. Dobby doesn't move through the procedure. In fact he's so deeply asleep he has to be carried out to Tinkerbelle on a little stretcher. We lay him on the bed, where Tally gently licks his mouth.

Back in the surgery, the vet asks if I can translate a few French words for him, as he has several English clients. Although he speaks a little of our language there are some words that fail him, like "*vomir.*" He talks about his son, who works in Marble Arch as a computer programmer. Once every fortnight, he tells us, he travels to Paris to meet all his other children. When they were little he'd spent too much time with animals and not enough with his family. Now he is making up for that lost time. He is a very sweet man. The bill for Dobby's treatment is more than twice our worst fears and represents two weeks of our budget.

We'd planned to visit Besançon's famous citadel, but it's suddenly become very hot, so instead we decide to drive until we find somewhere cool where Dobby can recover in peace. Our route leads eastwards to take us back on our track, into gently undulating countryside patched with wheat fields and large Comtois farmhouses. The hills become smaller and the landscape more open in this peaceful and prosperous part of the Doubs.

At Maîche we stop to restock our larder, and to stand at the gates of the 16th century Château de Montalembert, where General Charles de Gaulle and Winston Churchill met on the eve of the grand offensive towards Belfort and the Rhine.

Picking up the river Doubs at Saint-Hippolyte, we follow its course to Epomanduodurum as it was called in Gallo-Roman times or Mandeure as it's now known. Personally, I just love saying Epomanduodurum. At the spacious and peaceful campsite Tally has a good run and a game with his football while still-dozy Dobby watches through one half-open eye. They both eat their dinner enthusiastically, but Dobby seems to list to starboard every so often. We think it would be comforting for him to stay in bed with us tonight. The bed isn't particularly large; in fact it is particularly small, and it is like sharing it with a Shetland pony. Although he is quiet he still takes more than half of the available space. While he sleeps soundly, we barely sleep at all. He wakes up as lively as a cartload of

117

monkeys, and starts tearing off the expensive wrapping round his paw.

Epomanduodurum's main road is wonderfully adorned with the signs of the zodiac in huge floral designs, topiary and natural materials. We see many beautifully decorated towns and villages on our journey, but I think Epomanduodurum would take a lot of beating.

Montbéliard is the Peugeot stronghold. The dynasty's roots there go back to the 15th century, when the enterprising family was already established in the area as farmers, artisans, military men and builders of windmills. When the mills developed into steel mills they started manufacturing tools, coffee grinders, irons and steel armatures for corsetry like bustiers, brassières and crinolines. They progressed to hair clippers, ice skates, sewing machines and bicycles and from there, logically, to automobiles.

To atone for dragging Terry round the chocolate factory I suggest we visit the Peugeot Museum in Sochaux, just east of Montbéliard. I don't expect to be greatly interested in the history of the Lion, but the Peugeot Museum turns out to be far more than an exhibition of automobiles. It's a trip into the past, a look back to the age of elegance, and lots more beside. Beautifully laid out, the museum displays examples of Peugeot's earliest designs. Bicycles range from wooden ones made for children, through penny-farthings and tandems, tricycles and bicycles with wicker sidecars and children's seats to the very bicycle on which Richard Virenque won his fourth consecutive best hill climb in the 1997 Tour de France.

There are displays of marine and aircraft engines, sewing machines and divine old motor cars, their brass polished to a mirror finish, the leather glowing with elbow grease and good health. These vehicles must have been draughty, cold and quite uncomfortable, but their elegance is unsurpassable. In a small theatre a Columbo hologram – shabby mac, cigar, wonky eyes – relates the history of the company and the development of their cars over the last century. There are glass cases exhibiting Peugeot memorabilia and collectable items. Among the cars on display are East African Safari winners (I saw those actual cars during the events in the 1960s when I lived in Kenya and worked for the Peugeot agent), and the cars that won the Le Mans 24-hour race. There are examples of all the Peugeot models over the decades, and the latest outrageously futuristic concept car, as well as the Popemobile used during John Paul II's visit to the Alsace and Lorraine in 1988.

Ninety-nine per cent of the vehicles are in pristine condition, displayed against backgrounds of contemporary photographs, and films of rallying and racing. There's also an exhibition of 3,700 die-cast model Peugeot vehicles belonging to a private collector. In the centre of the open-plan museum is a restaurant from where you can continue admiring the exhibits while enjoying a very good meal.

It is filling up by midday, and we manage to squeeze into the last remaining table for two. Lunch is excellent and reasonably priced, and wouldn't be out of place in a superior hotel. Afterwards we're itching to play with the rally car simulators. As I settle behind the wheel an endearingly earnest little boy of about ten climbs uninvited into the passenger seat. He points out the controls of the car, and advises me which circuit to select. His grandfather tries to extricate him, but my co-driver explains that the lady is going to need somebody like him to help her drive the car. I agree that I'd appreciate his *savoir faire*. The boy can barely stop himself from snatching the wheel from me in his enthusiasm to demonstrate his driving skills. We agree he'll handle gear changes while I steer. It isn't an entirely successful partnership because apparently I keep doing something wrong. After a few circuits I hand over the wheel to Terry, who isn't quite so panicked by the boy's yelled directions, and he acquits himself rather better than me.

During the three very enjoyable hours we spend in the museum, Dobby has removed most of his bandage.

At Joncherey there's a memorial to Corporal Peugeot, who holds the unhappy distinction of being the first French person killed in the so-called Great War on the Western front, even before the formal declaration of hostilities between France and Germany. Although both countries were already mobilized, a tenuous hope remained that war might be averted at the very last moment, and the French troops had been ordered to withdraw seven miles from the German frontier. Corporal Jules Peugeot, a nineteen-year-old teacher, was washing his hands when a child alerted him that the Prussians were coming. Eight cavalrymen appeared, and responded with gunfire to Corporal Peugeot's order for them to halt. One shot mortally wounded the young corporal. Before succumbing he returned fire and killed Lieutenant Camille Mayer, a twenty-year-old from just south of Mulhouse (which at that time was part of Germany). The two young men died on 2 August 1914, at a few minutes after 10.00am. The following day, Germany notified France that they were officially at war.

Corporal Peugeot was buried with military honours at his home a few miles from Joncherey. During WWII German troops destroyed the memorial erected to mark the event; the French replaced it with a bigger one in 1959.

Hugging the frontier with Switzerland, we drive through a peaceful suburban landscape until the presence of storks' nests on houses indicates that we have reached the Alsace.

12

Alsace and Lorraine

Haut-Rhin

Fields of golden wheat and corn, and acres of baby trees in dense rows make up the landscape of the Sundgau. Village names become Germanic: there are *-dorfs* and *-lachs, -bachs and -kirchs, -ingens* and *-heims* and *-willers* everywhere. The architecture changes abruptly, and sprawling Franche-Comtois farmhouses give way to more modern, taller buildings, with steeper roofs, in wild colours. Intricately timbered houses are painted lime green, bright red, pale lilac, deep pink, daffodil yellow, various shades of blue, and ox-blood red. No colour seems too fantastic for local homeowners. On many of the houses the walls are painted with storks, milkmaids, birds and plants. Vivid geraniums and petunias spill from balconies. It's surprising how beautiful and how absolutely right these colours look. Just a few hundred yards away in the Franche-Comté they would seem garish, grotesque, but here in the Alsace they are perfect.

We make a brief stop in Ferrette, because Terry needs a haircut. The hairdresser wears black leather trousers draped with clinking chains, pointy-toed black boots, and a skimpy black top displaying his smooth brown arms with their spiked leather bracelets. He completes the look with pink-and-blond spiky hair. He gives Terry a painstaking haircut, snipping a tiny piece here, a little bit there until he achieves what they both agree is perfection.

From Folgensbourg the Swiss city of Basel spreads out before us. Cherry trees sag beneath the weight of fruit, and Europe's busiest waterway, the Rhine, pops up at Rosenau. Once a polluted nightmare used as a dumping ground for waste, the river is gradually being cleaned up. It's a paradoxical stretch of countryside along here: frequent ugly hydroelectric plants separated by patches of unspoiled bucolic landscape and thick woods. We're making a detour from here to visit Albert Schweitzer's birthplace, Kaysersberg. At the time of his birth in 1875 the

Alsace belonged to Germany, and he would always regard himself as German.

Although the outskirts of Colmar aren't anything you'd want to photograph, the old town centre is a ravishing panorama of technicoloured medieval buildings that managed to escape destruction during the war. A 40 ft. high replica of the Statue of Liberty stands on a roundabout on the northern edge of the town. It marks the centenary of the death of the sculptor who created the original – Frédéric-Auguste Bartholdi, a native of Colmar.

Each day by late afternoon our thoughts turn to finding somewhere pleasant to stay overnight. We have four sources of information, books and maps that I balance on my lap and search through at the same time as navigating, translating if necessary, keeping my eyes skinned for interesting features, and at this time also keeping a watchful eye on Dobby to prevent his removing the staples from his foot. This is a stressful period each day, when documents slither and slide all over the place, Terry fires questions and directions, and we frequently overshoot turnings because I don't see them in time.

Today we are all over the place, and already frazzled by the time we find Kaysersberg's campsite. It's full. One of the slithering guide books suggests a campsite a little further away, at Fréland, so that's where we go. It's a pretty village perched on a hillside in the foothills of the Vosges a few miles north-west of Kaysersberg. The campsite is beautifully located close to the forest. There is only one other vehicle there, which also belongs to English people. They display the same lack of interest in us as we do in them, in our strange insular English way.

After we've managed to bind a fresh dressing around Dobby's foot we take the dogs for a long walk through the nearby forest. Dobby runs happily with a hoppy-skippy motion. It is a chilly night up here, shaded by the Fréland pass, but peaceful.

It would be difficult to find a more picturesque town than Kaysersberg. Beautiful, ornate old buildings are buried in geraniums, the cobbled streets are immaculately clean, and the aromas of new-baked cakes and freshly brewed coffee perfume the air. Kaysersberg is seriously touristy and unbelievably quaint. In a patisserie I find an evil thing called *berawecka*, a Kaysersberg speciality. Sold by weight, its ingredients include dried pears and dried apples, figs, dates, candied citrus peel, plums, bananas, spices, hazel nuts, walnuts, almonds and kirsch. Texture-wise it is like an uncooked Christmas pudding, but heavier. Taste-wise it's a voluptuous mixture of sweet and spicy, rich and exotic that satisfies all the senses. It's divine, and a little goes a very, very long way. We also buy a delicious onion tart, a couple of pain raisin and some *kugelhopf*, an Alsatian speciality. As pleasant as *kugelhopf* is, it's not in the same

121

league as *berawecka*.

All around the hillsides are covered with tall vines in neat rows running in every direction from the crests of the hills down to the edges of the roads. They bask fresh and green in the ripening sunshine, and spread for as far as the eye can see, like armies massing for a decisive battle.

With the onion tart and the cakes filling Tinkerbelle with a heavenly fragrance, we follow the Alsace wine route to Mittelwihr and Riquewihr. As we drive through Zellenberg a pterodactyl-like shadow passes over Tinkerbelle's roof.

"Stork!"

We draw up on the side of the road to watch the dangly-legged bird circle and drop on to a heap of branches dumped on somebody's chimney. An adult bird and a juvenile sit peering down at us with scholarly interest, unperturbed by our presence or Tally's wild yelping. A few yards down the road another nest perches on top of a tree stump, with a crowd of sparrows happily cohabiting in the basement area beneath a stork family of parents and infant. There is something very endearing about these large birds choosing to make their homes upon the roofs of human houses. The nests are built of intertwined branches about seven ft. in diameter. We spend a happy half hour watching the birds preening themselves delicately with their long beaks while they watch us placidly, and talk to each other by clacking their beaks. At the beginning of the 20th century thousands of storks lived in Alsace, but by the 1980s only two couples remained. We are looking at what twenty years previously had represented the entire stork population of the region.

Hunawihr is a fairytale village of Hansel and Gretel gingerbread houses.

Glazed orange, green and maroon patterned tiles gleam from the bell tower of the Gothic church that since the 17th century has been shared between the Protestants and the Catholics under what is known as the 'simultaneum.' Each religion is allocated different times for its services. Whilst in life worshippers share the same church, the departed reside in separate parts of the fortified cemetery, so that in the hereafter never the twain shall meet.

We follow a sign leading to *'Parc des Cigognes'* and park Tinkerbelle under the watchful eye of a self-important car park attendant. He's immaculately dressed in black and white, with kohl-lined eyes and a long red bill, and he struts slowly along the lines of parked vehicles. A cluster of laughing children follow him, and he's clearly delighted by the attention.

When it opened in 1976 the park's objective was to save the white stork, which was on the edge of extinction. It's estimated that ninety per cent of storks die during their annual migration. The reason they migrate is not because of cold weather, but due to scarcity of food – mostly amphibians, insects and fish – during the winter. Travelling thousands of miles, they are electrocuted when they land tiredly on electric cables. In Africa they fall victim to hunters, droughts that deplete their food stocks, and poisoning from toxic chemicals used to combat locusts. They would be safer if they stayed where they are, nesting on Alsatian rooftops, so the *Parc des Cigognes* is working to breed out their migratory instinct. Each year the park collects some eggs from the nests. They incubate them and raise the chicks by hand. These baby storks spend the first three years of their life in a large, natural enclosure covered with netting, before being released into the wild, by which time their migratory instinct has withered. These birds will mate, either with other captive-raised storks, or with wild visitors. The wild ones will still migrate, but the captive-raised birds will remain, fed abundantly at the park. Their young will be born with the migratory instinct, and they too will be brought up in captivity for three years to ensure their safety. By 2001 more than 250 pairs of storks were nesting in the Alsace. And so the future of this beautiful bird is secure. That must be a good thing, yes? Because otherwise, who would deliver babies? The sound of dozens of stork bills clacking out messages to each other is almost deafening. They are everywhere around us, in the aviary, up in the trees, and flying overhead. The current year's crop of baby storks are in groups of three on man-made nests, large circular constructions of woven sticks covered with straw on tree stumps about three ft. high. The enchanting fuzzy-haired youngsters sit sunbathing and watching the world go by, their beaks still black, but their distinctive eye markings already evident.

With the storks out of danger, the park is working to safeguard the futures of two other creatures, otters and the giant Alsace hamster. Of course we know about otters, and spend an enjoyable half hour watching them swimming around and playing in their holts. But in view of all the jokes about giant hamsters, I am undecided as to whether they actually exist, or whether they are some kind of local joke. I contact an Alsatian wildlife association and they are upset that I might find anything amusing about the plight of the giant hamster. It's a very real animal, unique to Alsace, about eight inches in length, rather like a guinea pig, verging on extinction because its remaining habitat is being almost exclusively planted to maize. When the hamsters emerge from hibernation in late spring there is no cover for them, because the maize is not yet growing. And in summer, when the maize is irrigated, the hamsters' homes flood and drown them. Rapid urbanization is swallowing up land where the hamsters normally live. According to Stéphane Giraud of GEPMA – *Groupe d'Etude et de Protection des*

Mammifères d'Alsace – the general public doesn't really care. Next time you hear a hamster joke, please think about these threatened little animals.

The several hours we spent at the *Parc des Cigognes* is one of the most enjoyable visits of our trip.

Leaving the park we pass two small urchins off on a fishing expedition. They saunter along nonchalantly, rods made from sticks and string carried over their shoulders. Another Huckleberry Finn moment.

Bas Rhin

We want to visit at least one of the dozens of châteaux littering the hills, so we head to Haut-Koenigsbourg. Amid the vineyards we pass Bergheim's German military cemetery. Over 5,000 victims of WWII are buried there, their graves orientated to face their homeland, and maintained by an association funded by the German government.

What you notice here is the deep pink colour of the earth and the stone of the buildings. The confection that is Haut-Koenigsbourg castle dominates a craggy hill 2,500 ft. high, on the departmental boundary between Haut-Rhin and Bas-Rhin. From there it looks down across thousands of acres of beautiful Alsace landscape, over the plains to the Rhine, and almost as far as Switzerland. The original 12th century castle of Haut-Koenigsbourg was destroyed by the Swedish during the Thirty Years War. In the 19th century when Alsace was part of Germany, Queen Victoria's grandson Kaiser Wilhelm II took it upon himself to restore the castle. Whether the current version bears any resemblance to the original I don't know.

Despite its great size and robust construction – in places the walls are 20 ft. thick – there's nothing sinister about the place. You can't take a pink castle too seriously, and this one is seriously pink, built from the red Vosges sandstone. Not timid, pallid, pale maiden's blush pink, but deep-rich-almost-raspberry pink. It has a charmingly haphazard appearance, as if put together without any particular forethought, with turrets and towers and windows all over the place. There are no unpleasant dungeons or cramped stairways, and visitors are free to wander at will through the high-ceilinged rooms. On the top floor there's a collection of splendid cannons, almost works of art if you can forget their purpose, and the walls are pierced with slits and slots from which to shoot at invaders or drop scalding liquids upon them.

The wooden doors and ironwork are superbly crafted, and as for the salle de fétes – wow! Intricately carved wood, wonderfully painted murals, rich hangings: this room is so over the top. A wrought-iron fireguard round the pink fireplace bears the poignant words, *'Ich habe es nicht gewollt'* – 'I did not wish for this' – presumably referring to the war in which Europe was embroiled.

At the end of WWI Alsace reverted to France. It was retaken by Germany during WWII, and liberated by the Americans in 1944 and returned to France.

Whatever else the Kaiser might have done, in restoring Haut-Koenigsbourg I feel he created something rather beautiful in this romantic, fairytale castle.

We cross the canal linking the swan-covered Rhine to the Rhône and resume our drive, through the small town of Rhinau. Under a treaty of 1542 this French town owns almost four square miles of land on the German side of the Rhine. Uninhabited by humans, the land serves as a nature reserve. The ferry service that has linked the two sides since 1494 still runs today, every fifteen minutes.

Driving through Plobsheim we stop for a few moments to watch a newly-wed couple laughing their way out of church and through a guard of honour formed by pitchforks wielded by ranks of check-shirted yokels with straw in their hair.

We're going to camp in Strasbourg tonight, and arrive in the city in good time to find a campsite. Three hours later we are still driving around searching for one. It is the wifely responsibility to ensure smooth travel arrangements, secure comfortable overnight accommodation, produce edible food at regular intervals, maintain a supply of clean clothes, and navigate through unfamiliar territory. The husbandly responsibility is driving, vehicle maintenance and livestock management. In Strasbourg I fail quite miserably to find anywhere for us to stay. Round and round we drive, searching for the familiar municipal camping sign, or any camping sign: we are prepared to be flexible.

Terry becomes so frustrated at driving in circles that he stops in the middle of a road in the centre of <u>Strasbourg</u> and orders me to find the tourist office and make them tell us where the campsite is hidden. I trot obediently in the direction of an arrow pointing to the tourist office, which leads to the square where the magnificent cathedral stands. With a nimble piece of footwork and slight lunge I manage to squeeze through the doorway just as the office closes for the weekend. A helpful girl hands me a folded piece of paper with the name and address of a campsite on it, and a map of the city. She mentions that it is permitted to park and sleep in the city's streets and car parks if we wish.

Clutching my trophy I return to where Terry deposited me. There is no sign of him. We've made no contingency plans for where to meet. I wonder how I will survive in Strasbourg with no husband, no money, and nowhere to stay. After I've stood sadly on the pavement for a few minutes Tinkerbelle's rooftop appears in the distance over the oncoming cars. I climb back in and report my successful mission. We set off again in search of the campsite, and decide that once we've fed and walked the dogs, we'll come back into town to enjoy the sights and sounds. There's a brass band playing in a square, competing with the sound of the cathedral bells; the bars, cafés and restaurants are filling up, and we are excited at the thought of spending an evening in this lively city. We have the address of Strasbourg's only campsite, and four different maps of the city, but on none of them does the address appear. The map from the tourist office girl only shows tram routes. Up and down, backwards and forwards, round and round and round we go in search of the Green Mountain site.

Pedestrians shrug and shake their heads when we ask for directions.

By 8.30pm we are angry, hungry and barely speaking. We no longer care where we sleep, as long as we can stop driving, and we have abandoned the idea of spending a night in the city. We've already seen as much of it as we want to for today. I'm feeling seasick from reading the maps and guidebooks for so long, and have a tantrum. So we drive away from Strasbourg to seek somewhere, anywhere to stay. The road westwards leads through dozens of villages all called something or other –heim. One of them has a notice that forbids cycling within its precincts. I wonder what it must be like to live somewhere you are not allowed to cycle, and why.

At 9.00pm we arrive in the small town of Rosheim, about fifteen miles south-west of Strasbourg, where we find pleasant, spacious camping facilities in a small cherry orchard on a farm. We take the dogs for a walk – they've been trapped in Tinkerbelle for hours. Dobby bobs along happily on three legs. He's removed the bandage entirely, as well as one of the staples, and the wound is gaping. He will not let us rebandage it, and the best we can do is to splash and spray liberal quantities of Vetadine all over his foot.

It's almost 10.00pm by the time we have settled the dogs, and I don't feel like cooking anything elaborate. By a coincidence, when we shopped earlier today we bought a cheese called *Hansi au marc de Gewürtztraminer*, a variation of Munster that is produced in Rosheim. It was rather expensive but sounded exotic. The recipe on the wrapper says to enclose the cheese in aluminium foil and bake it until it becomes runny. That's what I do.

Never having eaten it before or since, I don't know if I cook it correctly. Unfolding the foil reveals a stinky slab of hot, grey, gluey mess. We smear it on a *baguette*. Terry says he enjoys it. I will eat anything except meat and uncooked or soft egg white. I'm easy to feed, and love cheese, but getting through the Hansi is a struggle. It tastes the way I imagine softened heated putty would taste with a dash of turpentine.

Our neighbours in the cherry orchard are a French couple who watch us through a crack in their curtains, and a friendly German couple on their way to Kaysersberg, who speak English and fall in love with the dogs. We invite them for a drink and spend a pleasant hour exchanging notes on the places we and they have visited. The farmer and his wife come round to collect the negligible camping fee and tell us to help ourselves to cherries, which are a welcome antidote to the heavy greasiness of our dinner.

In the morning we drive back to Strasbourg through hundreds of acres of maize fields, and the -*heim* villages growing out of the deep red soil. Terry wants to ride on one of the city's sleek trams, if we can find somewhere to park. We find a quiet shaded parking area where the dogs and Tinkerbelle will be safe and cool for a few hours. There's an automatic ticket machine on the tram platform, but we don't have a coin between us, only a few euro notes. And we don't know how much a ticket costs. A lady I ask trills, '*C'est gratuit!*' (It's free!), so when the next tram glides to the stop we jump on. As we slide through the outskirts of Strasbourg, we realise then that we don't know where to get off. While we are trying to correlate one of our maps to the plan on the inside of the tram, a gentle drawling American voice says, "If you want to get to the centre, the best place for you to get off would be here." He points to a blob on the plan.

"Then you just cross the street and you'll find yourselves facing the cathedral. Have a nice visit in Strasbourg." He touches a panel next to the door, which opens in silent obedience, steps out and is gone.

We disembark in front of the cathedral whose spire dominates the city, and gaze in awe at the intricate delicacy of the carved pink stone. Impossible to imagine how many hands, how many hours, how much skill and love went into this amazing work of art. Just for a few minutes we step inside to listen to Sunday Mass. The interior is ablaze with candles, and the walls reverberate with notes from the grandiose organ. Pagans though we are, it's still a moving spiritual experience.

Then we go to buy tickets to see the cathedral's illustrious astronomical clock.

In a tiny ticket office, no more than a cubicle, a woman is talking on the phone to her boyfriend. She glances up at us, and returns to her conversation. After two minutes of being ignored, I decide to match her rudeness with some of my own, and yell: "We want tickets to visit the clock, please!" She moves the receiver to her shoulder just long enough to say the clock is out of action. There is a long queue forming outside, unaware their wait will be fruitless.

We walk around the clean, smart city watching street entertainers. A

127

man wearing a dinner jacket and standing on a box is pretending to be a statue, and a couple of cheerful gentlemen are demonstrating puppets. Mouth-watering smells waft from every corner, and we settle at a table outside a restaurant just off the main square. Terry orders the fried Camembert and fried potatoes, and I have a *tarte flambée*, washed down with a small carafe of rosé, which is very dark red, and rather expensive.

The sun is blazingly hot, and by mid-meal we have to ask the waiter to move us under the shade of an awning. A couple sitting next to us move too, settling in the shade, fanning themselves and rolling their eyes. We are concerned for Tally and Dobby in Tinkerbelle, worried they may be too hot despite the closed curtains and all the vents open, so we finish our meal quickly and find our way back to the tram stop. When we reach Tinkerbelle the dogs are cool and sleeping peacefully.

For a couple of hours we drive around Strasbourg, through the pretty Petite France area and around the European Union buildings, and I feel it is a city where I could enjoy spending a few days if we did not still have many miles to go.

When WWII broke out in 1939, the French government evacuated to central France those inhabitants living close to the German border. However, those refugees were not greatly welcomed by the local population, and lived in rough conditions. When Germany and France signed the armistice of 1940, many Alsatians returned to their homes. The Germans promptly annexed the Alsace and forcibly conscripted 140,000 men of fighting age into the German army. These men, French by birth and at heart were put in the intolerable situation of being forced to fight against their own countrymen. They were known as the '*malgré nous*' (despite ourselves). Many died on the Russian front or spent long years imprisoned in Siberian labour camps. The French regarded those who survived and returned after the war as traitors. There is still a great deal of bitterness towards them, particularly those who were part of the German division responsible for the massacre at Oradour-sur-Glane.

The Alsace is a strange place, because it's so unlike any other part of France. Its history and geographical situation impart a strong German influence. While Alsace certainly isn't German, it doesn't really feel French, either. It's simply Alsace.

It was in this least French region that the French national anthem was born. In 1792, Claude-Joseph Rouget de Lisle (a strange name – a *rouget* is a red mullet) was asked to write a stirring piece of marching music for the French army, at that time engaged in war with Austria. He composed the music and wrote the belligerent lyrics overnight whilst garrisoned in Strasbourg. The first public recital of his work, called 'The Battle Song of the Army of the Rhine,' was given at a banquet hosted by the mayor of Strasbourg, M. de Dietrich.

The bloodthirsty song was an instant hit, quickly adopted by revolutionaries on their march from Marseille to Paris, and becoming known as 'La Marseillaise.' It's since been banned several times because of its association with the Revolution. And it's been suggested that the lyrics could benefit from being toned down, but so far it has remained true to Red Mullet's composition, and is the definitive French national anthem. (See the lyrics in English after the list of links at the end of this book.) Ironically, Red Mullet was a royalist who only just escaped the guillotine, unlike the less fortunate M. de Dietrich.

In the flat countryside north of Strasbourg anywhere not covered by a house or an industrial building is under maize. No carrots; no potatoes; no vines; no cabbages – just maize, maize and maize. We can see the giant hamster's problem.

From Seltz we snip a corner off our route and drive through a lot of -bachs and -willers until we reach Wissembourg, the northernmost town in the Alsace, where we are just in time to miss some major event. The town is heaving with vintage cars, chopped hogs, and German visitors. We squeeze into an ice-cream parlour-cum-cake shop, a scene of unadulterated pandemonium. One waitress and one waiter chase around with trays loaded with outsize sundae glasses piled high with ice cream, topped with mountains of whipped cream, cherries, paper parasols and sparklers. We have to be very determined and patient to get served.

Wissembourg was home for a while to Stanislas I, the on-and-off King of Poland during one of his 'off' periods. His luck changed when in 1725 his 23-year-old daughter Marie Leszczynski married sixteen-year-old Louis XV of France. She was a fruitful, quiet and dignified lady. After producing ten children, she withdrew to her own quarters and left her royal spouse to spend his time with his mistresses, Mesdames de Pompadour and du Barry. Marie's grandson, Louis XVI, and his wife, of whom more later, would spectacularly lose their heads one day. But by then Marie would have been dead for a quarter of a century.

As father of the Queen of France, old Stanislas did quite well for himself. Living in great style in France, he entertained up to 300 people to dinner each night. He met an unfortunate end in his ninetieth year when his dressing gown caught fire and he was engulfed in flames.

We follow the Franco-German frontier westwards, pausing at Lembach to visit one of the remnants of the spectacularly ineffectual and embarrassingly useless Maginot line. While Terry explores an old bunker, I search our guide books and maps for somewhere to stay the night, and settle on a campsite at Sturzelbronn. We drive through the green beauty of the North Vosges Regional Park, and a valley populated with Highland cattle with long fringes, long horns and long, rich-red shaggy coats.

Moselle

Sturzelbronn's campsite lies beside a lake in a wooded area. Most of it is occupied by mobile homes. They are not at all mobile because their owners have attached brick-built extensions with tiled roofs larger than the original buildings, patios, garden sheds and ponds. Children play on sandy beaches and adults swim in the lake. It is an ideal place for a quiet weekend.

To get in takes some time. New arrivals have to park behind a barrier and walk to the office up a long steep slope. Off I go, and find an old lady pushing a mop around. She points me to a stern woman sitting behind a desk, who agrees that we can stay the night. She isn't the friendliest person, though. She says they don't accept credit card payment, nor English cheques. I say that I will give her a French cheque.

"How is it," she asks, glaring over the top of her glasses, "that you have a French cheque-book?" I tell her I live in France and she says she will need proof. After showing her my driving licence, health insurance card and an envelope from an insurance company addressed to me, she is finally satisfied. But she wears the sour expression of somebody who has just lost an important battle.

We attract considerable attention as we install Tinkerbelle. The 'permanent' residents walk backwards and forwards peering at us and the dogs. Dobby adopts the role of guard dog and barks furiously at everybody who comes past, and even more angrily at any impudent dogs who look at him. People glare at him. If they would stop coming to examine us, he would stop barking. His wound is still open, but clean, and Terry is swabbing it several times daily with antiseptic.

Lorraine is famous for its quiche, its cross and its General Charles de Gaulle. Quiche, from the German word '*Küche*,' meaning cooking, was actually invented in Germany, in the medieval kingdom called Lothringen, which later became the Lorraine region of France. The double-barred cross of Lorraine was adopted as the emblem of the French Resistance as a riposte to the Nazi swastika. When Winston Churchill said during WWII: "Of all the crosses I have to bear, the heaviest is the cross of Lorraine," he was referring to his difficult relationship with larger-than-life Charles de Gaulle, a native of Lorraine.

Next morning I'm startled awake by Terry shouting: "It's nearly 9.00am. Come on, we've got to get going." I leap from the bed and check my watch, which reads just after 6.00am.

"Funny, my watch has stopped," I say, putting the kettle on. Except for one lone swimmer twirling around in the lake there is no sign of life. It occurs to me that maybe there is some form of curfew in operation to ensure residents a good lie-in each morning. I make breakfast as quietly as possible but as fast as I can, and we start packing up. There is still no activity outside. I switch on the computer to download some photos. The clock reads 6.58am. I look at my watch, which gives the same time.

"What time does your watch say?" I ask Terry.

"Nine forty."

"Then it's wrong," I say, rather irritably having been deprived of a couple of hours sleep. "It's not quite seven o'clock."

The office doesn't open until 8.00am. There is no way out of the site until somebody unlocks the barrier. We sit for an hour in these pleasant, tranquil and yet vaguely hostile surroundings.

As soon as the gate opens we are away, and in the small town of Bitche by 8.30am Vauban's magnificent citadel sitting on a hill at the centre of the town had not been sufficient to save the town from the ravages of two world wars. Eighty per cent destroyed in WWI, and again in WWII, most of the town is relatively new. We follow a sign to the Garden of Peace at the foot of the citadel. The theme of war and peace is demonstrated by collections of plants living in harmony despite their inherently antagonistic tendencies. Unfortunately the garden doesn't open until 11.00am, and entertaining ourselves for two and a half hours in Bitche is a challenge to which we don't feel equal. We drive away, past a roundabout adorned with brightly painted and decorated watering cans, towards Sarreguemines. The landscape is serene, pristine small villages surrounded by fields of wheat and straw stubble or dotted with rolled bales of hay. Like its neighbour Bitche, Sarreguemines has an attractive roundabout, depicting a life-sized gardener surrounded by garden tools and a wheelbarrow all made from plants.

We follow a small road to a sign announcing that we have crossed the frontier into the *Bundesrepublik Deutschland* (Federal Republic of Germany). In search of coffee and breakfast we drive through ten villages in this part of Germany's Federal Republic and all of them don't have a café, or a bakery, so we return to a rather scruffy but friendly old-fashioned bar in the centre of Sarreguemines, a pretty riverside town noted for its production of pottery. The establishment doesn't appear to have made any effort to keep up with the passage of time, or to slip into the twenty-first century. Neither does the cheery clientele, leaning against the bar sipping alcohol and puffing cigarettes. However, the coffee is excellent, and the mats on the battered tables are made from amusing laminated cartoons from the local newspaper.

The next town on our route is Saint-Avold, home to Europe's largest American military cemetery. More than 10,000 American soldiers lie here in beautifully landscaped gardens of more than 100 acres amongst the mellow hills of Lorraine, their headstones dominated by a huge white memorial. For the rest of our journey, until we are back in Brittany, we'll

131

be driving through land that has been a theatre of war for centuries. Cemeteries of different nationalities are as much a part of the landscape as the trees and hills.

Between Longeville and Zimming a metal pillbox protrudes from a grassy mound surrounded by conifers and weeping birches. Beside it stands a stone engraved with the cross of Lorraine, and the words "*Aux résistants et deportés 1939-1945: Leur chemin a été celui de sacrifice.*" Translations in German and English say: "Remember, passer-by, that their way was that of sacrifice and they struggled for your liberty." Simple, and poignant.

Lorraine's architecture and landscape are very different from its flamboyant neighbour, Alsace. It has a more sober air. There are plenty of flowers, but not the blinding displays of geraniums on balconies. The landscape is a patchwork of orderly, unspectacular wheat fields: a stolid, sensible part of the world. We decide to have lunch in Metz. We've invented a silly game of looking out for funny place names, Metz being one of them because it's pronounced "mess." We've found several Sillys, a Mad, an Orny, Charly and a Woippy.

Metz itself, capital of the Moselle *département* and the Lorraine region, is a dignified town of wide streets, pretty parks, huge churches and substantial, no-nonsense buildings. Dozens of swans glide along the Moselle river, necks bent so they can admire their reflections in the water. We head for an interesting-looking North African restaurant down a narrow lane. The tables are curiously positioned on the pavement on a slope so that cutlery, crockery and glassware are in danger of sliding off. It is extremely uncomfortable sitting on a lopsided chair that is several inches higher on one side than another and we begin to regret our choice. The menu, when it arrives, is all meat-based. We ask one of the beautiful waitresses whether they have any vegetable dishes. She goes to ask the chef. When she returns she says no, the chef says we'll have to eat meat. She doesn't seem to think this will present any problem, because she's come back with a carafe of water, basket of bread rolls and the wine list, and stands with her pencil poised over her pad to take our order. We say that we won't be staying, as we don't eat meat. The other lopsided diners stare wide-eyed and open-mouthed, knives and forks still, as if they cannot believe their eyes as we walk away.

We roam around until we find a truly delightful restaurant called Chez Mon Oncle Ernest, with a wonderful 1900s décor complete with an HMV wind-up gramophone. The food is excellent: roast salmon with vegetables and a potato gratin, and *pain perdu* for dessert. We ask if they will play a record on the gramophone. Our waitress says it makes a truly awful sound, but if we wait until the last customer has left they'll try it for us. The chef places a record on the turntable, starts winding the handle, and drops the needle on to the record, which emits a most terrible wailing noise. He winds faster and faster, but can only produce a frenzied yowl. His sister, who is standing in for the regular waitress who's been taken ill, tells us she has a teddy bear shop just up the hill, near the cathedral. When we've finished our meal we walk up there to admire her shop which is guarded by a seven ft. tall bear, and crammed with teddy bears big and small, old and new, dressed and naked – a teddy bear lover's paradise.

We had intended driving due north up to Thionville, following the Path of Freedom, the route taken by General Patton and his troops from France to Belgium via Luxembourg. However, we decide to divert to Briey to see Le Corbusier's celebrated *Cité Radieuse*, and from there to Valleroy's Russian cemetery which somebody has recommended we visit.

There are no directions to the *Cité Radieuse* until you are almost there. Maybe this is to deter visitors. Frankly we find this place simply hideous. It's a concrete block of apartments on pillars. The surrounding area is shabby, enclosed by gloomy woods where groups of young people are drinking from bottles and smoking. It may have been a wonder of its time, but in its current decaying state we don't even stop Tinkerbelle. I ask myself why we went there in the first place, particularly as I don't like modern architecture.

We head for Valleroy. Some towns are better than others at signage. Valleroy lacks directions to the Russian cemetery. Terry commands me to keep asking people where it is, and nobody seems to know. They look at me as if I'm insane. I've realised, since we set out on this journey, that if you ask a French person for directions to somewhere that they don't know, they will naturally regard you as mad. If somebody asks me for directions and I can't help, I feel apologetic. *Vive la différence!* When we see a man on a motorbike, I command Terry to do the asking. He is spectacularly successful, because the motorcyclist is visiting a friend in Valleroy and couldn't be more helpful. He disappears into his friend's house and emerges with a little map. As he is about to hand it to us he changes his mind and indicates we should follow him. Kicking his bike into life he leads us several miles down a country lane, to the entrance to the cemetery in a grove of trees. With a wave of his hand he wheels away.

Fifty or so Russians are buried in the cemetery, captured soldiers who were literally worked to death in the mines. Their graves are marked with simple white crosses, each bearing a name, except for one simply engraved *'inconnu'* (unknown), and another indicating three bodies buried together.

A sculpture of three emaciated figures standing in a group, one with his arm raised and pointing, maybe towards Russia, watches over them. There are wind chimes hanging from a post, and a few clumps of lavender filled with murmuring bees and butterflies rummaging in the blossoms. It is beautifully maintained, secluded and very peaceful. I've seen cemeteries far less inviting than this one.

We've heard of a place known as the Longwy concentration camp, the only such camp that existed on unannexed French soil. When we arrive in Longwy nobody there knows about the camp or its whereabouts. I eventually find a brochure, which says the camp is actually in a small town called Thil, several miles south-east of Longwy. I score no points at all for making Terry drive miles out of our way, and by the time we'd find Thil it's too late in the day to be able to visit the camp. The nearest campsite is at Thionville, due north of Metz by only a short distance, so going back on ourselves we head there having made a useless detour of fifty miles.

The municipal campsite at Thionville sits on the banks of the Moselle. It's next to the Parc Napoléon and shares its terrain with a kayaking club. A smiley lady indicates that Terry can go and park, and I wait to register. She is dealing with a thin little man who looks worn out and desperate. He has to keep making phone calls. It is impossible not to overhear that he is entirely without food or money. He implores whoever is on the other end of the line to send him some funds, and they apparently are not intending to do so. He is almost weeping. Twice he turns away as if he's finished his sad business, and just as I open my mouth to talk to the lady back he comes, pulling at his hair and asking to use the phone again. When he puts it down, he tells the *gardienne* that money is being sent, and he will be able to settle his camping fees within two days. She replies he isn't to worry, just to make himself comfortable. After he wanders away, she shakes her head and says sadly, "Poor man. What a terrible situation." Terry has chosen an excellent corner by the park and beside the riverbank. Just opposite the unfortunate little man, with a dog, is climbing out of a rather ancient campervan – even more ancient than Tinkerbelle! I tell Terry about his plight.

"Put some food together for him, and the dog. We'll leave it beside the van." Terry likes to pretend he's mean and hard, but internally he's as soft as an uncooked sponge.

So we make up a parcel of eggs, cheese, croissants, tomatoes, fruit, milk, coffee, sugar and some dog food, and wrap it in foil, place it in a shopping bag and hang it on the wing mirror of the camper. Several hours later it is still there, although the man and his dog returned long ago. Terry goes and knocks on the door. He hands the packet to the man, who shakes his head vehemently at first, saying he is fine, and doesn't need any help. Terry grasps him by the arm, pats him on the shoulder,

134

and says: "Take it – we want you to have it." So he accepts it, and we feel good and hope it is of some help to him.

Although the campsite is well situated, it isn't the prettiest we've been to. But the *gardienne* makes up for that by doing everything she can to make visitors welcome. She's bright and cheerful and even offered me a cup of tea or a cold drink when we arrived. Because the park attracts the town's young at night, she keeps the campsite sanitary blocks locked to prevent the revellers using them. Only residents have a key. Terry and I have one key between us, so when we both need the toilets at the same time, I unlock the gents for him and keep the key so I won't find myself locked in the ladies. The inevitable happens: while Terry is in the gents another person goes out and locks the door behind him.

I've been chatting by the washbasins with an English lady for about ten minutes, and when I come out I can hear Terry calling patiently. Yes, he is locked in the lavatory, causing great mirth to the surrounding campers, none of whom had thought to unlock the door for him.

When we leave after a rather disturbed night because of a long, loud, late party in the park, the *gardienne* asks whether we've enjoyed our stay. Can we suggest anything else she can do to improve the campsite? She asks us to sign her guest book, and gives us both a hug and several kisses. If you're ever in or near Thionville and looking for a really charming lady who takes pride in her work, do visit the municipal campsite. Sometimes I think back to all the places we've visited so far, and the people we have met. I wonder what makes most people friendly and helpful, and a minority quite the opposite.

We know nothing about Thionville, so we go to the tourist office for some brochures, and learn something of its history and legends. The town belonged to Germany between 1905 and 1914, when much of it was built to the design of a German architect from Cologne. It's a handsome town, with wide avenues lined with chunky elegant houses, the sort you find in places like Kensington, and solid, tasteful buildings in the town centre. In contrast is the 12th century *Tour aux Puces* – the Flea Tower.

The story goes that Charlemagne was particularly fond of Thionville, where he used to stay to indulge his passion for hunting. He kept a pack of 683 dogs. Now, we love dogs, and once had as many as six simultaneously, but 683 does sound excessive. Anyway, Charlemagne's vast pack of animals stayed in Thionville while he was elsewhere. The dogs were infested with fleas. When there was no more room on the dogs, the fleas migrated to Thionville's citizens, who were soon scratching vigorously. The situation became intolerable, so the citizenry wrote to Charlemagne, and a messenger was despatched to deliver their letter. Like all the inhabitants of Thionville, the messenger was flea-

135

ridden. One of his passengers sprang on to and bit Charlemagne's nose. The emperor instantly recognised the problem, and ordered the building of the tower to contain the dogs and their fleas.

Six centuries later, during the French Revolution, the Austrian army supporting the Royalist French besieged Thionville. For two months Thionville resisted calls to surrender. To underline their determination, they mounted a wooden horse upon the ramparts, with a bale of hay in its mouth and a sign reading: "We will surrender when the horse eats the hay." Meurthe-et-Moselle

In the afternoon we go back to look for that under-advertised place, the concentration camp at Thil. Following advice in the brochure, I telephone the Mairie to ask whether we can visit the camp. They say we can collect the key from them, and would we like a guide. We say we would prefer to wander around on our own. Although the Mairie vaguely indicates the general direction, we can't find it. There are no signs in Thil to the concentration camp. Nobody we ask seems to know where it is, or even that there is such a place. Finally we meet a man who shows us the way to the crypt, built by local volunteers and opened in 1946. It's tucked away up the hill from the town cemetery. Unlike the cemetery which is ablaze with flowers, the crypt is a bleak place. Terry unlocks the rusty gate beside a monument of a skeletal figure tangled in barbed wire.

Inside the crypt the main feature is the oven used to dispose of the bodies of dead prisoners. Beside it is a notice from the manufacturers disclaiming responsibility for the use to which the oven had been put. They installed it in the Villerupt abattoir before the war, from where it was dismantled by the Nazis and removed to the Thil camp. Three vases of roses stand in front of it; stone tablets on the wall bear the names of local victims. There's an urn containing ashes from Buchenwald, more flowers and ribbons and flags of various organizations. A prisoner's uniform of coarse striped material is surprisingly thick, like blanketing, not the thin fabric we'd imagined. On a table is a partly-finished scale model of the camp and factory.

After the Allied bombardment of the rocket development site at Peenemunde on the Baltic coast, the production of V2 rockets was moved to Thil, where thousands of prisoners of North African, Senegalese, Italian, and Eastern European origin were sent to work in the mines. They existed in appalling conditions on rations of watery soup, forced to march several miles to the factory from the barracks, carrying heavy rocks. While the Americans were entering Thil by road to liberate the town, the surviving prisoners were being shipped by train to concentration camps in Germany.

There's no sign today of the subterranean factory that lies beneath the grassy fields populated by grazing cattle. It is a sobering visit, and we

136

think of the horror this place has witnessed, just outside a small town where nobody knew about it, and where many apparently still don't. But somebody somewhere is still caring for the place and trying to keep its memory alive.

Meuse

We divert from the border again, to visit Verdun. Our trip isn't intended as a pilgrimage, nor as a morbid itinerary visiting battlefields and cemeteries. But so much of north and eastern France is steeped in warfare that if we want to understand the history, we can't ignore these places.

On the outskirts of the small village of Abaucourt-Hautecourt is a German military cemetery from the WWI, spick and span. We'll see many more German cemeteries in France, all as beautifully maintained as their Allied counterparts. In death, they are united in dignity.

Because the name of Verdun has always been synonymous with the horror of warfare – mud, blood, misery and despair – we don't know what to expect of the vast cemetery complex there. We've seen so many films about the battle, and read so many stories that I expect it to be sad, depressing, unbearable. What we hadn't anticipated is that on this bright, warm June day it is beautiful. Acres of white crosses stretching over the horizon, a red poppy at the heart of each. An ocean of crosses. Thousands and thousands of perfect rose plants, in full bloom. Birdsong and battalions of butterflies.

During 1916, in ten months 800,000 men died, disappeared or were wounded at Verdun. The town's symbolic importance comes from the 9th century, when the vast empire of Charlemagne was divided by a treaty between three of his grandsons to form the foundation of the future France, Germany and Lorraine, an event considered one of the most important in the history of Europe. The Germans believed taking Verdun would deal the French a demoralizing psychological blow. They'd keep killing until the French no longer had the heart to fight, until their very spirit had been bled to death. But the French fought ferociously. The battle cry of Verdun was: "They shall not pass!" Unlike their enemy, the French were able to resupply, rest and replace their troops for a few days every so often. Eventually the two sides were killing each other mindlessly, but Verdun, France's most decorated town, was never taken.

We drive around the monuments, past the sign to the village of Fleury, which no longer exists. The sign says simply: "This was Fleury." It is one of nine villages destroyed for all time and never rebuilt: the amount of unexploded ammunition amongst the ruins makes it too dangerous.

In the ossuary are the bones of 150,000 unidentified French and

German soldiers lying together in eternal peace.

In June 1916 a company of the 137th Infantry Regiment was positioned facing German artillery. By the end of the day, they'd all vanished. After the war bayonet tips and rifle muzzles were seen protruding from the ground. When the trench was excavated, the remains of the men were discovered beneath their weapons. An American gentleman named C. F. Rand, from Pennsylvania funded the building of a memorial to the men of the Trench of Bayonets. There's an imposing entrance inscribed, in French: "To the memory of the French soldiers who sleep upright in this trench, their guns in their hands. Their American brothers." A paved pathway leads to a mound of earth bearing crosses and wreaths, and small bunches of flowers, sheltered by a low concrete roof on pillars. The mournful atmosphere is emphasised by bats nesting beneath the roof.

What we notice at Verdun, apart from the pristine condition of all the monuments, memorials and graves, is the vast network of craters and shell holes pitting the contours of the ground. Out of them trees and giant hogweed grow as nature reclaims the land. The mud and barbed wire have faded into a peaceful green landscape. The overall feeling I am left with is how much love remains in this place, and how, although the events commemorated here took place almost a century ago, the dead have not been forgotten. And I feel too that the ghosts of Verdun might quite possibly sleep peacefully today. It is a very, very emotional place to visit.

We go into Verdun town and are pleased and surprised to find that despite the grim associations of its name, it's a town of charm, with medieval buildings as well as many memorials like the Victory Monument and the Monument to the Dead. The town's entrance is through the splendid 14th century Porte Chaussée, an archway within two crenellated stone towers. Verdun's streets are hung with baskets of vivid flowers and busy with cheerful pedestrians. There's a small harbour; the 18th century bishop's palace is now the World Centre for Peace and the theatre is a small-scale copy of the Paris opera house. We find a pretty good cup of hot chocolate in a pavement restaurant.

Verdun played a part in another wartime event when England broke the Treaty of Amiens and declared war on France in 1803. The treaty had only been an excuse for a short break in the irritating hostilities between the two countries. Napoléon Bonaparte ordered the arrest of British nationals living in France and their detention in various areas, one of which was Verdun. For eleven years between 800 and 1,200 English lived on parole in the city. They were free to lead their lives as they wished provided they gave their word not to escape. The military men amongst them received an allowance from Verdun's governor, and the poorer people were supported by charities in England. Many had their families and servants with them. Others married local ladies. One third of the births registered in Verdun between 1803 and 1814 were British. The 'prisoners' enjoyed balls and parties, horse races and show jumping, duels and gambling. Local commerce prospered; the natives would, for the right price, help people to escape.

Two English sailors escaped and managed to get as far as Boulogne. They made a tiny boat from small pieces of wood and a fragment of sail. With little chance of success they set sail towards what they hoped would be freedom, but was almost certain to be death. They were captured by the French, and would have been shot if the story of their daring and foolhardy adventure hadn't reached Napoléon. He sent for the men and their waif-like vessel, and was so impressed with their courage that not only did he have them safely delivered to an English ship, he gave them gold coins as well. Ah. I've always had a huge soft spot for Boney.

When the English were finally free to leave Verdun, they left behind a legacy of enormous debts, which the French government tried unsuccessfully to recover right up until the end of WWI. In June 2003 thirty descendants of the Verdun English called on the mayor of Verdun, and one of them paid a debt of twenty-one francs owed by his ancestor to a carpenter for a picture frame.

Pleased to find that the town has risen triumphantly above its grim past, we turn west towards our next port of call. Still a little off-track, but it's a small place that played a seminal role in France's history.

Although Varennes-en-Argonne is today just a sleepy village, it has two notable points of interest. The most visible is a gigantic memorial in the style of a Greek temple, erected in 1927 by the Pennsylvania Monuments Commission to honour the American troops who served in WWI and liberated Varennes in 1918.

More discreet memorials are dotted around the town, telling the fascinating tale of what happened there on a warm June evening in 1791. It was almost midnight when the door was flung open to the Bras d'Or tavern favoured by the Republicans. In came breathless Jean-Baptiste Drouet, the postmaster from the not-very-far-away town of Sainte-Menehould. He brought extraordinary tidings: the French king, Louis XVI, and his queen Marie-Antoinette were on their way to Varennes in a carriage, trying to escape from France. M. Drouet had recognized the king because of his likeness on a coin and had ridden at top speed to organize an ambush.

The mayor of Varennes, a grocer with the appropriate name of M. Sauce, sent his children into the streets shouting, "Fire, fire!" to awaken the sleeping citizenry. By the time the royal cavalcade reached the town, barricades had been set up and the royal flight was halted. After being questioned by M. Sauce the royal fugitives were invited to stay the night at his house. The next day they were returned to Paris, whence they'd been trying to flee to safety in Luxembourg.

Louis lost his head in January 1793; Marie Antoinette was parted from hers in October of the same year. The king's sister, also captured in Varennes, went to the guillotine the following year. Louis and Marie Antoinette's ten-year-old son Louis XVII died in prison in 1795, but Madame Royale, the king's daughter, did rather well for herself and lived to a reasonable age, serving as a councillor to her uncles, Kings Louis XVIII and Charles X.

After what must be rated as the most sensational event in French history, many of Varennes's wealthy residents left, and the town became impoverished. The inhabitants were divided over their part in the affair. Some commended the principal players, and others criticized them. Some made death threats against them. M. Drouet went on to lead a fairly exciting life until he died in Macon. Mayor Sauce and his wife left town when he was dismissed from his post. Mme Sauce fell down a well and broke both legs running away from invading Prussians. She died several days later.

A stone plaque marks the location of Mayor Sauce's house, where the royals lodged the night before their enforced return to Paris. The property was destroyed in WWI. Thank you to Varennes for the excellent noticeboards describing the event.

Back on the road north, we want Dobby to have his foot looked at to ensure that it is healing. Terry has been carefully cleaning it several times a day, but the wound is still gaping open. In Dun-sur-Meuse we find a veterinary surgery. Although the vet is just about to set off on his afternoon rounds, he obligingly agrees to see Dobby straight away. They strike up an instant rapport. Dobby is happy to show his foot to Dr Gressens, a tall, fair-haired Belgian vet of great charm. He tells us he owns a cottage in Scotland where takes his dogs shooting as often as he can. I ask whether it isn't an odd thing for a vet to go out killing wild birds. He smiles and says he kills very few, and only for the pleasure of watching and working with his dogs.

Dobby's foot is as well as we can expect, says Dr Gressens, given that it is a serious wound that will take a long time to heal. But it is clean and the best thing to do is to keep applying the antiseptic. He gives us a plastic bottle with a spout to make it easier. He refuses payment.

13

Champagne-Ardenne and Nord Pas De Calais

Ardennes

When the Crusaders and the armies of Julius Caesar and Napoléon rode to war, it was astride the forebears of the huge Ardennes draught horse. We pass a herd of these good-natured animals grazing peacefully along the banks of the river Meuse as we head to <u>Sedan</u>. The municipal campsite isn't remarkable in any way, fairly basic but pleasant and within easy walking distance of the town, so we settle there for the night.

The older part of town is elegant, and the public gardens and parks attractive and well cared for. There's a splendid WWI monument: a massive column topped by a bronze *poilu* (an affectionate term for a French soldier, meaning 'hairy' and regarded as being synonymous with masculinity and bravery), guarded by four beautifully cast wild boars, symbol of the Ardennes. It's all dwarfed by the immensity of Sedan's fortified château, the largest in Europe, towering seven storeys high, built on a hill, with a footprint of eight acres. Standing beneath its walls is to realize how small and insignificant a human being is. Paradoxically, for all its size the castle couldn't save Napoléon's nephew from a humiliating defeat by Bismarck's armies during the Franco-Prussian war. Taken prisoner at Sedan, Napoleon III was regarded as 'responsible for the defeat, ruin and dismemberment of France'. He's better remembered in France for that than for being the force behind the creation of modern Paris and the demolition of the slums.

Sedan suffered a second mortifying defeat when the Panzers broke through the French defences in 1940. As always, standing on the ground where such momentous events have taken place is a slightly surreal experience. In the sunshine, surrounded by the 20th century noises of car horns and radios, it is impossible to imagine it as a scene of battle. We'd like to tour the castle, but the queues are very long, and although there are plenty of enticing restaurants beneath the castle walls it is too early for lunch, so we decide to go and explore Charleville-Mézieres.

On the way we remark on the well cared-for municipal flower beds and roundabouts of the small town of Donchery. What we don't know is that at the exact moment we are driving through Donchery the police are digging in the grounds of a local château, excavating the remains of two young girls murdered and buried there by self-confessed serial killer Michel Fourniret. It's a pity that since we reached the Ardennes everything we've learned about it is rather gloomy, because the wooded and peaceful countryside is very beautiful.

Charleville-Mézières in appearance is solid, sensible, and spacious if rather austere. There are wide avenues lined with trees and robust three-storey buildings with mansard roofs. The central square, the Place Ducale, is absolutely gorgeous. But like Sedan, a splash of colour wouldn't do any harm. It all seems rather monochromatic after the colourful Alsace. It is as if these towns feel that anything as frivolous as tubs of geraniums should be frowned upon.

We end up on one of our anxious searches for a restaurant, seeking somewhere open and affordable where we can park in shade nearby, and a menu that doesn't consist wholly of meat. Time is running against us – it's 1.50pm and French provincial restaurants often won't serve after 1.30pm and we begin to panic. Eventually criteria give way to fear, and we're prepared to settle for just about anything. We plonk ourselves down at a pavement restaurant that doesn't look particularly attractive. However, it does feature fish on the menu and is willing to serve us lunch at 2.00pm. Although the fish isn't great, and neither is the wine, the place is redeemed by *crêpes* which the waiter drowns with a huge jug of Grand Marnier. He's a chatty fellow, and when we tell him about our drive all round France, he recommends we should visit Bogny-sur-Meuse, where we can see the biggest wild boar in the world – all fifty tonnes of it. I am not quite sure that I understand him. Wild boar don't normally grow to fifty tonnes, even in the Champagne-Ardennes. Maybe it's a local joke. No, he insists, it's true. The boar called Woinic is a metal sculpture almost 30 ft. high, and an amazing sight. It still sounds like a tall story to me. He sloshes some more Grand Marnier over our *crêpes*. We leave a generous tip, and in high spirits.

Carolomacériens, as inhabitants of Charleville-Mézières call themselves, are proud their town was the birthplace of wild child Arthur Rimbaud. However, the dazzling young poet, who led a bohemian and dissolute but exciting life, did not reciprocate this affection. The town loves Arthur very much more than Arthur loved the town. As a youth he ran away four times from the provincial ambience he despised. He abandoned poetry when he was just twenty to become a wanderer, an explorer, and maybe even an arms dealer and slave trader. Rimbaud died rather horribly in Marseille from complications after having a cancerous leg amputated. He was only thirty-seven. Ironically, he's buried in his birthplace, when he'd probably have chosen to remain in the vibrant and exotic atmosphere of Marseille.

Charleville-Mézieres is home to the International Puppet Institute, and hosts the World Puppet Festival every three years. We are too early by ten days to celebrate the most unlikely event you would expect to find in this dignified town – the Boomerang World Cup. The town's rather staid façade seems to hide a great sense of fun.

Bogny-sur-Meuse, home of Woinic, is seven miles north, and you might think that in a small town with a population of under 6,000 a fifty-tonne stainless-steel pig would be easy to find. It must be difficult for its neighbours not to notice. We drive around for half an hour, asking pedestrians where we can see the giant boar. They shake their heads, and hurry away. I telephone the local tourist office for help.

"No, you won't be able to see it. It's been put away." I explain politely that we've travelled to Bogny-sur-Meuse on a personal recommendation to see their pig. Is it not possible for her to make a phone call? We don't want a guided tour of Woinic, but would love to be able to take a quick look. If I ring back in five minutes, she says, she'll do her best.

But when I call back, the answer is no: the pig isn't available for viewing.

Terry insists I find out where the pig is hidden. Reluctantly the tourist office lady explains where we should go. We arrive at a tall iron gate. Standing inside is a magnificent ten ft. high stainless-steel sculpture of a pop singer. Beside it stands a knight in armour; but there's no sign of any pig. Next door to the yard a fat man is sitting in a deckchair in a small garden. We call out to him, smiling, and ask if he knows how we can get a glimpse of Woinic. He heaves himself out of the deckchair, spits on the ground, and says, "It's closed. They're busy. Goodbye." He goes through a door and slams it behind him.

Still optimistic that the Ardennes will reveal its better side to us, we follow the serpentine coils of the Meuse through the valley of legends. This is the lair of all kinds of gremlins and ghoulies; the naughty *pie-pie-van-vans* lure unwary travellers into the forest where they get lost, while benevolent *nutons* will mend your shoes and saucepans during the night.

Just before Tournavaux we stop to visit the four famous sons of Aymon. It is a steep hike up a hill to where a monumental statue of the robed knights stand beside their magical horse Bayard, overlooking the valley and the river winding through it.

Bayard could, when asked, carry all four of the brothers at once. When one of them killed a nephew of Charlemagne in a dispute over a game of chess, the emperor pursued them implacably through the

Ardennes forests. Bayard saved the brothers by leaping across the river Meuse in one great bound. However, nothing would pacify Charlemagne or stop his pursuit of the brothers except for the sacrifice of the horse. Bayard was thrown into the river with a millstone round his neck, but he survived, and can still be heard sometimes whinnying in the forest.

The Meuse twists its way through the wooded, steep-sided valley between Bogny and Revin. Every rock along the valley seems to host a legend. At Monthermé there's a heap of rocks known as the Devil's château. The story here is that the lord of nearby Thilay made a bargain with Satan. He would exchange his soul if the devil would build a magnificent château in one night, and complete it before cockcrow. Satan summoned all the goblins and elves and they worked through the night. Just before they could lay the final stone, the cock crowed. In a fit of rage, Satan kicked the walls down.

On the opposite side of the river lounge the Dames de Meuse, three sisters married to three brothers. Whilst their menfolk were Crusading in Jerusalem, the women were consoling themselves in the arms of their lovers. God punished them by turning them to rock, destined to lay there forever in their shame.

Then there's the Dame des Roches, married against her will to a man she didn't love. During his absence, the Devil changed her into a green bird so she could visit her true love. But one sad day her husband came home unexpectedly and the bird couldn't get back into her home because of a blocked grille. She regained her human form and fled to her lover. The husband caught her, killed the lover, fed him to the dogs, and hanged the errant lady. Sometimes people still see a green bird that changes into the shape of a woman.

Isn't it interesting, by the way, that in all the tales and legends of infidelity, it's always the wife who's to blame? But then until the middle of the 20th century French wives were regarded as their husband's chattels. While an adulterous husband might be punished with a fine, a wife could be sentenced to imprisonment.

The summit of Mont Malgré Tout offers a beautiful panorama of the river and valley. Mount "Despite Everything" earned its name in the 18th century when a local land-owner wanted to build a house there. The forestry would not give him permission, but he insisted that he would build his house, *malgré tout*. And a house appeared one morning, where the night before there had been none. The gentleman had built a demountable framework and, with the help of friends, put it into place during the night. *Malgré tout*, he had his house. Good: finally a story with a happy ending. Oh, but maybe not. During WWII, 106 Resistance fighters were massacred by the Germans on Mont Malgré Tout.

After a heavenly afternoon exploring the ravishing countryside, by

144

late afternoon we reach the small town of <u>Rocroi</u>. All we know about this town is that it is only half a mile from the Belgian border, and that it has a campsite. We are delighted to discover that not only is Rocroi is a wonderfully preserved, star-shaped fortified town, but the lovely campsite is safe enough for the dogs to run freely as much as they wish.

Schoolboys from the City of London School are staying at the site to do their silver and bronze Duke of Edinburgh awards. I ask one of their teachers why they've chosen Rocroi. He tells us that in the past they'd always gone to the Brecon Beacons; but when foot-and-mouth disease put the Beacons off-limits, they had to look for somewhere else. They chose the Ardennes because it's an excellent area for walking, and having enjoyed Rocroi so much the previous year they've returned.

Rocroi's campsite feeds directly on to the grassy ramparts of the fortifications that surround the town in a perfect 10-point star. Dobby's foot is still unhealed, but he needs to run, so we let him loose for an hour to run up and down the paths and mounds. Tally, who never tires, spends several hours playing football with the schoolboys while Dobby watches with his usual befuddled expression.

In the early evening the boys set off on one of their trials. While they're away a group of giggling local girls come strolling nonchalantly about the site, laughing loudly. They settle down on the banks of the ramparts, turn on their radio and sit drinking beer. During the night, when the boys have come back from their exercise and are asleep in their tents, the girls creep up and release all the guy ropes.

No fortified town would be worth its salt if Vauban hadn't had a finger in it somewhere. In 1643 Rocroi hosted a battle between the French and the hitherto invincible Spanish army. Led by the 22-year-old Duc d'Enghien from the powerful Bourbon dynasty, the French won a resounding victory. The young duke would come to be known as the Great Condé. Vauban began his military career when he joined Condé's regiment in 1651. When in a fit of pique Condé went to fight for the Spanish, Vauban went with him. Both men subsequently returned to France, were pardoned and went on to enjoy glittering careers. Vauban, who, as we know, was never one to twiddle his thumbs, supervised the modifications of Rocroi's defences.

It's a chilly morning with a sharp little breeze and rain is forecast. A two-minute walk from the campsite leads to the town whose streets radiate symmetrically from an old well in the centre of the square. We enjoy a nice hot drink with some excellent pains aux raisins and blue chocolate 'slates', a regional speciality. If it wasn't cold and raining, we could have been persuaded to stay in delightful Rocroi. It's a perfect place for the dogs to enjoy themselves, and the local hotel has on its lunchtime menu the wonderfully named potato-and-onion dish *cacasse a cul nu* — bare-arsed potato stew, a peasant dish of onions and potatoes, that does not contain meat. It is the only opportunity we have had so far on our journey to try a regional French savoury dish suitable for vegetarians. Unfortunately, lunch is four hours away, and in tiny Rocroi there is not a lot to do in the rain.

Picardy

Aisne

Terry wants to visit Aubenton, about 12 miles south-west of Rocroi, just over the departmental border in Picardy's Aisne *département*. Nothing of its calm and modest appearance gives any hint that it has been the setting for famine, plague, leprosy, and invasion by Cossacks, Prussians, and the Germans during both world wars. In 1340 the town was beseiged, pillaged and burnt to the ground during the Hundred Years War. There's a superb illustration of the Siege of Aubenton in Froissart's Chronicles. In 1960 the town council tried unsuccessfully to rename the *Ruelle du Sang* (Blood Alley), and the *Ruelle du Sac* (Pillage Alley), but the inhabitants wanted these reminders of their turbulent past to be preserved for posterity.

The reason Terry wants to come here is because Aubenton is home to the Jean Mermoz museum. We go to the Hotel de Ville to ask how we can visit the little museum. The mayor and his staff are the friendliest, smiliest and most helpful people we've met so far on our travels. The mayor picks up the phone and five minutes later the caretaker arrives, an elegant grandmother named Mme Schlienger. She has left her lunch preparations and come immediately to the town hall with her two young granddaughters to open up the museum.

The Musée Jean Mermoz is a shrine to France's dare-devil, record-breaking airman and pride of Aubenton. It's filled with posters and photographs, medals and certificates, newspaper articles and books, models of aeroplanes, his cradle and tiny christening robes and silken bonnet. Terry is fascinated by Mme Schlienger's tales. Mermoz, she tells us, was raised by his grandparents just outside Aubenton. He joined the military and learned to fly, returning to Aubenton at weekends to visit, sometimes flying overhead on a Sunday morning during Mass, to signal his arrival. People would run from the church crying, "Ah – it's Jean!" More and more people would follow until only the priest was left inside. Finally, he'd join the rest of them as they stood watching Mermoz land and taxi his plane.

Mermoz's career was the stuff of comic-book heroes – breaking records and crashing aeroplanes in deserts and mountains, being captured by tribesmen and arrested as a spy. A legendary aviator like Saint-Exupéry and Roland Garros, Mermoz was the first pilot to fly over the Andes. He shortened the route between Argentina and Santiago in Chile by almost 1,000 miles. In 1936 he vanished over the Atlantic. Charming Madame Schlienger, whose husband has written two books about Mermoz, knows all there is to know about the man and his exploits and is happy to patiently answer all Terry's questions.

Once we've finished admiring her museum, she says she expects we'll be visiting Montcornet. Why, what is special about Montcornet, we ask.

"But – it's where de Gaulle fought the tank battle!" she exclaims, as if everybody in the whole world must know of this event.

"You must see it!"

Montcornet is about twenty miles from Aubenton, diametrically in the opposite direction to where we are heading. But Terry doesn't get stampy-footy about the extra mileage. Even without de Gaulle he'd have been on fire to see the site, as he did his National Service in the 5th Royal Tank Regiment as a tank driving instructor.

We set off in good spirits, through fields of wheat in varying stages of evolution from short and green to waving tall and golden in the sun. French signposting can sometimes be very frustrating. It leads you along towards where you want to go and then suddenly runs out, usually at a crossroads, as it does today. But unlike many other elusive destinations we have sought, as soon as we mention Montcornet to a passing cyclist he replies: "Ah, Montcornet! You want to see de Gaulle's tank, yes?" He puts us on the right road. We lunch at a busy restaurant in the small town. The place is so packed that we have to perch on wonky chairs at a lopsided table almost in the gutter. When we get to the monument, it isn't quite what we expect. A smart 1960s tank stands on a raised platform on the corner of the main road next to the Citroën garage and outside a building belonging to a plumber. There's a plaque describing the heroism of the French tank regiment led by a Colonel Charles de Gaulle, fighting the German invaders in the battle of Montcornet on 16-17 May 1940.

Colonel de Gaulle, who'd been wounded and captured at Verdun in the previous war, was a hero, a maverick, a proponent of mechanized war and, *surtout*, a Frenchman. A month after the battle of Montcornet he leapfrogged the ranks to become a General, and was on his way to London. From there he rallied the Free French Army with his legendary Appeal of 18 June, calling on the French people to reject Pétain's surrender and join his army to fight for their country. In July and August he was court-martialled for treason in his absence, and condemned to death.

After the war it was Pétain who was tried and condemned to death for

147

treason. General de Gaulle pardoned him, and he died in prison.

Nord Pas de Calais

Nord

We retrace our steps through Aubenton towards Cambrai. A heavy truck loaded with aggregate has toppled into a ditch and ploughed into somebody's neat laurel hedge, from where a digger is trying to extract it. The apt name on the truck is Dropsy Transport Co.

Cambrai was the theatre for the first large-scale use of tank warfare. In November 1917 a contingent of 381 British tanks made the greatest gain in a single day in the history of the trenches, breaching the German lines and advancing almost five miles, an event commemorated annually by the Royal Tank Regiment. On our way to Cambrai we pass the communal cemetery at Ors, where Wilfred Owen, English poet of WWI was killed just one week before the Armistice.

Something nice had happened in le Cateau-Cambrésis – Henri Matisse was born there in 1869. In the midst of all the death and destruction that has afflicted this picturesque and unfortunately-placed area of France, it is heartening to come across, every so often, an event that isn't related to it.

Because its name has rather bleak connotations, being associated with tank warfare, Cambrai is a pleasant surprise. The town, birthplace of French aviation hero Louis Blériot, is an attractive and lively mixture of 17th and ornate 18th century architecture with elegant squares and beautiful parks. Once belonging to the Spanish Netherlands, Cambrai's tourist office lives in the last remaining Spanish-style timbered building.

Crowning the Town Hall is the splendid clock, the hours struck by giant mechanical Moorish characters known as Martin and Martine. They are subjects of two legends regarding their origins: one is gruesome tale involving someone bashing somebody's head in with a hammer, so I've chosen the second and more positive one. This tells of Hakem, a Muslim Moor, and Martine, a Christian who fell in love with each other. Because neither would change their religion, their relationship was illicit. They were condemned to imprisonment in the clock tower and made to strike the hour every hour with a heavy hammer. A sympathetic priest pleaded for clemency for the pair, and the court agreed they could be released just as soon as the priest found two replacement Moors. He built two Moorish automatons that performed the striking duties with perfect precision, thus releasing the prisoners. Hakem was so pleased he converted to Christianity and adopted the name Martin. Martin and Martine were married and lived happily ever after, producing hordes of children.

Immediately outside Cambrai we are back amongst tranquil wheat fields, with here and there flowery spick and span little villages of brick-built houses smothered in Picardy roses. We follow the Chaussée Brunehaut, the old Roman road named for the powerful Visigoth queen, and settle down to roost for the night at Saint-Amand-les-Eaux. Set in an apple orchard, the campsite is very pleasant in the hot evening sunshine, but next morning we wake to teeming rain, and a grey and grizzly day.

Our plan is to reach Dunkerque tonight, following small roads running along the Belgian frontier. Very soon we are lost. There are no road signs, only spindly lanes through fields of spinach. A few potatoes here and there, but mostly spinach. An occasional field of wheat or rye, but mostly spinach. Serious quantities of spinach. We drive around seeing spinach for a long time. Then we discover we are no longer in France, but somewhere in Belgium. Not anywhere on our map, but definitely in Belgium because the road signs are different.

Through the spinach there is a network of lanes that don't tell you where they go, nor where they come from. Every so often notices signal déviations, with no indication of where they deviate to. The road surface is silver in the rain, the sky bright white above it. There is nobody around; no vehicles, no people, until we arrive in a small village where it is still raining nice and steadily. Outside the village bakery several large metal trolleys stacked with loaves are standing in the rain. We find a small café/bar, where they don't have hot chocolate. But wait a moment: the waitress has an idea. She takes a bottled milky chocolate drink from the fridge, pours it into a cup and puts it in a microwave. What comes out isn't the best hot chocolate I've ever had, but it isn't the worst, either, and it was very kind of her to try and satisfy me.

We'll easily find our way back to France, she says. It's quite simple. In fact we don't, and it isn't, but we do manage to shake off the spinach and reach an area of hundreds of acres populated entirely by *pépiniéristes* (market gardeners) growing infant trees and shrubs. The road seems to be made of rectangles of concrete glued together.

The landscape is very flat, and we keep finding ourselves one minute in Belgium and the next in France. We can't pinpoint our position because none of the road signs in either language corresponds with anything on our map. So we drive around, admiring the scenery, the white-painted brick houses and some cattle grazing in the wet fields, their brilliant white coats broken by patches of blue-grey.

We pass the great menhir called la Pierre Brunehaut that marks the site of Queen Brunehaut's frightful death. Resisting the merrily named *Café des Morts* (Café of the Dead), we finally find our way back to France just east of Lille. Through vertical sheets of rain we manage to

149

circumnavigate the town surprisingly easily, and arrive in Armentières, where the mademoiselle came from. The monsoon-like rain makes it impossible to see anything of the town.

Clinging to the small roads on the Belgian border we continue northwards, managing to stay within France. At Boeschepe we stop to admire the splendid Flemish windmill called, for some reason that we do not discover, the Mill of Ingratitude. Next to it is an *estaminet* (simple bar/restaurant) where we decide to have lunch.

This is our first experience of an *estaminet*, and of a typical Flemish meal. We are given a wooden plank heaped with slices of cheese, slabs of wonderful wholemeal bread, a wooden pot of potatoes smothered in garlic butter, a generous pot of mustard, and a dish of gherkins. Washed down with a large ceramic cup of cider, it is delicious, filling and extremely indigestible.

The décor is fascinating: flagstoned floor, old metal bird cages and milk crates hanging from the beams, antique agricultural tools and lace-edged ladies' bloomers pegged on to ropes. The walls are covered with family photographs from the early 1900s: First Communions, babies in cumbersome and extraordinary prams, couples getting married, men with moustaches and flattened hair parted in the centre, women with thick eyebrows joined in the middle, wearing plain dark clothes and long white veils. There are proud young men, small boys with sticking-out ears, and pretty little girls. Did all the pretty little girls grow up to have huge eyebrows? The background music is like an Irish jig, and if you close your eyes you can imagine yourself in a Bruegel painting.

With the bread and cheese lodged stubbornly halfway down our digestive tracts, we drive on. The rain has stopped, but a strong wind buffets Tinkerbelle all over the road, pushing the trees horizontal, and the road is covered with debris. Ahead, sitting calmly in the middle of the road is what looks from a distance like a small rock, but which as we drive past I see is an owl. I jump down into the road, flapping my arms like a flying machine and leaping around to stop a car that is almost on top of the owl. The driver brakes (they don't always – I've had to jump out of the way on many occasions when a driver has continued driving at me) and I pick up the bird. One eye is closed and both feet are curled up beneath it. It sits placid and unmoving in my hand. The car's occupants are intrigued and pleased; their little girl strokes the feathery head with one finger.

The owl presents a dilemma. It is clearly injured, and with a bitter hurricane-force wind blowing, it will not survive if we leave it here. There is nowhere sheltered or safe to put it. I stick it inside my fleece. There isn't much in the way of urban development around this part of Flanders, right on the north-eastern edge of France, and it's fifteen miles before we find a village with any commerce. Terry goes into a pharmacy to ask where we can find a vet, while I sit warming the bundle inside my fleece. Out come a lady pharmacist and a young boy, delighted to be involved in our small drama; it doesn't look as if much happens in these sleepy parts. The nearest vet, they say, is in Ghyvelde, right up on the coast.

This is a very low-lying area. The altitude at les Moeres is 8 ft. below sea level! In Ghyvelde we find the blue cross of a veterinary surgery. The lady vet, Dr Deliessen watches curiously as I delve into the fleece and try to untangle the owl's claws from it. She is enchanted when I place it on the table. Both the bird's eyes have opened, but its claws are still tightly clenched so it can't stand. Dr Deliessen telephones a nearby animal refuge that handles wild animals. I hear somebody bellowing down the phone. The vet replaces the receiver and pulls a face. She says the shouter is angry we have taken the bird from where we found it. We should have left it there. It's very difficult to nurse owls, he said. They always die. We are to take it back immediately and leave it where we found it.

We all look at the bird, sitting dozily in her hand.

"It can't hunt, or avoid predators," she says. "If you do take it back, it's going to die." "Could you perhaps keep it for a few days until it recovers?" She looks dubious. "I've no experience with owls." We have looked after a couple in the past. I say I've successfully fed them on raw liver, tinned cat food and once a mouse that the cat caught.

"OK," she says. "I'll try."

She places the bird in a large cage at the back of the surgery. There is no charge.

Three days later I telephone to enquire how the owl is doing.

"She's doing well. Her legs are fine, and she's eating. But I want to find a mouse, and see if she can eat it before I release her," says Dr. Deliessen.

A few weeks later, once we are home, I phone again.

"I let her go about a week after you brought her in. One of the cats caught a mouse," (it's almost as if the cats know, I think) "and she ate it straight away. That evening I took her to the woods at the back of my house, and released her. She flew straight off into the trees. That's the last I saw of her, and I'm sure she's fine."

14

The Northern Coast

Nord

We reach the Channel at Bray-Dunes by mid-afternoon. In the wind ghostly snakes of sand slither across the road. Inshore the sea is murky green and violent; further out white horses top the grey waters. It looks particularly uninviting, but the sailboarders are out there shooting along at breakneck speed.

Beside the road hoardings show pictures of dragons and promise '1001 shivers for all the family' at the popular amusement park, Plopsaland, just over the Belgian border. I wonder why it has a name that sounds like a children's lavatory.

The area around Dunkerque isn't the prettiest in the world, nor is it chic. My Uncle Bill is somewhere there. He's one of the thousands who didn't make it back in 1940 during the evacuation Winston Churchill described as 'a miracle', when a heroic flotilla of little boats sailed from England to rescue the English and French troops stranded on the coast. Dunkerque's shallow beach prevented large vessels from getting close inshore, and the ragtag-and-bobtail little craft played a vital role ferrying the trapped soldiers out to them. A theory as to why the Germans allowed this massive evacuation of fighting men is that Hitler thought the British had been taught such a good lesson that they'd be prepared to surrender, whereas an all-out slaughter would provoke a fearsome reaction. Whoops! We may never know if this was the reason, but 338,226 men were rescued from Dunkerque and lived to fight another day.

Pas-de-Calais

Crossing the river Aa into the Pas-de-Calais *département* we drive to les Hemmes d'Oye, where the tide is out and the beach covered in a slimy carpet of bubbly green weed. For the dogs it is heaven, the opportunity to play on sand and for Dobby to run in the healing salt water. A vicious wind lifts the top layer of sand, lashing it into a fast-flowing torrent that stings the backs of our freezing legs. We climb back into Tinkerbelle until the dogs come back panting, wet, covered in sand and thoroughly pleased with themselves.

Heading west now, we drive along the Opal Coast through Calais and past Sangatte, once a major refugee camp, now just a small French coastal town. Just by Cap Blanc Nez – France's version of the white cliffs of Dover – is a monument to aviator Hubert Latham, standing appropriately windswept on a large chunk of rock. Son of a wealthy English merchant and a wealthy, aristocratic French mother, Arthur Charles Hubert Latham was a keen amateur aviator who spent most of his short life flying aeroplanes and killing wild animals. At the age of twenty-nine a wounded buffalo brought an end to his adventures. Buffalo 1: Latham 0.

At Cap Blanc-Nez the sea is so wild it seems at any moment it could leap right from its bed and fly around in the sky. It's impossible to stand upright in the wind. We spend the night at a campsite in Wimereux sitting in Tinkerbelle reading with the heater on, buffeted by the gale. The dogs refuse to go out. All through the night the storm rages, rocking Tinkerbelle and slashing at her windows.

The weather is still foul next morning, the Channel ugly and mean under scudding grey clouds. In Boulogne the sea hurls great spumes over the harbour wall; a group of intrepid kite-boarders fly above the waves, heedless of the despicable conditions. As France's largest fishing port, the first thing you notice is the stench of fish, and then the shriek of thousands of gulls, perching on rooftops, strutting on the harbour front, hovering over the water or dangling in the skies.

Posters of pyramids and sphinxes advertise an exhibition of pharaohs in honour of Auguste Mariette, the 19th century Egyptologist who discovered the Serapeum Sphinx – the tomb of the Apis bulls worshipped by the ancient Egyptians. Having located this priceless treasure, he found he couldn't actually excavate it from the implacable sands. As we arrive the exhibition is closing. There are a only few traders left, selling plastic souvenirs and hookahs, and although the street market is lively we can find nowhere to park, so we drive on looking for somewhere the dogs can run.

Equihen-Plage does not allow dogs on the beach, and in any case the breakers are laden with thick brown-green scum. So we continue to Hardelot, past fields of horses and cattle undisturbed by the weather, concentrating on munching the lush grass. No wonder it is lush if it is always this wet.

By the time we reach Hardelot the wind is at near-hurricane strength. As I climb out of Tinkerbelle a gust wrenches the cab door off its hinges.

I try vainly to hang on as my baseball cap is whipped off and tumbles up the street. Terry gives chase. The cap lies still until he is within a fraction of an inch of grasping it, and then flies off again. It keeps on happening. We are both laughing, tears streaming down our faces as the pink cap rolls around Hardelot's streets with Terry in pursuit. Once he's managed to catch it he has to fix Tinkerbelle's door back on to its hinges. It takes our combined strength to wrest it from the wind's grasp.

Unsurprisingly the streets of Hardelot are deserted. A few people in restaurants and bars gaze forlornly out of windows coated with a fine layer of sand and salt. We find a modest restaurant where the food is unremarkable but entertainment is provided courtesy of two English couples at the adjacent table. The women both wear white stiletto heels and tight white jeans, and their menfolk lots of heavy gold bracelets and neck chains. From what we understand from their loud conversation, one couple are estate agents who have just finalised selling a property to the other couple. They are celebrating with numerous pints of beer. A small child is eating spaghetti Bolognese with its fingers. The new house-owners suddenly realize the time and have to rush to catch a ferry. As they drive away the remaining couple look at each other meaningfully and clink their glasses.

After lunch we take the dogs to the beach, which on a fine day would be glorious, but the sea is too violent and the wind drives sand into our eyes. It's disappointing that the beastly weather means we can't enjoy the beautiful beaches on this part of the coast. Tally and Dobby look reproachful and want to get back in Tinkerbelle. That's when we notice that one-quarter of her rear bumper has vanished. We attribute this to Dobby, who'd been hitched to it the previous evening. He's also tipped his water bowl over on the floor so the carpet squelches.

The roads are becoming crowded with long queues building up, in contrast to when we'd set out seven weeks earlier. We pity holiday-makers arriving this week, the first week of July, to such dismal weather. Even elegant le Touquet with its extravaganza of architectural styles doesn't look much seen through icy driving rain.

Whoever is in charge of the town's greenery in Merlimont has been up to something odd: the lateral branches of a long avenue of beech trees are nailed and roped to wooden structures so they resemble the crucified Christians in Spartacus.

By the time it stops raining we are just coming into Fort-Mahon where we decide to drop anchor for the night at a mobile-home park. The *gardien* is most welcoming and helpful, and we can let the dogs run around freely. Dobby's foot is finally starting to heal.

Next morning is icily cold, and the sky and seas are a uniform grey. We are a few miles east of Crécy where the outnumbered English archers

154

defeated the French cavalry so soundly. Having seen enough battlefields recently, and with Normandy's landing beaches ahead, we decide to just drive round the calm, flat marshes of the Somme bay. It's an area of peaceful backwaterliness, seemingly overlooked by time over the last few decades. Swans and herons weave and wind their way amongst the reeds and marshes.

Picardy

Somme

From the comfort and warmth of Tinkerbelle's cab we explore the Marquenterre bird reserve that is also home to the Henson horse, a sturdy breed perfectly adapted to life in its marshy environment.

According to legend, the Henson was made by God. He blew upon a handful of sand to create a magnificent mare whose coat was golden like the sands, her pride that of the great winds, and her black-and-gold mane rippled like the waves. He ran a finger down the length of her back, leaving a long black mark, his stamp of approval. If ever the Somme bay should disappear, its image will remain forever embodied by the Henson horse.

The more prosaic truth is that the Henson is a man-made breed, developed in the 1970s by enthusiasts M. Bizet and M. Berquin. They took over God's work by crossing Fjord ponies with Anglo-Arab and French saddle horses. Decades of hard work and love produced a breed that was finally recognized by the French National Stud in 2003. Henson horses are docile, versatile and handsome, and used for riding holidays in the Somme bay. At the riding centre a dozen small children in anoraks are scurrying around with bits of saddlery and pieces of paper, while a rather distraught young woman tries to keep them all in the same place at the same time.

We continue driving around the tranquil, drizzly marshes until we come upon two pop-eyed white marble temple dogs standing guard at the small hamlet of Nolette, from where we follow a sign to the '*cimetière Chinois*'. It's just outside the village, surrounded by fields and enclosed by a natural stone wall and portico designed by Lutyens. The atmosphere is *très, très* Zen. Simple stone tablets inscribed with names and numbers, or sometimes numbers alone, stand in neat rows of flower beds surrounded by manicured lawns. Headstones bear inscriptions like: 'A good reputation endures for ever', 'Faithful unto death', 'Though dead he liveth still', 'A noble deed faithfully done'.

In the field next to the cemetery a group of black-and-white cattle are swiping up mouthfuls of grass. Along comes a farmer who leans on the wall and is happy to pass the time of day. He tells us the cemetery's upkeep is the responsibility of the Commonwealth War Graves Commission, but it's local French people who actually do the work. They usually come on Tuesdays.

All 842 inhabitants of this tranquil little colony were part of the 100,000-strong Chinese Labour Corps shipped to France in 1917. Their purpose was to undertake building, road repairs, recovery and burial of the fallen as well as general labouring, releasing British soldiers to go and fight. The Chinese mostly came from the northern provinces, lured by the prospect of earning four times what they could in their own country. Under the command of British officers, but segregated in their own camps, with their own hospital, each wore an identification bracelet riveted round his wrist. They arrived in their Chinese peasant clothing with their bamboo tools and mostly died of cold and disease. Difficult to imagine how these men felt so far from home, in a strange country, surrounded by the horror of a war whose cause they knew nothing about. And what of the families they left behind? Did they ever wonder what had become of their loved ones? Did they ever find out? Does anybody ever visit this pretty cemetery to talk to their ancestors? Despite the damp and cold we are enjoying this quiet, unspoilt part of the world and decide to take a train ride on the little Somme bay steam railway from Noyelles to Saint-Valéry-sur-Somme. We share a carriage with an elderly lady and her small grandson. The seats are of polished wood, and the heavy windows raised and lowered by sturdy leather straps. We listen to the old lady telling the little boy how she used to travel on these old trains sixty years ago, and how uncomfortable they were for long journeys. I can imagine that. Wooden seats are hard even over short distances! The engine chugs through marshes and flat fields of wheat and corn. Frequently it whistles and emits clouds of steam and smoke, attracting stares of mild interest from cattle and indignant glares from geese. We stand on the platform of the carriage, holding the wrought-iron railing as the train rocks and rolls. It feels as if the wheels are square, the way they thump over the rails. Sometimes the old, long-remembered whiff of dirty coal smoke floats around us, reminding me of long-ago journeys to boarding school. Disembarking in Saint-Valéry-sur-Somme we follow our fellow passengers in search of food. The first restaurant, the Drakar, is packed with diners, an indication that the food is good. We join a long queue of other damp people. A few lucky ones are led to spaces as they become vacant. Others are turned away and wander off despondently. When we reach the head of the queue, the *maitre d'* asks whether we have booked. We shake our heads, and he suggests we return in fifteen minutes, which we do. This time when he asks if we've booked we say yes. Of course, this isn't really true, but we don't want to be sent away for another fifteen minutes. We squeeze into a tiny table just inside the door next to a couple with lank wet hair and dressed in old sacks.

The staff run around as best they can through the crush, trying keep up with the ever-changing customers. Condensation flows down the windows and personal clouds of steam rise from moist customers. A party of four old people come in with a small white poodle on a lead. As they follow the *maitre d'* another little dog shoots out from beneath a table, where it is tied to the leg, and tries to kill the poodle, which stands its ground. The table is jerked about on the end of dog No. 2, as the two set about each other snarling and yelping. A waitress carrying a heavy tray has to leap over them. It is a wonderful scene straight from Fawlty Towers.

The food is excellent, and we crush a brief guilty pang seeing people still queuing in the rain. The impromptu entertainment continues. For no apparent reason one of the waitresses drops a tray piled with dirty plates and glasses, which crashes to the floor and makes a spectacular mess. A lady appears from the kitchen with a mop and bucket and cleans it up, while the waitress stands red-faced and almost in tears before vanishing into the kitchen. Five minutes later she reappears with another large tray containing two buckets of moules marinières. She manages to empty these over the head and shoulders of a small boy at the table next to us. The poor little chap is drenched, with mussels in his hair and clinging to his woolly jumper; slices of onion and fragments of herbs are draped over his ears, and he is saturated with hot liquid. An adult carts him off into the washroom, while his mother berates the clumsy waitress and the rest of us sit and stare. The bewildered child reappears a few minutes later in a jumper far too big for him, and the *maitre d'* arrives and presents a bottle of bubbly to the diners and a large ice cream to the boy. The waitress disappears.

We surrender our table to a wet couple and go to walk around the pretty Picardy town. There is much activity, with a host of marching bands, from the Rexpoede brass band dressed in black smocks and caps and red kerchiefs, and the bagpipes of the Premier Val de la Somme from Pont-Rémy, to the local Boy Scouts (*scoots*, as it's pronounced in French). Led by a *scoot* who is seventy if he's a day, with a ferocious moustache and heavy spectacles, they look magnificent in their scarlet tunics. In the medieval part of town we meet troubadours and knights, queens and jesters, and our sack-clothed lunchtime neighbours.

There's a stone plaque on the harbour side commemorating an event that took place here nearly a thousand years earlier. A Norman noble known as William the Bastard had assembled an army and fleet to go and fight the English. Shortly after sailing from Dives-sur-Mer they were caught in a heavy storm and forced to take shelter in Saint-Valéry-sur-

Somme to repair their ships.

On the 29th September 1066, with the wind in their favour the fleet of over a thousand ships and around 50,000 men sailed to England. The Bastard's army gave the English a thorough thrashing at Hastings, and killed King Harold. After that, they didn't call William the Bastard any more. Wey hey! They called him William the Conqueror. Quite why he'd felt compelled to undertake such an aggressive venture is something we've never previously considered, but shortly we'll find out.

Each year at the beginning of July, Saint-Valéry-sur-Somme, now amicably twinned with the town of Battle near Hastings, celebrates the *Fêtes Guillaume*, parading a giant model of William through the streets. By pure and unusual coincidence we have arrived on the day of the event. On our return journey the pretty red-and-turquoise train stops momentarily on the swing bridge. As I stare idly out of the window into the canal, where the yachts sit obediently side by side at anchor, I find myself gazing into a pair of limpid eyes, over a fine set of whiskers all capped by what looks like a German helmet. Before I've had time to call to Terry, who is looking from the opposite window, the seal has slid beneath the water and vanished.

We clatter, thump and toot our way back to the terminus at Noyelles, where somebody named Gérard hasn't switched the points in time, earning a loud and irate reprimand from our driver. We only just avoid colliding with another train occupied by several dozen very old people, sitting with their chins on their chests, or heads tilted back, open-mouthed. They are all asleep and happily unaware they've been within seconds of being involved in a train crash.

Back in Tinkerbelle we go to find somewhere for the dogs to have a run, and stop at Cayeux-sur-Mer's pebble beach lined with bathing huts. Concrete ramps lead down to the water. The dogs are unimpressed; they walk halfway down the ramps and sniff over the edge, then stare at us despondently. Their expression says: This isn't at all what we have in mind. Where is the sand? They can't be persuaded into the grey foamy water creeping furtively through the pebbles and trickling back out again. On the outskirts of the village there are mountains of shingle in different colours and calibres: big, medium, small, grey, white, brown, and huge boulders. If you need shingle or pebbles, Cayeux is the place to go. I wonder if the name is a corruption of the French word for a pebble – *caillou*, as there is a vague similarity in pronunciation.

We drive on to Mers-les-Bains and find a pleasant campsite there. The buildings are designed like bunkers with grass growing over them, and it looks somewhat like a converted wartime facility. However the *gardien* says it was actually designed like that. It's peaceful, and it finally stops raining.

15

Normandy

Seine-Maritime

Next day we cross into the region of Normandy at le Tréport. From the Tourist Office we pick up a brochure of local attractions, including a local red-herring factory. I'd like to visit it, because I've never seen a red herring, and who knows when one might come in handy. Terry adamantly refuses, so instead we head for Dieppe in search of lunch.

The sun is out in full force; there's a yacht race in progress, and the harbour front is crowded with stalls selling marine clothing and nautical gadgets. The collectes de sang are looking for new donors. In England we prefer to think in terms of donating blood; in France you often see notices for blood collections. To me this conjures up images of sinister white-coated men forcibly attaching tubes to the veins of the unwary and draining them into tankers. English people would be safe though: we can't donate blood in France in case we are carrying mad cow disease.

Dieppe being a major fishing port, we expect a good lunch and are spoilt for choice in choosing a restaurant. On the harbour side we manage to find what is probably the worst restaurant in France, or even the whole of Europe. We both order freshly grilled sardines. The waiter spins around and within twelve seconds places in front of us two plates of microscopic cremated skeletons. Hair-thin ribs poke through gaping wounds from beneath a blackened coating. Sad white eyeballs gaze blindly at the ceiling from small charred faces. I am famished, so I push a forkful into my mouth. These sardines are unquestionably grilled. Fresh they are definitely not. It is a gastronomic experience unequalled by anything I can remember. The fish have not been scaled. Chewing them is like chewing and trying to swallow a mixture of burnt straw and flakes of crisp plastic. Somewhere inside them is something soft, slimy and bitter. I think it might be a liver or a spleen.

Terry's sardines seem to have fared slightly better than mine. He says he's enjoying them, but I give up after the first mouthful. Anybody who knows me will tell you that I eat anything except meat, and am probably one of the least-fussy eaters alive. But I can't eat these. Instead I chew the lemon slice and a hard bread roll. Terry asks if I want to complain and order something else, but my gullet is already choked and I've lost my appetite. A seagull comes to our table and accepts a morsel of bread politely. It refuses the next piece, spits out a sardine, and wisely waddles away to the next restaurant.

Despite the shocking food we enjoy sitting in the sun watching the yachts and their crews bobbing around in the harbour. As we are walking back to Tinkerbelle a man wearing a loose and violently patterned shirt with tattoos on his neck falls into step beside us. He is slightly off his head, but harmless. As Terry says, I always attract oddballs. Uninvited, our new companion strikes up conversation. He asks whether we are English, German or Dutch. He seems satisfied, even pleased, that we are English, and says, "Yes, I thought so!" What makes us look so specifically English, I wonder? He points to the TransManche ferry sitting outside the harbour, and warns us never to go on it. The captain, he says, is a drunk. He makes the characteristic French gesture of a fist twisted on the end of his nose to illustrate his point. You should watch the ferry if it leaves port after lunch, he says. Weaving from side to side, and one of these days, just wait and see, there'll be a frightful accident. We thank him for the advice, and discourage him politely but firmly from climbing into Tinkerbelle with us.

Along the Alabaster coastline the sea is calm and beautiful in shades of green. Down a narrow peaceful road through a tunnel of overhanging trees we arrive in genteel Varengeville-sur-Mer, perched on the cliffs. The spectacular beauty that attracts artists from both sides of the Channel has absolutely no impact on the dogs, who are unimpressed by the narrow strip of noisy shingle that passes for a beach.

Ravishing is the best word to describe the landscape: on one side the sea and on the other lush hedges and beautifully kept gardens. Chocolate-box pretty Veules-les-Roses is home to France's shortest river, little more than half a mile long. It pops up magically from its source just outside the village, from where it wends its way to the sea between fields of cress, ancient thatched cottages and old mills.

Saint-Valéry-en-Caux is an artists' paradise of colombage and narrow shuttered houses. Pot plants dangle from wrought-iron balconies overhanging the sleeping yachts in the harbour. The beaches are still shingle, and officially out of bounds to dogs in les Petites Dalles, but as it is very hot and we have the beach to ourselves we let them out to explore the foot of the cliffs. Tally disdains the water, but Dobby throws himself down and lies with gentle waves sweeping backwards and forwards over his head.

The road leads through the small village of Sassetot-le-Mauconduit, whose château has an interesting history. In 1875 the intriguing and sad Empress Elisabeth of Austria (Sissi), a central figure in one of the greatest scandals in the history of Austria, came here with her small daughter and large entourage to benefit from the bracing air and waters of the Normandy coast. Sissi was the wife of Franz-Joseph and mother of Crown Prince Rudolf who died at the hunting lodge in Mayerling, in an apparent suicide pact with his young mistress, Marie Vetsera. He seemingly shot her through the head, and then killed himself, although there were rumours that he had been killed for political reasons. The official version of his death claimed at the time that he was mentally unbalanced. This exonerated him of murder and suicide, so that he could be buried in the Imperial tomb. Poor Sissi had already lost an infant daughter, and was herself stabbed to death in Geneva.

I like standing in places where historic events have taken place, or famous people have breathed the air, but we don't stop at the château because according to one critic, 'inside is not that nice, nor is the food'.

Instead we drive to the superbly located campsite at Yport. From a terraced hillside it overlooks the glorious seascape that has inspired so many great painters. As soon as we have settled down there I am gripped by an urge to set up my easel and dig out pots of paint and brushes to capture the shades of blue of sea and sky, the white of the cliffs, and the houses of Fécamp just along the coast. Then I remember that I don't have an easel, or any paints, because I can't paint.

While Terry takes the dogs for a walk I go down to the sanitary block for a shower. They are all occupied, and another person is waiting ahead of me. He is carrying a red umbrella. I think it is odd to take an umbrella to the showers, or indeed to be carrying one at all on a hot sunny day without a hint of cloud in the sky. Although we are standing side by side, his body language indicates that he isn't receptive to any kind of social intercourse. I am bursting to know what the umbrella is for, but I don't ask. It might be a weapon. The shower outside which we are queuing becomes vacant, and he marches in leaving the door open, and hooks the umbrella on to a rail. He looks at it for a couple of seconds, removes it and walks a little way to stand outside another occupied shower. I gratefully take the one he's abandoned, which suits me well as I don't have an umbrella to worry about. To this day I am still wondering why anyone would take an umbrella into a shower.

This morning the sun is already hot and high by 10.00am. The sea is very, very blue, and it would be hard to find a prettier part of the world. We decide go to Etretat for lunch. It's a mistake because we drive straight into a traffic jam where nobody can move. The narrow streets are blocked with vehicles coming from every direction. We are trapped behind a butcher's delivery vehicle. The back door opens and a youth dressed like a monk in a white cloak and hood emerges with half a pig, neatly sliced from snout to tail, slung over his shoulder. He delivers it to the boucherie next to where we are stuck, and returns for the second half. His white outfit is now streaked with blood and he looks like a surgeon who's cut through somebody's artery. I can say with certainty that there is nobody in Etretat today who could be more revolted than we are being stuck next to a shop full of dead animals in bits and pieces, or hanging by their feet from hooks.

Once we escape Terry spots and sprints towards a newly vacated parking space and we find ourselves going the wrong way up a one-way street. A line of furious people hoot and wave us back to where we've come from. But other vehicles have unwittingly followed us. We all stick our heads out of the windows and shout to the person behind to reverse into the main street, which is still at an impasse. Charming as Etretat is, and it's very charming indeed, we've just about had our fill and are ready to abandon our planned visit. Then Terry spots and snaffles a tiny parking space and manages to squeeze Tinkerbelle in.

The busy town with its wealth of old, timbered properties has been home to painters, presidents and writers. Guy de Maupassant wrote a particularly disgusting story entitled 'The Englishman of Etretat in which the hero is reputed to eat nothing but monkeys. We find a table at a simple hostelry, where over *moules marinières* in cider we sit and watch the frantic tourist world go by in its endless search for a parking space.

After lunch the dogs play on the pebbly beach, while we admire the cliffs. The tides of centuries have scooped great arches through the chalk, leaving beautiful works of nature immortalized by artists like Monet and Gustave Courbet.

From the Tourist Office we pick up a brochure about a nearby farm that produces goat's-milk chocolate and ice cream, so off we go, arriving at le Valaine goat farm just as the guided tour begins. It's in French, but as it's the last tour of the day we join ten other people and our guide, Bernard. Before entering a large barn we all have to wipe our feet carefully on a mat just inside the doorway. Being an organic farm le Valaine doesn't use disinfectants, but the special mat will destroy any bacteria on our shoes. And we are not to touch the goats, please, in case we pass germs on to them.

Our visit starts with an explanation of hygiene, and the difference between a virus, a bacterium and a protozoon. Bernard isn't only an expert on his subject, he is also a skilled entertainer, punctuating his talk with frequent jokes. We learn that the goats are fed on an assortment of foodstuffs including barley, corn, straw, hay and lucerne. Lucerne is also known as alfalfa and was first introduced into Europe by the Moors.

162

Goats love it because it's sugar content is as high as chocolate.

With our new knowledge of hygiene and nutrition, we move into an airy barn where the female goats spend their time when they're not out at pasture. Two of them approach Bernard and search his pockets for pieces of dried bread, a great delicacy. They are completely docile while he moves them around to display their salient points. Some have horns, and some don't. This is purely down to nature – he hasn't cut any of their horns off. Back in the mists of goat-time, their horns served as cutlery to help them break branches and strip bark. As they evolve through the centuries, becoming increasingly domesticated, they are losing the need for horns, which are slowly disappearing. Likewise the dangly things beneath their necks – these are vestigial remains of tusks, Bernard explains, once used for self-defence and, like the horns, becoming obsolete. In time, apparently, goats will have neither horns nor danglers.

The next thing we learn about goats is that every herd has a dominant female. We are introduced to her, and then we meet her little daughter, the only baby amongst the herd. When the kids are born they only stay with their mothers for a few weeks before being separated. The young females are grown on until they're ready to supply milk and replace the older goats, and the little males – here Bernard rolls his eyes and rubs his hands together – are made into pâté.

Recently female goat No. 2 challenged the dominant female, and stuck her horns into her foe's belly, causing goat No. 1 to lose the kid she was expecting. She was successfully mated again and her young baby is still with her because she is much younger and smaller than the other kids, and because her mummy is top of the tree. Maybe one day, says Bernard, she'll take over her mother's crown.

We move to view the cheese-making room through small windows. Do any of the ladies in our group make cheese, asks Bernard. We all shake our heads. He points at a woman with two young children.

"When your children were babies, did you feed them on milk?"

"Yes, of course," she replies.

"And afterwards, did you put them against your shoulder and bounce them up and down?"

She nods.

"And did they then spew up sour white stuff all over your clothes?"

She agrees.

"Well, then – you made cheese! That's what it is – curdled milk."

There are trays of cheeses in various stages of ripeness, and the discussion turns to spores and mushrooms. I admit I get a little lost here, because my French has its limitations, but it is something to do with the dusty black stuff that builds up on the outside of cheeses. Bernard takes a dusty-coated cheese from a tray, wipes his finger over it, and smears it

163

over the eyelids of an embarrassed teenage girl.

"*Et voila!* The original eye shadow, as used since the days of Cleopatra. Non-allergenic, waterproof, and free of heavy metals, unlike modern cosmetics." "It won't come off with water," he continues. "The only effective way of removing it is," – he pulls out a clean white handkerchief, and licks it – "saliva!" He reaches towards the girl's face with the spitty handkerchief as she recoils in horror, and then laughingly replaces the hanky in his pocket. Then he herds us outside to meet the ram, a handsome bearded animal tethered on a patch of long grass. Bernard explains that he and this fine male goat have something in common, a little thing that is special to them. Would we like to see what it is? The crowd shuffle their feet nervously as Bernard's hand seemed to hover at the front of his trousers. Then he grabs the goat's beard, and strokes his own.

"The goat urinates on his beard. Me, I don't! But let me explain why the goat does." By peeing on his beard, and rubbing it on the neck of the nannies during mating (a nanny goat can produce eight distinct smells to encourage him), he leaves his distinctive odour on their necks. This reminds him if he hasn't mated with them. Although I personally love goats and we have three, I don't find the smell of a working ram, or his urine, appealing in any way. But according to Bernard goat's musk is one of the ingredients in 4711 Eau-de-Cologne.

We buy ice cream – it's delicious, with no hint of goaty flavour – as well as a few packets of le Valaine's excellent cheese and a box of chocolates. We carefully avoid looking at the jars of pâté.

It's mid-afternoon and we don't know where we are going to spend the night. We drive slowly along the coastal road, through the small town of Sainte-Adresse, base of the Belgian government in exile during WWII. We've never visited le Havre, only ever driven off the ferry terminal and been on our way as fast as possible. The area around the terminal isn't the most attractive, so it is a pleasant surprise to see rows of bathing cabins on the beach, a flotilla of yellow yachts in the harbour and the promenade crowded with holidaymakers licking ice cream and strolling about, unfazed by strong winds whipping the flags. The port is neat and tidy; fishing boats doze on their moorings before their next shift, and only the rather sorry state of the potted palms indicates that this is very much a northern seaside resort.

We cross the Seine estuary by the Pont de Normandie. Meandering around pretty, dozy villages of thatched cottages topped with irises to bind the thatch and draw up the moisture, we find our way to Berville-sur-Mer, the Seine-Maritime's only coastal village. Terry inspects the construction of the fifty-year-old boats, now just rotting hulks that are all that remains of a once thriving port.

Calvados

On to Honfleur, exquisite, hot and crowded, the harbour-front houses seeming as if they're straining to reach the sea. We join several thousand other motorists in Trouville-sur-Mer and beautiful neighbouring Deauville, watering hole of poseurs and horse-racing fans, in an hour-long traffic jam during the afternoon rush. It's far too hot to be sitting in a van with two large panting dogs. I feel some sympathy for a blonde woman in a green hat, trying unsuccessfully to cross the road and screaming abuse at scooters and bicycles weaving through the traffic.

A benevolent life-sized topiary dinosaur (a brachiosaurus, I think) and her elephant-sized green baby stand on a roundabout in Villers-sur-Mer to signify that this is a particularly rich palaeontological area. It's a paradise for fossil-hunters who scour the sands of the Black Cow cliffs for ancient bones.

I haven't the slightest idea where we settle for the night, because we drive for miles and miles and miles trying to find a campsite that isn't full. By the time we find somewhere we are dizzy from driving and too tired to care where we are. After showering in modern, claustrophobic cubicles like vertical plastic coffins, we eat a snack and talk for half an hour to our neighbours, a Canadian girl and a Dutch man who met in China and are going back there to work.

Overnight yesterday's excessive heat turns to torrential rain, propelled horizontally by a saw-toothed wind. Our calendar says it is the first week of July. From wherever it is that we are we return to Villers-sur-Mer. The town straddles the Greenwich Meridian, which is represented by a line of dots painted on the road. A telescope on a low wall points across the Channel to Greenwich.

On the windy, rain-battered beach a man in a black baggy tracksuit is entertaining a group of small children. They are playing happily and apparently oblivious to the weather. He has them jumping up and down, raising their arms above their heads and stamping their feet in the sand. Two little girls play on a trampoline; one is cautious, just bouncing a few inches, but the other leaps higher and higher, kicking up her heels as she flies into the air. Old people sit on benches in raincoats, huddled under umbrellas; gum-booted pedestrians tuck *baguettes* into fleeces, anoraks or raincoats. Water flows in streams along the gutters and down the shop-front canopies, and drips from peaked caps. We squash into an already crowded restaurant, steamy from wet clothes, and sit sipping hot drinks, wiping condensation from our spectacles. More drenched people try to get in, squeezing even closer at tables to make room for other refugees from the weather. Yet again it is raining so hard it is funny. The drumming noise on the roof is so loud it makes conversation impossible.

165

Then it grows even louder, as if somebody is physically turning up the volume. We all start laughing; what else is there to do? There's no point going out, so we stay for lunch, a plate of piping hot *galettes* followed by strawberries and cream, washed down with a pitcher of cider. When we've been here for three hours, and the weather doesn't show any sign of improving, back we splosh to Tinkerbelle, where the dogs look at us mournfully as if we are responsible for the weather.

We drive off along grey roads beside a grey sea under a grey sky. We are heading for Bénouville, home of the historic bridge that was the first objective captured on D-Day by British Airborne troops, landing in gliders in a daring nocturnal operation. In recognition of this coup, the bridge was renamed Pegasus after the winged horse that is the insignia of the British Airborne forces. By the mid-1990s the bridge was no longer suitable for modern traffic and had to be replaced. British veteran associations bought the original Pegasus bridge for the symbolic price of one pound, and it now stands a few yards from its previous situation over the river Orne, a prized exhibit of the Airborne museum.

Parked alongside the bridge is a replica of a Horsa glider, bearing the black and white invasion stripes that identified it to Allied aircraft spotters. Primarily constructed of wood, components of the Horsa gliders were built in furniture factories around London. It has all the elegance of a garden shed, but did a first-rate job. Another glider named the Hengist was manufactured as a back-up in case the Horsa failed. In a rather neat twist, the original Horsa and Hengist were two German warriors who invaded England in the fifth century.

Beside the legendary bridge is the historic Café Gondrée, the first house in France to be liberated after the invasion. It's still owned and run by Mme Arlette Gondrée, a little girl at the time of the liberation, whose parents were members of the Resistance. They supplied vital information to the British regarding the German forces on the bridge. Memorabilia covers every inch of the tiny café's walls: photographs, medals, letters, helmets, flags, and certificates. Mme Gondrée doesn't seem to have made any concessions to the twenty-first century in her café, which happily looks as if nothing has changed in the last sixty years. It's the modest, scruffy simplicity of the place that gives you the wonderful sense of stepping back in time. We queue at the counter for coffee, and force ourselves on to a table occupied by an old English couple who reluctantly move their paraphernalia to allow us space. Soggy bikers queue with helmets slung over their arms, ahead of a group of debonair French Air Force officers in creaseless khaki raincoats.

As we drive on to our next destination, the roads and villages are almost deserted. It is the sort of weather to be tucked up in front of a log fire with a book, a plate of crumpets and a nice warm drink. The wintry conditions haven't deterred the sailboarders though. They're skimming over the scummy foam on the murky waters of the Côte de Nacre.

On the five miles of beach code-named 'Sword' during the Normandy landings, stretching from west of Ouistreham to Lion-sur-Mer, the sands are cowering beneath torrential rain. It's bleak, and many of the seafront properties are sad examples of immediate-post-war architecture at its ugly worst.

Adjacent to Sword on the western side is Juno beach, the objective of Canadian forces. The weather then was as unseasonable as it is today, which was a major factor leading to the Allied success: the Germans would not have expected them to attempt landings in such appalling conditions. 'Operation Overlord' had already been delayed by twenty-four hours due to bad weather. If they'd waited any longer it might never have been launched: the worst Channel weather for twenty years was on its way. Today the weather is thoroughly detestable, perfect for visiting the landing beaches to imagine what it would have been like for the men on their journey from the landing craft to the beaches, struggling through cold, rough waves, beneath cumbersome loads, in saturated clothing and under fire.

At appropriately named Graye-sur-Mer we take advantage of a break in the rain to walk the dogs on the beach. Two hundred yards from Tinkerbelle the grey skies tip their load on to the grey waters, the sodden sands, and us. We all rush back to the vehicle frozen, shivering and drenched to the skin, appreciating what it must have been like on that longest day of 6th June 1944.

In almost-deserted Courseulles-sur-Mer a brave carousel is spinning anoraked children astride horses, fish and aeroplanes. There are many monuments and memorials here, including a Sherman tank recovered from the sea in 1970 and the La Combattante stone in memory of the Free French Forces' destroyer of the same name which delivered General de Gaulle to France on 14th June. A 60 ft. high cross of Lorraine marks the spot where he set foot back on French soil after the liberation; and plaques commemorate the Canadian regiments who took Juno beach.

You can't visit these places, especially on a miserable day, without being chilled by the thought of all the lives lost in the immediate area. You look at the choppy waves and think of the landing craft and the men they spewed out. You think of the midget submarines that had lain on the sea bed gathering information and guiding in the landing craft. You marvel at the whole enormous task of planning 'Operation Overlord'. The French holiday guide books, holiday snaps and sailing books that gave vital information to the planners. Colonel Sam Bassett landing secretly at night to test whether the sands could bear the weight of the tanks. The building of the 'funnies,' tanks designed for strange tasks.

167

And the delicate question of how much information about the planned invasion could safely be given to the Resistance, whose cooperation was critical, but whose ranks contained suspected traitors.

That an operation of such magnitude could be successfully launched and accomplished without word reaching the enemy is almost beyond belief. We try to imagine the mutual euphoria of the locals and their liberators when they met in the shattered villages and shared celebratory pots of cider and calvados.

On an old, thatched windmill a short distance from the beach a cormorant sits upon one of the sails, preening itself. We continue along the coast, passing through the oddly named Ver-sur-Mer (*ver* means worm in French). 'Gold' beach, the middle of the five landing beaches, and the British troops' second objective, extends from west of Courseulles to Arromanches, where we cast anchor for the night. The campsite *gardien* assures us that although Normandy is France's wettest region, it almost never rains for two consecutive days. We can expect seasonal summer weather tomorrow. This is encouraging news, because travelling in a small campervan with two big dogs is more enjoyable if you can all get out of the vehicle from time to time without getting frozen and drenched.

We wake to something rare in Normandy – a second consecutive wet day. Contrary to the *gardien's* assurance we are treated to intermittent heavy showers punctuated with periods of icy drizzle. Perfect weather for being indoors, so we go to visit Arromanches's 360° cinema, to watch a film of the events of D-Day, shown from the perspective of the people who were there. It's an ingenious blend of original war correspondents' archives interlaced with colour film taken of the same spots now, in peacetime. The eighteen-minute long film is projected on to nine screens encircling the auditorium; there's no commentary, just background sound and music. The noise of the guns is deafening. Men run through collapsing buildings; tanks rumble; men fall; and on a pile of rubble a soldier binds a dog's injured paw. When the film ends we leave in silence. It feels as if we've personally experienced this momentous event. Out in the sea the remains of the Mulberry harbour are visible. It's one of the things my mind always has difficulty in getting to grips with, the concept of floating concrete. I realize it works, because I've seen the result, but despite Terry's patient explanations I still don't truly understand how. More than 150 concrete caissons, some 200 ft. long, nearly 50 ft. wide and 60 ft. high, weighing up to 6,000 tonnes, were manufactured in England and towed across the Channel by tugs. You have to be astounded at the ingenuity and optimism of those who believed this project could succeed. It had to: to supply the Allies with the reinforcements and equipment they would need following the landings, there had to be a means of unloading supplies on to the beach whilst the ports were still in German hands. The Mulberry harbour at Arromanches known as Port Winston would do the job for ten months. Its brother at neighbouring Omaha Beach was destroyed by the violent storms, like the one raging today.

Emerging into the familiar rain, we do something unusual, being not very good at museums: we go to visit the Bayeux tapestry. It is Terry's idea. I agree, expecting to be bored, but willing to do almost anything to keep dry. We fight our way into a parking space in Bayeux, and to the front of the queue to see the tapestry.

"Come back in one hour," says a cashier. "There are too many people at the moment." We devise a cunning plan. We'll have a very early lunch, then double back to the Centre Guillaume le Conquérant and have the place to ourselves whilst everybody else is eating. In a quaint street of timbered buildings we find a restaurant making the transition between morning coffee and lunch. The staff are sitting down having a smoke and a chat. They aren't absolutely thrilled to be disturbed at 11.30, but they install us at a table and ask us to wait, which we do patiently, until the chef arrives.

An American family takes the table beside us. There are mother and father, an aunt, a grandma and two engaging teenage girls bursting with vitamins, perfect skin, excellent teeth and manners. They express an overwhelming desire to see grandma eat snails which they are certain she is going to love. Although she isn't convinced, she obligingly agrees. The girls and their father speak French reasonably well; mother, grandma and aunt don't speak it at all, but they are all enthusiastic about French food and France in general. That's pleasing after the general breakdown in relations between the two countries over the Iraq war. With more than 116,000 Americans dying on French soil during the Second World War, nearly 11,000 in Normandy, it seems a tragedy that the old allies have subsequently fallen out so bitterly. Thankfully not all Americans are boycotting France. I can in one way understand their resentment at the outset of their assault on Iraq, how they feel France owes them a debt of allegiance that should override its own sentiments. But I hope fervently that seeing the appalling Iraqi debacle, the Americans may no longer feel so sure France was wrong.

While we eat I discreetly watch granny battling with the snails. The girls show her how to clasp the shells in the miniature forceps and prise the inhabitants out. She puts one in her mouth. After a lengthy chewing and a gulp, she says they are very nice, but she thinks she'll just eat the sauce. She endorses what I've always believed: snails are just an excuse for mopping up melted garlic butter with a bread roll. As fish-eating vegetarians, we're confused about snails: while they're clearly not a fish,

169

they're not really a meat, either. We've probably eaten them twice in the last twenty years, and I don't really know why, because they wouldn't be anything without the garlic butter.

Our cunning plan has worked. When we return to the tapestry exhibition we only have to queue for five minutes, before being given an electronic guide rather like a large mobile telephone and allowed through the doors into the darkened room where the original Bayeux tapestry lives. For a moment I panic, feeling claustrophobic, but the moment I see the first panel, I forget my surroundings.

I've been expecting a gigantic, gloomy woolly picture, like those hanging in the dining hall of Pierre Loti's house, but this is really something else. It isn't a tapestry at all. No. It is an absolutely mind-blowingly wonderfully crafted cartoon of simple stitchwork on a linen strip 230 ft. long, but only 28 inches high. It explains why William the Bastard went to England to attack Harold and become a conqueror. It wasn't an act of wanton aggression, but to claim the throne that Edward the Confessor had intended William to have, and Harold, perfidious creature that he was, tried to steal from him.

The text on the not-tapestry is in crude Latin, and the electronic guide explains the words and actions so exquisitely depicted in simple stitches. It is a pity that the queue ahead moves at a slower pace than the guide, which can't be turned on and off. While listening to an explanation of panel No. 11, we are stuck in front of panel No. 7, trying to store up all the information to correlate to the pictures when we eventually reach them. Behind us are people even more distant from what they are listening to. But it doesn't matter because as we edge along in the darkness watching the scenes unfolding in the glass case housing the embroidery, we are lost in time, sailing with William's fleet across the Channel. What is extraordinary is how a few threads of wool perfectly convey the emotions of the characters. They aren't anonymous people, but soldiers and sailors, farmers, dogs and horses, sometimes mythical animals, fleets of ships, Normans and Saxons. We hear the snort of the horses, the ribald shouts of the soldiers, the lapping of the waves on the sides of the boats, and the whooshing of arrows and clashing of sword and axe. And for heaven's sake – there's Halley's comet making one of its periodic appearances, shortly after Harold's coronation: a foreteller of doom if ever there was one! You're not looking at history – you're living it! And the amazing thing is this work of art was created more than nine hundred years ago! Could the people who made it have ever imagined it would last so long? They were not going to leave the momentous event that was the battle of Hastings to word of mouth. They wanted it chronicled so that every man could see why and how it took place.

Even more amazing is that it has survived through the centuries, almost intact apart from the two final missing panels. It's come close to disaster several times. After resting in obscurity for four hundred years following its creation, it was mentioned on an inventory of Bayeux cathedral in 1476. Another three hundred years passed then the French Revolution broke out. Somebody decided that the cloth would come in handy to cover a munition wagon. Fortunately a gentleman named Lambert Leonard Leforestier had the foresight to retrieve it and replace it with something more suitable.

Bayeux's burghers established a council to protect the tapestry, which was just as well. Not many years later somebody suggested chopping it up and using it for decoration. This unthinkable idea was thwarted, and then along came Napoléon who carted it off to Paris. He believed that studying the tapestry would give him insight into how William had successfully invaded England. Failing to do so, he returned it to Bayeux. There it was displayed in between various wars, and locked away for protection during them.

The tapestry's craziest adventure is recounted in Andrew Bridgeford's book "1066: The Hidden History of the Bayeux Tapestry." At the outbreak of WWII the cloth was treated with insecticide and locked away beneath Bayeux cathedral. Once the Germans arrived, it wasn't long before they found it. Like Napoléon they believed it held the key to the secret of William's successful invasion and conquering of England.

The French suggested that it should go into safe storage to Sourches château at Saint-Symphorien, west of le Mans. The Germans agreed, but the only vehicle the French could lay their hands on for the transport of this invaluable treasure was a lorry fuelled by charcoal. It really wasn't up to the job being asked of it, and needed pushing to start it after the driver's lunch break. Very soon it conked out completely, and had to be shoved up the many hills along the route. Reaching the crest of a hill, it careered crazily down the other side, with the pushers chasing frantically after it until its impetus was halted by level ground. It took ten hours to cover the 115 miles, but at least its priceless cargo remained safely in Sourches for most of the duration of the war. Herr Himmler had it in his acquisitive eye, and ordered it delivered to the Louvre. When the Allies landed, he wanted it moved to Berlin. It was thanks to the deliberate prevarication of German commander Dietrich von Choltitz, called the 'Saviour of Paris' that Himmler didn't get his avaricious hands on the cloth.

At the end of WWII it returned to Bayeux, where it has remained undisturbed ever since. I feel I could sit and look at it for a whole day. When we reach the final panel, an explanation of which we'd heard five minutes before we arrived there, I am disappointed that you can't go back to the beginning; you have to keep moving onwards, rather like sheep queuing for the dip, as more and more people move up behind you. However, upstairs in the Centre Guillaume le Conquérant you can visit a replica at your own pace, and I think without charge.

The last thing I expected was to enjoy this visit, because I'm a self-confessed philistine whose idea of hell is wandering around a museum looking at bits of pots and obscure relics of past ages. It's just the way I am. But in Bayeux I find something I could look at again and again and again. I want to buy it and pin it up all round the walls of our house. It does what all the tedious hours of droning teachers with their dry, meaningless facts and dates never could: it puts passion, drama and life into history.

How accurately does the not-tapestry tell the tale? Is it biased, told from the Norman perspective? Who sewed it? Was it William's wife Mathilde, having nothing better to do than to sit stitching with her ladies in a draughty castle? Or was it worked by accomplished English hands? The English were talented needlewomen with all the requisite skills to create such an embroidery at the time of the Norman invasion.

Over eight hundred years later a group of Englishwomen, the Leek Embroidery Society, would sew a replica. A lady named Elizabeth Wardle had seen photographs and drawings of the Bayeux tapestry, and made up her forceful mind that England must have its own version. She formed a group of thirty-nine embroidering ladies, one of whom used photographs to trace the pictures on to linen. Elizabeth was married to Thomas Wardle, whose family business was fabric dyeing, so she was well placed to have the threads coloured to match the originals. Within a year of starting their work, the industrious ladies had completed it, more or less true to the original apart from an understandable desire on their part that their labours should not go unsung: each of them embroidered her name on to their section of the tapestry.

The other differences between the two cloths are certain omissions. When you see the original, there is a great deal to take in visually while trying to retain the audio information. However, you will quite likely have time to notice the well-defined distinction between male and female horses, and also the fact that amongst the figures frolicking and crouching in the border some of them are emphatically masculine, as can be seen because they are stark bollock naked. Imagine how this could have affected the sensibilities of Victorian embroidering ladies, especially if there were maidens in their midst. They circumvented this distressing situation by simply obscuring the offending appendages. The lady who laboriously traced the original design on to the linen pencilled in little pairs of shorts to protect the modesty of the ladies and their subjects. But a Miss Margaret Ritchie seems to have been something of a rebel and less sensitive than her fellow embroiderers, or else a purist.

172

Miss Ritchie did not dress her males in the modest shorts. Imagine the blushful tuttings, whisperings and comments that must have gone on behind her back! Would those masculine parts that discomfited the English ladies have been a reason for giggling and sly jokes by their French counterparts all those centuries ago? By the time we reluctantly reach the end of this splendid visit, it is still raining. It has been raining ceaselessly for nearly forty-eight hours, but as we reach Omaha beach the sun finally breaks through.

'Omaha' is the six mile stretch of beach where everything went so horribly wrong during the invasion. Aerial bombardment designed to weaken the German defences was ineffectual. Specially adapted floating tanks didn't float – they sank. Unhelpful currents and winds landed American troops everywhere but where they should be, making them easy targets for the well-entrenched and numerous German artillery emplacements overlooking the beach. Trapped on the beach without the tank support they expected, it was only by super-human determination and effort that the Americans succeeded in their objective, sustaining enormous casualties, an event graphically portrayed in the film Saving Private Ryan. It is difficult to visualize now, on a peaceful day, in the sunshine. There are almost 10,000 American graves at the immaculate Saint-Laurent-sur-Mer's American cemetery, and a truly beautiful 22 ft. high bronze sculpture The Spirit of American Youth rising from the waves. All American cemeteries in France were given to America by France in perpetuity. A few miles down the road is the German cemetery, a reminder that it wasn't only Allied soldiers who died. Among the 21,500 German soldiers buried there is legendary German hero and Panzer ace Michael Wittmann, commander of the Tiger tank Bondesquely numbered 007. When he was killed in August 1944 he was just thirty years old.

People stroll around in the sun among pillboxes and memorials on the grassy hillside, and Tally and Dobby run on the narrow sandy beach. We can't imagine this peaceful, pleasant strip of sand and grass as a bloodied battleground, but the few seafront houses are bleak and sullen. They overlook the beach drearily, as if afraid to offend the ghosts of the past by any frivolous decoration. I find this place unbearably sad.

Our next stop is Pointe du Hoc, the strategic site which had to be neutralized before the landings, because from there German cannons could dominate both Omaha and Utah beaches. The American Rangers tasked with disabling the cannons had to land on the narrow beach, which was becoming ever narrower as the tide came in, and scale a 32 ft. perpendicular cliff.

They used extending ladders supplied by the London Fire Brigade, mounted on amphibious vehicles, and rocket-fired ropes fitted with grapnels. A British commando, Colonel Travis Trevor, strolled around the beach encouraging the men. When asked whether he wasn't afraid of being shot, he replied that he took two short steps and three long ones, so the snipers always missed him. No sooner had he spoken than a bullet hit his helmet and knocked him down. Thereafter he stopped taking short and long steps and crouched down on the ground like everybody else.

When the Rangers succeeded in scaling the cliff they found the cannons they'd been sent to destroy had already been removed from the casemates and replaced with telegraph poles. They found the guns and put them out of action, but were cut off from support for 48 hours, sustaining terrible casualties.

The hilltop is pitted with craters up to 30 ft. wide and 10 ft. deep, surrounding dozens of concrete bunkers and casements. Some of these are intact, and some in ruins with fingers of twisted metal pointing accusingly to the skies. In a swallows' nest in a dark corner fledglings hang over the edge with gaping beaks as their nervous parents skim the heads of sightseers. The craters serve as playgrounds for children sliding and rolling to the bottom, then heaving themselves back up clutching clumps of grass.

Looking down from the cliff's edge beside the tall dagger-like obelisk erected by the French to honour the Rangers, I try to imagine what it was like for the men hauling themselves up there, under fire. How they did so, and still had the strength to arrive fighting at the top. I think that of the battlefields we have seen, this is the one that portrays most vividly the actuality of warfare: the sheer size of the bunkers and the craters brings home what the men on both sides were faced with.

We leave Pointe du Hoc in a contemplative mood, and don't have much to say until we reach the outskirts of Grandcamp-Maisy. Pale sunshine reflects from the 30 ft. steel sculpture The Statue of World Peace, in the shape of a young girl releasing a dove from her upraised hands. This beautiful work is a gift to France from Chinese artist Yao Yuan. The original sculpture stands in a square in Beijing. Forced to work in a factory during the Cultural Revolution, Yao Yuan now devotes himself to working for world peace. It is a change to see something that has a positive significance rather than a memorial to the dead: we've seen so many memorials, so many graves.

'Utah,' the westernmost of the landing beaches is a particularly desolate stretch of coastline. Mean seafront houses stand dourly taking the brunt of the weather. Trees bend like bows beneath the driving rain and the spiteful wind whipping off the sea.

When I asked Mr Colin Bruce at the Imperial War Museum the significance of the code names given to the beaches, he said they were chosen to be deliberately meaningless. He told me too that a sixth landing area for the Allied invasion, code-named Band, was designated to the east of the river Orne, but was never used.

This is the final lap of our odyssey, and we have mixed feelings. On one hand we are looking forward to seeing our home and animals and I'm longing to sleep in a full-sized bed and cook in a proper kitchen. Sometimes I've felt like Alice through the Looking Glass in Tinkerbelle's tiny cooking space, and we are both bruised black and blue from the sharp corners of her splendid oak joinery. On the other hand each day brings new and wonderful experiences, forming a kaleidoscope of memories, and we feel we would like to travel ad infinitum until there isn't a nook and cranny that we haven't visited and explored.

Manche

We're on the Cherbourg peninsula, and the weather is worsening by the minute. Unripened wheat looks as if it has been flattened by a steamroller; the fields, still fallow, are saturated oceans of shiny mud. Ploughs lie idle on the boggy land, where people in coloured rainwear are diligently picking lettuces. A woman with glowing, fluorescent crimson hair walks beside the hedgerow, towing a wet, bewildered-looking little boy in a hooded anorak. At Quettehou we see a man sitting in the rain in a field on a low three-legged stool, milking a cow into a galvanized pail, watched by another man and a small boy. A solitary rainbow-sailed dinghy bobs just off the exotically named Île de Tatihou, and fishing boats lie on their sides in the mud in pretty Barfleur, where the air smells deliciously salty and seaweedy.

The compensation for the rain is, of course, the richness of the vegetation that produces Normandy's most beautiful crop – horseflesh. Every lush field holds burnished beauties grazing unfazed by the weather. And that same grass feeds the cattle that produce Normandy's delicious cheeses – Camembert, Livarot, Pont l'Eveque, and creamy Neufchâtel.

As we follow narrow little lanes past small granite cottages and wild, rocky land smothered in deep-pink heather, the Gatteville lighthouse peers through the gloom. The tide is coming in rapidly, gaining inches with every sweep.

Avoiding the uranium processing plant at Cap de la Hague, and the nuclear plant at Flamanville, we cut down from Cherbourg to the western coast of the peninsula to a beautiful sandy bay surrounded by grassy dunes and smooth chunks of cushion-like black and blue-green stones. The dogs race around while we tramp the damp, tightly packed sand whirling our arms and stamping our feet in the glacial wind. To Tally's joy a group of people are playing with a ball, and off he runs to join in.

Unfortunately they aren't inclined to play with him. One woman snatches the ball and clutches it possessively to her chest. Tally stares and wags his tail hard. He's very nonplussed by her behaviour. Normally people playing ball welcome his participation.

After lunch in the teeny toytown-by-the-sea village of Carteret, we go to Lindbergh beach, named for the American aviator, where the dogs help a couple of young men flying stunt kites. The sun comes out and the skylarks sing, and clumps of wild orchids and patches of wild thyme grow along the roadside. On the road we come up behind a boat being towed by a tractor. Within the boat stands a very old man directing the traffic. He signals vehicles past energetically and with no reference to the oncoming traffic. Despite almost causing a collision, he continues merrily waving people past and we scrape by unscathed, notwithstanding his best efforts.

It's been a while since we visited a château, so we follow a sign to the small, picturesque Château de Pirou. Built on an artificial island surrounded by a moat, the château is like a toy castle. From the battlements we look out over the marshes towards the Channel Islands, then go to admire the Pirou tapestry. Made during the 1970s in the same style as its more famous Bayeux relative, it relates the tale of an earlier Norman conquest – that of Sicily and southern Italy.

Like all good châteaux, Pirou has its own legend. While the Vikings were besieging the château in the 9th century, after some time the assailants became aware there was no sound coming from within the walls. When they stormed the castle they found only one old man. All the inhabitants and the garrison had vanished. If the old man would tell them how the people had escaped, they promised to spare his life. He said they'd used a magic spell to transform themselves into geese, and had flown away. The enemy recalled seeing a large flock of geese overhead the previous evening. In time the geese returned, but were unable to find the spell needed to return to their human form, because the spell-book had disappeared. They still return each year in the hope of finding it.

We continue driving along the coast until we find an empty sandy beach in a place that seems to have no name, where we park Tinkerbelle behind the dunes and spend several hours enjoying a respite from the weather. The dogs run through the water, over the sands, and up and down the dunes. Tally is inexhaustible, but Dobby returns every so often and flings himself down to recharge his batteries. After his recent forays into the salt water, his paw is almost healed.

Because where we are is so sheltered and peaceful, and ideal for the dogs, and as there is nobody around, we decide we'll do some '*camping sauvage*' just this once. At nightfall we put the dogs into the cab with their beds, and draw the curtains around them. We settle down in the back with a DVD and a bottle of wine.

Engrossed in 'Master and Commander,' I am pondering how a slightly overweight man with a Cupid's bow mouth and long hair can be as devastatingly attractive as Russell Crowe, when a car draws up nearby and we hear men's voices. I remember the warning we were given all those weeks ago about being careful where we stay at night. Torchlight plays on Tinkerbelle's windows, followed by a rap on the door. Terry opens it to find two *gendarmes*. They are friendly and polite, but say we cannot stay here for the night. Not just for one night? No, *désolé*, not even one night. There is a designated place for les campingcaristes half a mile down the road. They give us directions and drive away.

"Well," says Terry, "we'll have to move. You stay where you are and I'll drive us round there." He climbs into the cab with the dogs, and follows the *gendarmes'* directions to a car park on the edge of a small village where several other campervans are parked. I hear a brief exchange between Terry and someone else, and when he rejoins me he is almost crying with laughter.

As he drove into the parking area, the *gendarmes* signalled him towards a vacant place. When he halted Tinkerbelle, one *gendarme* walked up to what he thought was the driver's side – but Tinkerbelle is an English vehicle with the wheel on the opposite side. Instead of Terry, the *gendarme* found himself face to face with a huge black dog. His expression froze in shock and disbelief as he struggled with the thought that the dog had driven the vehicle. Terry says he'll never forget the *gendarme's* momentary open-mouthed amazement, nor Dobby's puzzled look at being stared at in such horror.

Terry is still laughing the next morning. It is a blue-sky day, with clouds on the horizon and armies of scarlet poppies patrolling the coastal road. We drive through Granville, a pleasant, sturdy little town, birthplace of one of the great couturiers, Christian Dior. The tide lies far out beyond a vast expanse of golden sand dotted with small pools and beds of seaweed. In the distance blue, red and yellow sails of flotillas of small boats bob on the flat water.

Although this part of France's coastline doesn't show many signs of warfare, Vauban hadn't neglected it in his tireless quest to fortify his country. At Carolles a stony and uneven path leads from the car park to la Cabane Vauban, one of several lookout posts built under his direction at the end of the 17th century to keep an eye on the English enemy across the Channel. Sentries watched shipping movements and signalled to each other by means of fires, smoke or sirens. The Vauban cabin is a stocky single-roomed building of thick stone walls beneath a stone roof; there's a chimney and fireplace, and spectacular views across the bay of Mont-Saint-Michel. It's a great bird-watching site, too. On our way back to

Tinkerbelle we detour through a field smothered in flocks of goldfinches singing as they strip seeds from the plants.

For lunch we go on to <u>Avranches</u>, where Henry II of England crawled around in penance seeking absolution for the rash words that caused the murder of Thomas Becket in Canterbury. The town is renowned for its beautiful medieval manuscripts, and an enterprising Avranches *chocolatier* advertises that they create chocolate manuscripts. I think what fun it would be to produce a 100,000-word manuscript in chocolate and send it to my publishers by refrigerated juggernaut. I imagine the editorial department sitting around eating their way through it, and somebody saying: "Gosh – did anybody ask Susie if she has a hard copy?" However, the advertised manuscripts are in fact only chocolate tablets engraved with a single letter. They'd be too laborious to assemble and impossible to read.

Burnished fruit and vegetables shine like jewels in a treasure chest in the lively street market. We buy punnets of blackberries, raspberries, strawberries, blueberries and gooseberries. Laden with berries, as we walk through the back streets of the marketplace we find old people with simple trestles displaying small bunches of their home-grown fruit and vegetables. We wish we had found them first. In Avranches after trying half a dozen restaurants that are full, we find in an alley a tiny place called le Pouc. While it's empty of diners, there isn't a square inch that isn't wonderfully decorated. A stunningly slim, pretty girl swathed in exotic silken clothing tells us it was previously an Indian restaurant belonging to a Briton. That explains the elephants and Himalayan mountains, the minarets, tigers, jungles and palm trees painted on the walls, even in the toilets. The girl and her partner retained the original decoration when they bought it. It would be sacrilege to destroy such wonderful work, but they have added their own style to it, painting fairies diving into the lakes and hovering over the mountains. The lampshades are made of feathers and paper. The effect is enchanting and the food is excellent.

While Terry sits savouring his coffee, I skip round the corner to the church of St Gervais to have a look at the skull of St Aubert, an 8th century bishop of Avranches who invoked the wrath of the Archangel Michael. On the rock known as Mont Tombe where a Christian settlement had existed since the 5th century, Michael told Aubert to build a church. The bishop did nothing. Michael reminded him. Aubert still didn't start building. When St Michael's patience and normally good temper ran out, he poked the dilatory bishop in the head with his finger, leaving a large hole in the cranium. This encouraged St Aubert to undertake the building of an oratory where the Archangel had suggested.

Over the centuries it grew into a Benedictine monastery, and between

178

the 13th and 16th centuries the stupendous abbey called '*la Merveille*' arose. Used as a prison during the late 18th and 19th centuries, today Mont-Saint-Michel is France's most popular tourist attraction.

The bishop's holey skull reposes in the treasury of St Gervais's church. I have never seen a skull pierced by a finger, so I want to have a look. The treasury houses a collection of ecclesiastical riches: gold and statuary, religious clothing, and the relics of St Suzanne, an unfortunate maiden from Rome who refused the marriage proposal of an emperor's son, and had her head cut off instead. St Aubert's head, or what's left of it, lives in a glass cage, and the extraordinary thing is this: when I saw it, although the skull certainly had a finger hole in it, it wasn't made of bone like yours or mine, but gold-plated copper! Now how do you explain that? Pondering this miracle, I collect Terry and we walk round Avranches's public gardens, a collection of manicured lawns, tapestry-like flower beds, towering trees, ponds and a magical view of Mont-Saint-Michel across the serpentine estuary. A large sinuous sculpture looks as if it's made from metal, but when you get close you read that it is carved from a giant sequoia tree felled by the great storm that ravaged France in 1999. It's called very appropriately *La Fille du Vent* (Daughter of the Wind), and was created by a local sculptor named Fabienne Campelli.

A restored Sherman tank named Thunderbolt and the great monument to "the Glorious American army of General Patton" is a reminder that it was from here that the revolver-toting Patton (whom Hitler referred to as the 'General-cowboy') began his victorious march across France to the German border. General Patton died just after the end of the war, ostensibly from injuries sustained in a car crash. However, since then there have been claims that he was assassinated by his own government and/or the Russians to silence him from disclosing unsavoury war secrets. He is buried in Luxembourg.

Heading for the coastline where we'd first begun our journey, we make a brief detour to the château at Ducey, family home of the Montgomerys. Gabriel, Earl of Montgomery was captain of the Scottish guards of King Henri II of France. It was his great misfortune to be responsible for the monarch's death during a friendly joust. Precisely as Nostradamus had predicted, a splinter from his lance found its way into the king's eye, causing the monarch a lingering and painful death. Probably served him right: Henri had a nasty way with Protestants – having them burned alive or cutting out their tongues. Banished in disgrace, Montgomery converted to Protestantism – could there be a better example of adding insult to injury? Subsequently he was captured and executed on the orders of Henri II's widow, Catherine de Medici. Nostradamus predicted all that, too.

There's every possibility the Château Montgomery is wondrous to behold inside. However, it is closed and it might rate as one of the ugliest châteaux of all time: a tall, grey and foreboding granite building patched in places with brick, with insufficient and far too narrow windows. It looks like the ancestral home of the Addams family.

16

Full Circle

Ahead sits the incomparably beautiful sight of <u>Mont-Saint-Michel</u>, straddling the regional boundary between Normandy and Brittany. Although the abbey features heavily in Brittany's publicity, administratively it falls under Normandy. All that separates us from it is the causeway, several thousand cars and sightseers. Today we decide to enjoy the scene as a whole rather than struggling around the streets. We sit happily in Tinkerbelle, gazing at this beautiful jewel glowing in the sunshine, the cherry on the cake of our journey.

Once more in Brittany, we drive along the flat landscape edging the bay, past fields of horses and people selling garlic and onions by the roadside, until we arrive at le Vivier-sur-Mer, where the farming of *bouchots* – cultivated mussels – started in 1954.

The mussels at le Vivier-sur-Mer are grown from spats attached to ropes wound round stakes planted in the sand. The little mussel babies hang round for eighteen months, growing nicely and contentedly. Then one day along comes a special wheeled boat that enables the mussel farmers to reach the breeding grounds at any time, tide in or out. The mussels are picked off, boxed up and end up on our plates.

At Cancale we complete our journey around France's outer limits, 6,000 miles from where we started out. Our trip is over. We have encircled the whole wonderful country. Turning south, we head for home.

By the time we reach Combourg it's late afternoon, so we decide to spend one last night in Tinkerbelle at the local campsite. Next morning while we are enjoying a leisurely breakfast in town our waiter urges us to visit Combourg château – it's incredible, he says. Terry says he's seen enough châteaux to last for several years, but I can't pass up the opportunity to visit Chateaubriand's childhood home.

The ticket-selling lady at the gate says I must move with the speed of light to catch up with the tour. I sprint along the curving path between neat lawns and up the stone stairs leading to the central part of the building, which is guarded on either side by circular towers topped with witches' hats. The guide hands me a German translation of her script. I ask for an English one, which she gives me with a funny look. Maybe I look more German than English. Anyway, I am grateful, as it means I'll understand more than I usually do when the commentary is in French.

I don't notice whether there is a motto over the front door, but if not I'd like to propose 'Abandon Hope All Ye Who Enter Here'. The château of Combourg is the very embodiment of gloom.

In the hallway is a bust of Francois-René de Châteaubriand. Above is the ancestral coat of arms originally given to one of his forebears during the Crusades. It bears the cheery slogan: 'Our blood stains the banner of France.' When the crusading knight returned, his wife was so overjoyed she died of happiness. I'm sure we heard the same story at the Château de Joux.

A graphic, jolly painting depicts Cardinal de Richelieu's siege of la Rochelle where he starved 15,000 people to death. In what is now the lounge, there are portraits of Marie Leszczynski (remember her from Wissembourg?) and brave, noble Guillaume-Chrétien de Lamoignon des Malesherbes. He was the grandfather of Châteaubriand's sister-in-law, and he defended King Louis XVI at his trial. Doing so, he knew, was signing his own death warrant. He could not have known that he would be forced to watch his daughter, her husband and their children all guillotined before his turn came.

There's a bust of King Francois I's defiant mistress, Countess of Châteaubriand, in the dining room. When he dispensed with her services he asked her to return the jewellery he'd given her. What a cheapskate! She returned it melted into ingots. Bravo.

There are various items of furniture and *objets d'art* but the only thing I would want, offered a choice, is the silver tea service ordered by Châteaubriand during his stint as ambassador in London in 1822. It's beauty lies in its absolute simplicity, which I find a pleasant contrast to the other ornate, depressing paraphernalia. In his book 'Memories from Beyond the Grave' Châteaubriand describes his father pacing around this room by dim candlelight, casting ghostly shadows.

Leaving the dismal dining room we move to the archive room, a small museum housing personal documents, family portraits, souvenirs from foreign travels, and his deathbed. There's also the inkstand in the shape of a black cat, commissioned by Châteaubriand as a reminder of the cheery legend of the long-dead count of Combourg whose wooden leg tapped itself up the staircase, followed by a black cat. What a fun place this is turning out to be!

From the east and south battlements there are views over the town, and the old fairground where once a year, wrote Châteaubriand in

Memories from Beyond the Grave 'something resembling joy' could be seen in Combourg. In the Cat Tower we admire a mummified cat, exhibited in a glass showcase. According to tradition, the animal would have been walled up alive when the château was built to ensure good luck to the inhabitants. Doesn't seem as if it worked here.

The writer described the room at the top of the turret he occupied as a child. Flitting owls, rustling winds and creaking doors convinced him of the presence of ghosts until he was immune to fear. He wrote: 'I could have slept with a corpse.' We traipse on to the western battlements giving views on to the gardens, where a stone cross marks the favourite spot of the writer's melancholic sister, Lucile.

According to Châteaubriand the château boasted secret passages and dungeons 'and everywhere silence, darkness and a face of stone: such was the château of Combourg.' Indeed it is. For the rest of his life he'd suffer 'a vague sadness,' and who can be surprised? Most of us would probably have gone stark raving mad had we had to endure the horrors of Combourg. Nevertheless he did very well for himself both as the founder of Romanticism in French literature and as a career diplomat. And for the gourmets, it is in his honour that the Châteaubriand steak was invented. Visiting this château has been an experience. Maybe not a cheery one, but nevertheless another to add to our collection.

After a final hot chocolate, we leave behind the fertile greenery of Brittany. The nearer we get to home, the drier the terrain. Driving through a dustbowl of pale-beige grass withered by drought, a landscape of wilted plants and weary trees, we feel a wave of nostalgia for Normandy's persistent rain.

We've learned so much from this adventure. We've learned that France is not one country, but a collection of regions as different from each other as Japan is different from Iceland. Each region has its own identity, culture, customs, cuisine, landscape and architecture. Of the coastlines we loved Brittany most, more than the turbulent Atlantic and the somnolent Mediterranean.

We preferred the rolling hills of the Jura and the grassy crags of the Pyrenees to the menacing peaks of the Alps. We found the Alsace the most picturesque region, and enjoyed the quiet peace of north-eastern France. Frequently we trawled estate agents' windows, discussing idly what we could afford in a particular area.

It was easy to succumb to quaint stone cottages, modern apartments overlooking the sea, alpine refuges, narrow houses in colourful city back streets. Almost everywhere we've been held the hint of new pastures. But driving up the lane to our home we know that for now this is where our hearts lie.

We have learned, too, that circumnavigating France in six weeks was more of a challenge than we expected. We've learned that a small camping car is not the ideal way to tour with two dogs, one the size of a Shetland pony. And we have learned that given the opportunity, we'd do it all again, ropey vehicle and destructive dog notwithstanding.

For the first week after our return, Tally and Dobby sit beside Tinkerbelle every day, nearly all day.

Acknowledgements

We owe thanks to Tinkerbelle, of whom we asked much more than we should, and who in return gave all that she could. Despite her varied ailments she responded to our needs valiantly and with good humour. May she enjoy a long, happy and gentle retirement.

Vivien Prince has been my friend since we were both horse-mad teenagers in Kenya. Over the years (decades, in fact), and over the seas our friendship has endured. Without her, our journey would not have been possible. She looked after our animals with total dedication and enthusiasm, just as I knew she would. I hadn't expected her to transform the weed-cluttered wilderness into a garden and reorganise my chaotic house into something manageable, but she did. That's the kind of person she is: she will always go the extra miles.

Asante sana, Vivien.

Links

CHAPTER 3
Le Croisic aquarium
http://www.ocearium-croisic.fr/
La Maison de l'Ane
http://www.bourricot.com/maisondelane/index.html

CHAPTER 4
The Marais Poitevin
http://www.francethisway.com/places/marais-poitevin.php
Brouage
http://www.fortified-places.com/brouage.html

CHAPTER 5
Blaye
http://www.tourisme-blaye.com/index.php?
option=com_content&view=article&id=54&Itemid=39&tmpl=en
Château Pichon-Longueville
http://www.pichonlongueville.com/en Dune du Pilat
http://www.dunedupilat.com/english/

CHAPTER 6
The la Rhune cog train
http://www.rhune.com/pages/en/17/le-petit-train-de-la-rhune-train-
touristique-sur-la-chaine-pyreneenne.html
Antton Chocolaterie
http://www.chocolats-antton.com/index.php?
option=com_content&view=article&id=42
The transhumance at Lourdios-Ichère
http://www.pierremm.com/2011/lourdios-ichere-transhumance Falaise
aux Vautours
http://www.falaise-aux-vautours.com/index.html?L=1 Col de Portet
d'Aspet campsite
http://www.portet-d-aspet.mnei.nl/

186

CHAPTER 7
Villefrance-de-Conflent
http://www.villefranchedeconflent.com/index.php?lang=en

Conservatoire de la Fourche
http://fourchedesauve.free.fr/

CHAPTER 8
La Ciotat
http://en.tourisme-laciotat.com/

CHAPTER 9
St-Martin-Vésubie
http://www.saintmartinvesubie.fr/
Guillestre
http://www.guillestre-tourisme.com/guillestre-
tourisme.com/Tourism_Office_of_Guillestre_alpss_Queyras_Ecrins_Gui
l_Montdauphin.html
St Véran
http://www.saintveran.com/

CHAPTER 11
Absinthe distillery in Pontarlier
http://pontarlier-anis.com/
 (Click Union Jack flag for English translation) – Besançon
http://www.besancon-tourisme.com/ The Peugeot Museum
http://www.musee-peugeot.com/Front/index.aspx?
numfiche=1679&langue=3&cc=03ec2f5814edcdef19662c39310e0f34

CHAPTER 12
(Click drop-down next to French flag to select English translation) –
Kaysersberg
http://www.kaysersberg.com/
Parc des Cigognes (French site)
http://www.cigogne-loutre.com/
Haut Koenigsbourg castle
http://www.haut-koenigsbourg.fr/en Strasbourg
http://www.otstrasbourg.fr/?lang=en

CHAPTER 13
Château of Sedan
http://www.chateau-fort-sedan.fr/

Rocroi
http://www.fortified-places.com/rocroi.html
CHAPTER 15
Etretat
http://www.frenchmoments.com/Etretat.html Le Valaine goat farm
http://www.levalaine.com/home.htm Bayeux tapestry
http://www.bayeuxtapestry.org.uk/ Pointe du Hoc
http://www.theworldatwar.info/pointeduhoc.html Château of Pirou
website, in French and English http://www.chateau-pirou.org/
Avranches
http://www.ville-avranches.fr/english/histoire/histoire_abrincates.htm

CHAPTER 16
Mont St Michel
http://www.ot-montsaintmichel.com/index.htm?lang=en

PHOTO ALBUM
If you'd like to see the photo album of Susie's trip, please go to:
http://goo.gl/hcngw0

Tally

The lyrics of La Marseillaise
Courtesy of: http://www.marseillaise.org/english/english.html

Arise children of the fatherland
The day of glory has arrived
Against us tyranny's
Bloody standard is raised
Listen to the sound in the fields
The howling of these fearsome soldiers
They are coming into our midst
To cut the throats of your sons and consorts
To arms citizens Form your battalions
March, march
Let impure blood
Water our furrows
What do they want this horde of slaves
Of traitors and conspiratorial kings?
For whom these vile chains
These long-prepared irons?
Frenchmen, for us, ah! What outrage
What methods must be taken?
It is us they dare plan
To return to the old slavery!
What! These foreign cohorts!
They would make laws in our courts!
What! These mercenary phalanxes
Would cut down our warrior sons
Good Lord! By chained hands
Our brow would yield under the yoke
The vile despots would have themselves be
The masters of destiny
Tremble, tyrants and traitors
The shame of all good men
Tremble! Your parricidal schemes
Will receive their just reward
Against you we are all soldiers
If they fall, our young heros

France will bear new ones
Ready to join the fight against you
Frenchmen, as magnanimous warriors
Bear or hold back your blows
Spare these sad victims
That they regret taking up arms against us
But not these bloody despots
These accomplices of Bouillé
All these tigers who pitilessly
Ripped out their mothers' wombs
We too shall enlist
When our elders' time has come
To add to the list of deeds
Inscribed upon their tombs
We are much less jealous of surviving them
Than of sharing their coffins
We shall have the sublime pride
Of avenging or joining them
Drive on sacred patriotism
Support our avenging arms
Liberty, cherished liberty
Join the struggle with your defenders
Under our flags, let victory
Hurry to your manly tone
So that in death your enemies
See your triumph and our glory!

About the Author

Born a Londoner, Susie Kelly spent most of the first 25 years of her life in Kenya, and now lives in south-west France with her husband and assorted animals. She's slightly scatterbrained and believes that compassion, courage and a sense of humour are the three essentials for surviving life in the 21st century. She gets on best with animals, eccentrics, and elderly people.

Connect with Susie

Keep up to date with all Susie Kelly news and new titles, join the Susie Kelly Mailing List http://eepurl.com/zyBFP (All email details securely managed at Mailchimp.com and never shared with third parties.)

Susie's Facebook:
https://www.facebook.com/SusieKellyAuthor

Twitter:
@SusieEnFrance

Terry

More Books by Susie Kelly

US Amazon Top 100 Title*

#1 TRAVEL
#1 TRAVEL BIOGRAPHY
#4 MEMOIR
#5 NONFICTION

I Wish I Could Say
I Was Sorry...

250 US REVIEWS
Av 4.00 STARS
55 UK REVIEWS
Av 4.7 STARS

SUSIE KELLY

*#35 Paid Chart Jan 2014

I Wish I Could Say I Was Sorry
'*A Child Called It* meets *Out Of Africa* in this stunning memoir of a woman's 1950s childhood in Kenya. Filled with candid humor and insights, this authentic tale captures one woman's incredible coming-of-age journey.' BookBub

Safari Ants, Baggy Pants and Elephants: A Kenyan Odyssey
The long-awaited sequel to *I Wish I Could Say I Was Sorry.* More than 40 years after leaving Kenya, Susie unexpectedly finds herself returning for a safari organised by an old friend. With her husband Terry, Susie sets off for a holiday touring the game reserves, but what she finds far exceeds her expectations. This is the link to the online album and slide show of Susie's safari: http://bit.ly/2rhZF1k

Best Foot Forward – A 500-Mile Walk Through Hidden France
(Blackbird 2011) A touching and inspiring tale of the Texan pioneering spirit, English eccentricity, and two women old enough to know better. Ebook, paperback & audiobook.

The Valley of Heaven and Hell – Cycling in the Shadow of Marie-Antoinette (Blackbird 2011) Novice cyclist Susie bikes 500 miles through Paris and Versailles, the battlefields of World War 1, the Champagne region and more. Ebook & paperback.

Swallows & Robins – The Guests In My Garden (Blackbird 2013) Susie stays at home and attempts to run two holiday gites, not helped by the cleaning lady from hell.

Two Steps Backward (Bantam 2004) The trials and tribulations of moving a family and many animals from the UK to a run-down smallholding in SW France. Paperback. Revised edition out in 2018

The Lazy Cook (1) Quick & Easy Meatless Meals
The first of Susie's delightful round-ups of her favourite quick, simple, easy recipes, sprinkled with anecdote and humour.

The Lazy Cook (2) Quick & Easy Sweet Treats
'I like a dessert to make me feel slightly guilty about eating it, but not enough to make me stop.

Dobby

More from Blackbird

The Dream Theatre (2011) by Sarah Ball
The Widow's To Do List (2012) by Stephanie Zia
That Special Someone (2014) by Tanya Bullock
On Foot Across France (2014) by Tim Salmon
The Modigliani Girl (2015) by Jacqui Lofthouse
The Road To Donetsk (2015) by Diane Chandler
Love & Justice (2015) by Diana Morgan-Hill

blackbird

The #authorpower publishing companhy

Rights-reverted and new titles by established quality writers alongside
exciting new talent.

http://blackbird-books.com

12937289R00118